Prestholme Island Ormeshead point
St. Sirian chap   Llandidno
Llandrigile
The Sound mouth   Penryn
                                         Eglos reste   Brynyryn
                                         Llangustennyn
                                         Bedskrethlin   Llandlas
Sevadon Cast.   Aberconwy
Pennenbian   Llansanfraid   Llanehan
Pennen maur   Dowy
                     Gouilchye   Guffin

Part of

Denbygh

Llanvaier
Vachan   Llanghenayn
Bodsyllyn   Caierhean
                     Castet flu.   Eglos vach
Llanaber   Llanbeder   Kennyn
Llandigaio
Llanlleghya   Mananah
Mynkeggil   Llynyga
                     Porlant flu.   Llanrust
          Llynydulyn   Swider   Glyn flu.
                     Llanrughwen   Coyde flu.
          Llyn Conlwyd
Chapell Kerig   Llegave flu.
                     Bettus Seyrion ython
Llytinumber
Flinnon   Llegoe   Brinmoyle
          Dolathelan Castell   Lledder flu.
                     Llanpenmachno
          Llyn Dolathelan   Conwy flu.
                                         Spitie
                                         Eian
          Drurid flu.
                     Llyn Canwy
          Teshniog

PART OF MERIONETH SHYR

Llanvrothen
     Mainturog
          Llandechwyn
Strat the maure
Skyen Ille
Llanthan gle ytrath
Harlech
Llandanog   Llanbeder flu.
          Artro flu.

CAERNARVON
BOTH SHYRE AND
Shire-towne with the ancient
Citie BANGOR described.
Anno Domini 1610

HONI SOIT QUI MAL Y PENSE

BANGOR

The free Schole

history · spectacle · romance
CASTLES
IN WALES

history·spectacle·romance
CASTLES
IN WALES

CONTENTS

The road map section of this book is based on the Ordnance Survey maps, with the permission of the Controller of Her Majesty's Stationery Office. Crown Copyright Reserved.

Maps reproduced by the Cartographic Department of the Automobile Association. Motor tours compiled and driven by the Publications Research Unit of the Automobile Association with the help of the Wales Tourist Board.

Special thanks for assistance in compiling this book to the National Museum of Wales, the National Trust, the Welsh Office (Ancient Monuments Division).

The contents of this book are believed correct at the time of printing. Nevertheless, the Publishers cannot accept any responsibility for errors and omissions, or for changes in details given.

Phototypeset by Tradespools Ltd, Frome, Somerset
Reproduced by Mullis Morgan Ltd, London
Printed and bound by W S Cowells Ltd, Ipswich, Suffolk

Published by the Automobile Association, Fanum House, Basingstoke, Hampshire RG21 2EA and the Wales Tourist Board, Brunel House, 2 Fitzalan Road, Cardiff CF2 1UY.

Distributed in the United Kingdom by the Automobile Association and the Wales Tourist Board and overseas by the British Tourist Authority, 64 St James's Street, London SW1A 1NF.

standard edition: ISBN 0 86145 125 2   56478
de luxe edition: ISBN 0 86145 126 0   56481

Produced jointly by the Publications Division of the Automobile Association and the Wales Tourist Board
Written and edited by **Roger Thomas**

Managing Editor **Donna Wood**   Art Editor **Peter Davies**
Editorial Contributors **Professor Glanmor Williams** CBE, MA, D Litt, FR Hist S, FSA, Professor of History, University College of Swansea, **Peter Humphries** AMA, **Jeremy Knight** BA, FSA, **Derek Renn** PhD, FIA, FSS, FSA
Illustrations by **Terence Dalley** ARCA, **FD Graphics**, **KAG Design**, Introductory Map Illustrations by **Arka Cartographics Ltd**

All photographs, other than those listed on page 192, are copyright Wales Tourist Board

The paintings on pages 66, 84, 109, 111, 116, 147 and 150 are reproduced from original prints by **Alan Sorrell** RWS

FOREWORD

The late Professor R T Jenkins quoted from a school book on the history of Great Britain; when the author reached Edward I he said: 'The history of Wales now comes to an end.'

It was undoubtedly Edward's intention, in building his castles, to enclose Gwynedd and put an end to Welsh political independence. Professor Glanmor Williams suggests in his introduction that the Edwardian castles were to ensure the permanent subordination of Gwynedd to English authority and they were so regarded for centuries. Thomas Pennant (1726-98), the great 18th-century antiquary and naturalist, described Caernarfon Castle as 'the magnificent badge of our servitude.'

After seven centuries, it would surely be wrong to regard the remains of Edward's castles as nothing more than symbols of past defeat and oppression. Seven hundred years after the killing of Llywelyn ap Gruffudd in 1282, Gwynedd remains a stronghold of the Welsh language and culture. In this context, the castles, like the cathedrals of Wales, are superb visual aids to understanding a turbulent, and often cruel past. They are also magnificent examples of military architecture at its best which have survived into a Wales which retains a viable Welshness. This book is a valuable introduction to understanding that Welshness.

WALES THROUGH THE AGES

An introduction by Professor Glanmor Williams

TIME CHART

Wales has been the home of man since prehistoric times. Throughout the centuries, its many settlers have experienced the major forces of invasion, resistance, warfare, religion and, in relatively recent times, industrialisation. This time chart does not look at Wales in isolation. It highlights important events in both Welsh and English history, relating the one to the other. Its content, spread over thousands of years, also places in context the medieval period (11th-15th centuries) on which this book concentrates.

Each time band reads chronologically from left to right.

200,000 BC

Man was in Wales a few hundred thousand years before the birth of Christ. In these times — the Old Stone (Palaeolithic) Age, he was a primitive, cave-dwelling food gatherer.

By the Middle Stone (Mesolithic) Age c5,000 BC, man the hunter develops better tools and weapons.

The New Stone (Neolithic) Age starts c4,000 BC. Man in Wales becomes a farmer growing wheat and rearing sheep and cattle. He also acquires skills in pottery-making.

3,000 BC

3,000-2,000 BC. Parts of Wales are occupied by the builders of Cromlechs (stone burial chambers). Many can still be seen today. At this time Wales was also settled by the 'Beaker' people, so-called because of their pottery.

A beaker from the Bronze Age.

A Bronze Age shield, discovered at Harlech, on display at the National Museum of Wales, Cardiff.

c2,000 BC — the Bronze Age. Metal objects become more and more sophisticated. By c550 BC the Iron Age arrives. With iron came the Celts and the building of hilltop forts.

Birth of Christ

In 43 AD the Romans invade Britain. By 74-78 AD they conquer Wales. The Romans establish powerful strongholds — at Caerleon, Chester and Caernarfon, for example — to control the native tribes.

A Roman tombstone from Caerleon. Here, they built a great fortress for 6,000 legionnaires; also a magnificent amphitheatre.

At nearby Caerwent the Romans founded a town — 'Venta Silurum', where this 2nd-century bronze plaque was found.

1000

1066. The Normans invade Britain, as depicted in this scene from the Bayeux Tapestry.
William I ('the Conqueror'), who reigned from 1066-1087. This Norman magnate, a fierce but calculating warrior, led an invasion that was to change English and Welsh history.

After their victory at the Battle of Hastings (1066), the Normans turned their attention to Wales. Soon they were firmly established in the borderlands, building one of their first stone castles at Chepstow.

1200

Giraldus Cambrensis (d 1223) wrote of Wales's princes, politics and people. He set the scene for the struggle for independence under Llywelyn the Last.

The Treaty of Montgomery 1267 — the high point of Welsh power before Edward I's invasion.

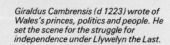

Edward I launched two successful campaigns against Wales in 1276-77 and 1282-83. From 1283 he began to construct his massive castles to dissuade the Welsh from ever rising again.

Seal of Edward I, who ruled from 1272-1307.

1400

In 1400, Wales rose once again under a charismatic new leader, Owain Glyndwr. For a time he was successful, capturing English strongholds and holding Welsh parliaments. But hopes of permanent independence were soon dashed and by 1412 Owain had disappeared, leaving Wales in a weak state.

Owain Glyndwr (1344-1416) led Wales in the last uprising against England. Gradually, the English monarch Henry IV (d 1413) won back his territories.

In 1404, Owain captured Harlech Castle. This martingale (horse-harness), found on the site, carries his coat-of-arms.

Harri of Monmouth — later to become King Henry V — was born in Monmouth Castle in 1387. During his reign (1413-1422) he won the famous Battle of Agincourt with the help of Welsh Longbowmen.

1600

Elizabeth I, born in 1533, reigned from 1558-1603. She is depicted here on a medallic portrait (1565).

During the Civil Wars (1642-1649) many of the Welsh castles saw action as Royalists (supporting Charles I) and Parliamentarians (for Cromwell) did battle.

Charles I, King from 1625, was executed in 1649. His main protagonist, Oliver Cromwell, died in 1658.

Cromwell left his mark in Wales. During the conflict, he personally took charge of the siege of Pembroke Castle and many other Welsh castles were damaged.

The Methodist Revival started in Wales in the 1730's, a reaction against a pro-English church. With this upsurge in Welsh Non-conformist religion came a great spate of chapel-building.

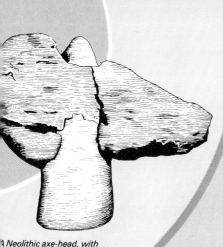

A Neolithic axe-head, with part of the handle preserved.

An iron sword found amongst bronze objects at Llyn Fawr (Mid Glamorgan).

By 383 AD, the Romans, their empire crumbling, were forced to leave Wales.

Richard I ('the Lionheart') reigned from 1189-1199. Here he appears in heroic pose on a wax seal.

After Richard came John (1199-1216). In Wales, Llywelyn the Great (d 1240) built up his power at the time of a weak English monarchy.

Dafydd lived in the calmer, more settled times of the 14th century. His Welsh verse celebrates love, not war. He is buried under a yew tree at Strata Florida Abbey, Mid Wales. The abbey, once an important Cistercian monastery, is now a peaceful ruin.

An ornamental bronze plaque from the Celtic period of 1st century BC.

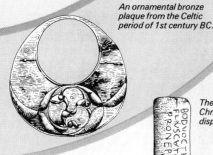

The medieval Welsh bard, Dafydd ap Gwilym (d 1380?), who wrote of nature and romance.

The Bodvoc Stone, an early Christian memorial, on display at Margam Abbey.

Henry II (1154-1189) allied with the Welsh prince, The Lord Rhys, to their mutual benefit.

400-600 AD, the 'Age of Saints'. Christianity spreads across Wales. St David, the patron saint (d 589?) founds a monastery in West Wales. c784 Offa builds his earthen dyke along the Welsh/English border as Celt clashes with Saxon.

William II ('Rufus') died in 1100. He was succeeded by Henry I (1100-1135), depicted here on a silver penny minted during his reign. Henry was the power behind the Marcher barons who ruled much of Wales.

Llywelyn ap Gruffudd ('the Last') was killed by an English trooper in 1282. All hopes of Welsh independence died with him. This Stone, near Builth Wells, marks his place of death.

After Harri came Henry VIII (1509-1547). The Act of Union was passed in 1536, linking Wales and England as never before.

The 13th century in Wales was dominated by the age of the two Llywelyns — 'the Great' and 'the Last'. Under the former, Wales achieved some measure of independence. With the accession of a strong English King — Edward I — Welsh fortunes were reversed.

Seal of Llywelyn the Great (Llywelyn ab Iorwerth).

Harri Tudur, the Welshman who became King Henry VII of England (1485-1509).

1455-1485. The Wars of the Roses. These wars ended, a mere 80 years after the Glyndwr revolt, on an unexpected note — a Welshman became King of England. Harri Tudur, the Lancastrian claimant, defeated Richard III at

Bosworth to become Henry VII, first of the Tudor monarchs. The days of a separate Wales were now numbered.

The start of the Industrial Revolution was the second crucial force to affect 18th-century Wales. In 1759, the Dowlais Ironworks was established at Merthyr Tydfil. By 1801, Merthyr was the largest town in Wales and the iron-producing 'capital' of the world.

By the 1850s, large-scale coalmining arrived in the South Wales valleys. Hundreds of mines produced millions of tons of coal a year.

Cardiff became, by 1913, the world's premier coal-exporting port (10 ½ million tons per annum). The wealth from this coal trade had enabled the Marquess of Bute, a few years earlier, to build his fantastic Victorian castle at Cardiff.

WALES THROUGH THE AGES

PREHISTORIC PEOPLES AND THEIR MONUMENTS

For 50 centuries at least, Britain has been subjected to the incursions of successive waves of invaders and migrants. During the New Stone Age (c4,000–2,000 BC) the first farmers made their appearance. Spreading outwards from western Europe, they brought with them the arts of growing crops and taming livestock. The most notable monuments bequeathed by their culture are those vast stone burial chambers, known as cromlechs, built for their chieftains and liberally sprinkled over many parts of Wales, from Tinkinswood in South Glamorgan to Barclodiad-y-Gawres on Anglesey.

About 2,000 BC the farmers were followed by the 'Beaker' people, so called after their distinctive form of pottery. These Bronze Age folk knew how to work metal, from which they made their weapons and tools of copper and bronze. They may have been the first to introduce the Celtic language into Britain. As a mark of distinction their chiefs were buried in the characteristic round barrows still outlined against the skyline of many moorland ridges.

Though it was perhaps the Bronze Age people who first began the building of hillforts, the bulk of these splendid fortifications were built during the Iron Age (c550 onwards). At places like Llanmelin in Gwent and Pen Dinas near Aberystwyth, these superb defences dominate the hilltops and the surrounding countryside. From behind their carefully-designed girdles of ramparts, palisades and ditches, Iron Age warriors, armed with their metal swords and other weapons, were able to withstand fierce attacks. Yet these forts may also have been just as useful as peaceful social and economic centres, controlling a neighbouring territory of farmland and grazing.

A farming settlement in prehistoric times

THE COMING OF THE ROMANS

It was this Iron Age culture which confronted the Romans when they came to conquer Britain in the 1st century AD. The Roman legions brought with them the whole panoply of military might and cultural distinction associated with a great imperial civilization, epitomized by the boast 'Veni, Vidi, Vici' ('I came, I saw, I conquered'). However, Roman Wales lay for the most part within the military zone of highland Britain and so was not as intensively Romanized as the south and east of Britain.

Although never conquered in the fullest sense, Wales was systematically covered by a network of military roads designed to link the two important legionary fortresses of Chester and Caerleon and the series of lesser forts placed along the roads as strategic points. Caerleon's magnificent amphitheatre still stands where the Romans built it, and other impressive remains are to be seen in many of our museums.

St David, patron saint of Wales

Yet Wales did not remain untouched by more peaceful Roman influences. There was a Roman town at Caerwent, civilian settlements near bases like Caerleon or Carmarthen, and many villas on fertile lowland sites such as the Vale of Glamorgan. Roman gold mines at Dolau Cothi show how trade and industry were fostered. The Christian religion was also introduced, though it made less headway than might have been expected.

CELTIC SAINTS AND SEAWAYS

The Romans' eagle-standards were finally withdrawn from Britain after AD 400. During the next two centuries the most significant development in the history of the Welsh was their conversion to Christianity. The men responsible were the 'Celtic saints', a dynamic band of monk-missionaries. Working unceasingly for the conversion of all the Celtic lands, they tirelessly voyaged the western seaways between Brittany, Cornwall, Wales, Ireland and Scotland in their frail-looking curraghs. Preaching, evangelizing and teaching, founding monasteries and schools in all the Celtic countries, they achieved astonishing success.

Their names are perpetuated in all the oldest parish names of Wales as a monument to their fruitful labours. The first syllable of so many place-names, 'llan', meaning 'church', is followed by the name of the saint to whom it was originally dedicated – Dewi (St David), Teilo or Padarn.

Hence the place-names Llanddewi or Llanbadarn.

Their zeal left a further mark on the many Christian stone monuments of Wales dating from the 5th to the 10th centuries. These commemorate the names, burial places and Christian allegiance of the rulers of those little kingdoms which emerged after the Romans had left.

THE 'DARK AGES'

The departure of the Romans was a prelude to growing encroachments by new invaders, the Angles and Saxons. Battles between them and the native inhabitants of Britain were hotly contested and each side produced its heroes. Foremost amongst the ancient British was the peerless Arthur. His name and reputation have since attracted so many myths and mystical associations that he has sometimes been dismissed as a mere figure of legend. But he really seems to have existed and by his generalship to have won a number of famous victories. By his prowess he held back the Anglo-Saxons for half a century.

Eventually, however, the Anglo-Saxons extended their control over most of the lower ground in England. They penned the Welsh back within their hills and mountains and cut them off from their fellow-Brythons in North West England and Cornwall. By the latter half of the 8th century, Offa, ruler of the Midland kingdom of Mercia, built the famous Offa's Dyke, much of which can be walked even today. For centuries, this massive earthen barrier served as a rough Welsh/English borderline.

From the 9th to 11th centuries a new threat pressed grimly on Welsh and English alike in the shape of raids by the Vikings. These ruthless Scandinavian warriors in their long, speedy, graceful dragon ships terrorized the shores of Britain. Sweeping on the coastline without warning and raiding fast and deep inland, they plundered farmsteads and churches, disrupting the life of whole communities.

The general effect was to keep Wales politically divided and undeveloped. Its numerous kingdoms were torn among themselves and hostile to one another. As Giraldus Cambrensis, Gerald of Wales, later wrote of them: 'From this cause brothers continually kill brothers ... whence arise murders, burnings and almost a total destruction of the country'. Fortunately for Wales, the Saxon kingdoms, too, were divided, and though strong enough to threaten the Welsh, not powerful enough to overcome them. So far, the mountains of Wales, difficult terrain for any would-be invader, had ensured its people's independence.

A penny from the reign of Offa Rex, King Offa of Mercia

THE NORMAN CONQUEST

The danger to the Welsh from the Norman kingdom established in England in 1066 was qualitatively different from anything they had ever faced before – and much more threatening. The first Norman king, William I, was a powerful monarch, the last man to tolerate quietly any threat along his western border from the Welsh rulers.

He himself was fully occupied in ruling England and his Duchy of Normandy. But he had willing vassals to whom he could delegate the responsibility for holding the frontier. These men were a warlike élite, an aristocracy organized for combat and battle-hardened by experience of feudal warfare in its most advanced and deadly form on the Continent. Its two most decisive characteristics were already thoroughly familiar to them: the private fighting-force of armed knights to win their battles, and the essential stronghold of the castle to hold their gains.

Soon after the conquest of England William planted a number of these lieutenants along the Welsh border. Their task was to defend that frontier securely. But they were not long in coming to interpret their role more aggressively. Having once scented weakness or division among the Welsh, they pressed forward in campaigns of conquest.

Yet they were not destined to complete the conquest of Wales swiftly. Whereas the fate of England was settled by the one decisive battle of Hastings and a few years of consolidation, overcoming Wales would take 200 years. That long-drawn-out struggle left behind it a legacy of castles. Indeed, no part of the British Isles was more thickly peppered with Norman castles than South Wales. The remains of about 80 stone castles can still be seen here together with some two dozen in the north. Many times that number of early timber castles have disappeared.

A NORMAN PIONEER: WILLIAM FITZOSBERN

As early as 1067 William the Conqueror installed at Hereford one of his ablest and most trusted lieutenants, William FitzOsbern. FitzOsbern overran the Welsh-speaking part of Herefordshire before penetrating into Wales proper, building a number of castles along the line of the Rivers Dore, Monnow and Wye. Before his death in 1071 he had pressed deeper into South East Wales and seized much of the country west of there.

His exploits pioneered a typical pattern for the conquest of much of South and East Wales by ambitious frontier lords, each with his own force of knights and retainers, all rewarded, fed, clothed, and equipped at his expense. These attackers were the medieval equivalent of panzer divisions, to whose hard, swift strike the Welsh had no immediate answer.

Their successes were consolidated by the building of the vital strongholds, those castles which the Normans took care to put up at all strategic points. Having thus seized the territories of Welsh rulers, they also took over the right to rule the population that went with them.

EARLY LORDS OF THE MARCH

Farther north in the March (from the French word 'marche' meaning 'frontier') early success in Mid Wales was achieved by Roger of Montgomery, who was created palatine Earl of Shrewsbury in 1071. He and his brood of fighting sons thrust up the Severn valley into Powys. There they set up their base at Montgomery and threw up supporting castles in Mid Wales. By 1086 they were poised to strike down into South West Wales.

Another formidable figure was Hugh of Avranches ('Hugh the Fat'). He entrusted the conquest of North Wales to his kinsman, Robert of Rhuddlan. By 1073 Robert had reached Rhuddlan, the vital fording-place on the River Clwyd. Here, where the marshy estuary formed a natural barrier protecting the heart of North Wales, Robert built his castle.

Soon afterwards, he had moved forward to Deganwy, an equally crucial crossing-point on the Conwy estuary, where in 1075 he set up a castle as his forward base. Robert's bold and far-reaching successes led William I to recognize him as his lieutenant of all North Wales.

When Robert died in 1088, Earl Hugh took up where his aide had left off. He advanced far into Gwynedd, building a castle at Aberlleiniog and another at Caernarfon. The latter was a crude earth and timber forerunner of Edward I's mighty stone fortress which now stands on the site.

PRESSURE ON THE WELSH

Down in South Wales, meanwhile, a native prince, Rhys ap Tewdwr, succeeded in gaining William I's recognition of him as a vassal. This gesture turned him into a kind of southern Welsh counterpart to Robert of Rhuddlan, a shrewd stroke, for it was instrumental in keeping the Normans at arm's length for some years. But when Rhys was killed in battle in 1093, the dam, which had held back the flood, broke.

The invaders now poured through from all sides. The Montgomery clan, led by Roger's son, Arnulf, swept like a whirlwind through Ceredigion as far south as Pembroke. Near Carmarthen, William FitzBaldwin, Sheriff of Devon, was making conquests in the king's name. The de Braose family moved into Radnor, Bernard of Neufmarche conquered Brecon, and Glamorgan was swiftly overrun by Robert FitzHamon.

The extreme rapidity of these victories suggests a preconcerted Norman plan. In fact, they may have been brought about solely by adventurers acting on their own initiative, all simultaneously exploiting weakness caused by Rhys ap Tewdwr's death. The resultant gains were again systematically underpinned by a network of motte and bailey castles.

MOTTE AND BAILEY CASTLES

In this first tide of Norman conquest, castles played a crucial role. The earliest ones were not the massive and elaborate stone buildings we normally associate with the word 'castle', but usually earth and timber structures known as motte and bailey castles. Though they could be put up relatively easily and cheaply, they represented some of the most versatile and advanced fortifications of the age and served their purpose admirably.

The motte consisted of a mound some 20–30ft high. It was either a natural hillock, shaped and made steeper, or else an artificially-constructed

Detail from a medieval manuscript, with two knights preparing to joust

Willelm – William the Conqueror – as he appears on the Bayeux Tapestry

mound of heaped earth. This was surrounded by a moat, wet or dry, and defended by an embankment. Turning round the top of the motte was a palisade, 10–12ft high, with a sentry-walk. Inside this was erected a strong wooden tower, possibly three-storeys high and often brightly painted.

Adjoining the motte were one or more baileys. The bailey was an oval or right-angled structure with one gateway at the farthest point away from the motte. It, too, was defended by a ditch and rampart and by a stockade. Within the bailey were located those buildings necessary for the maintenance of life in the castle – kitchen, barn, retainers' quarters and chapel.

Access from bailey to motte was gained only by means of a sloping bridge, part of which, on the motte end, was a drawbridge. The whole area of such a castle might encompass about one-and-a-half acres, increasing in some instances to about three acres. It was the kind of castle so graphically illustrated in the Bayeux Tapestry, which shows lively scenes of men busily engaged in building them.

A variation of this kind of defence-work was known as the ring-motte. In this case, the circular area of the motte, on which the wooden tower was built, was not raised above the general level of its surroundings but was protected by steep banks of earth dug out from the encompassing ditch.

SURVIVALS OF MOTTE AND BAILEY CASTLES

At Cardiff, the original motte, now surmounted by a stone tower, is plainly visible. Some distance from the present castle at Rhuddlan rises the Norman motte known as the 'Twthill', while at Kidwelly remains of the motte are preserved in the mound in front of the gatehouse.

A few of the timber castles were later rebuilt in stone and sometimes keep the outlines of their origins as motte and baileys. At Cilgerran, the

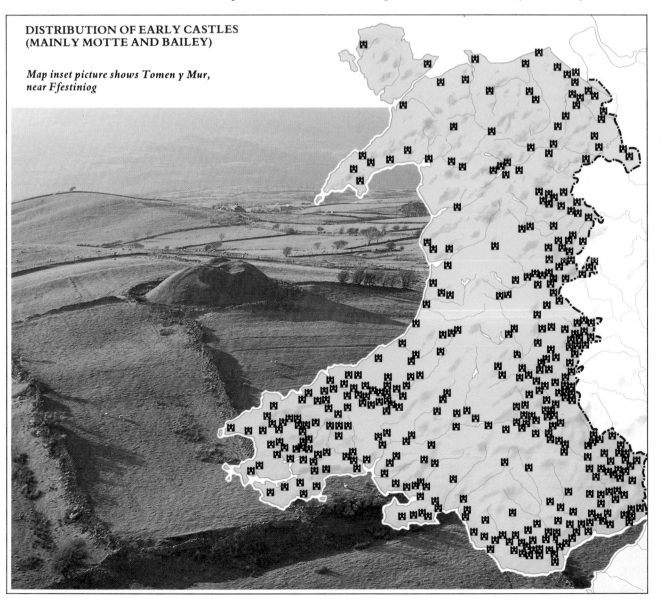

**DISTRIBUTION OF EARLY CASTLES
(MAINLY MOTTE AND BAILEY)**

*Map inset picture shows Tomen y Mur,
near Ffestiniog*

inner ward occupies the site of the motte, the outer ward that of the bailey. Caldicot Castle is another that maintains the plan of its original timber structure. The motte survives at Skenfrith where we know that money was being spent in 1187–88 on its surrounding timber defences.

Most of these motte and bailey castles, however, were simply allowed to fall into disuse and were eventually abandoned in favour of more comfortable and commodious stone castles or fortified houses. Nevertheless, rudimentary as they may have been by later standards, they had served their purpose extremely well as citadels whose occupants were not easily dislodged. Invaluable for subduing territories already won, they had also acted as springboards for further expansion.

Even in those rare instances where a Norman lord took possession of Welsh land by means other than conquest, castles proved their value.

WELSH RESISTANCE

The Normans had initially taken the Welsh by surprise. The latter had not at first realized what a menacing enemy now confronted them. They had been glad to see their traditional Saxon foes humiliated and had optimistically supposed that they might even make use of the Normans as allies in their own endless feuds with one another. Such illusions were brutally shattered by the speed and extent of Norman encroachment into Wales. It seemed as if the whole country might fall like a ripe plum into the invaders' rapacious hands.

These setbacks, however, acted like shock-therapy on the Welsh. Drawing again on their reserves of pride as masters and defenders of their mountain land, they took full advantage of their own rugged terrain of hills, moors and woods, so admirably suited for operations by hardy, lightly-armed guerillas. So the Welsh countered with furious uprisings aimed at ejecting the invaders, and between 1094 and 1098 there were fierce onslaughts against the Normans in most parts of Wales. The fight-back to defend Welsh independence had begun and would continue for centuries.

Rallying to their leaders among the ruling families of Wales, they achieved considerable success. Castles were besieged and many destroyed; Norman forces were beleaguered and reduced to desperate straits. Giraldus Cambrensis relates how his ancestor, Gerald of Windsor, sorely-pressed at Pembroke, resorted to hair-raising stratagems to mislead his besiegers, worthy of the diplomatic bluffs of today. He threw some of his last remaining provisions to his enemies to give the impression of plenty, and planted a letter in which he pretended to have no need for reinforcements.

By the courage and spirit of their response the Welsh could undoubtedly exert heavy pressure. But they lacked the resources and the organization to keep the Normans out of the lower and more easily penetrable country of the south and east. When the waves of Welsh uprisings subsided, the strongest rocks of Norman power reappeared intact. In particular, their main castles had not been overthrown.

THE CREATION OF THE MARCH

Behind his frontier lords stood King Henry I (who ruled from 1100–1135), so masterful a figure that he seemed to a Welsh chronicler like 'the man with whom none may strive, save God himself, who hath given him the dominion'. Henry's 'divinely-ordained' power was certainly felt in much of Wales. In Pembroke, Cardigan, Carmarthen, Kidwelly, and Gower, his clients, including a large colony of Flemings, were firmly implanted.

By this time the March of Wales, ruled by Norman lords on behalf of the King, was clearly taking shape. It swung in a rough arc south from Chester to Chepstow, and then west to Pembroke. At some points, between Hereford and Llandovery, it was as much as 50m wide; at others, between Cardiff and the northern limits of Brecon lordship, 50m deep. Carved out by the persistent enterprise of a couple of generations of tough lords, most of it had been won by the sword and held by the castle.

Along with the land its native ruler's rights had been usurped. These rights had previously been based on the Welsh cantref or the commote, the territorial units within which authority in politics, administration and justice was exercised. The Norman lord now transformed cantref or commote into his new lordship. Within its boundaries he ruled like a miniature king. He enjoyed the privilege of parcelling out land to vassals

Giraldus Cambrensis – Gerald of Wales – whose chronicles describe Welsh life

Map inset picture shows Conwy Castle and walled town

Mounted knights preparing to do battle

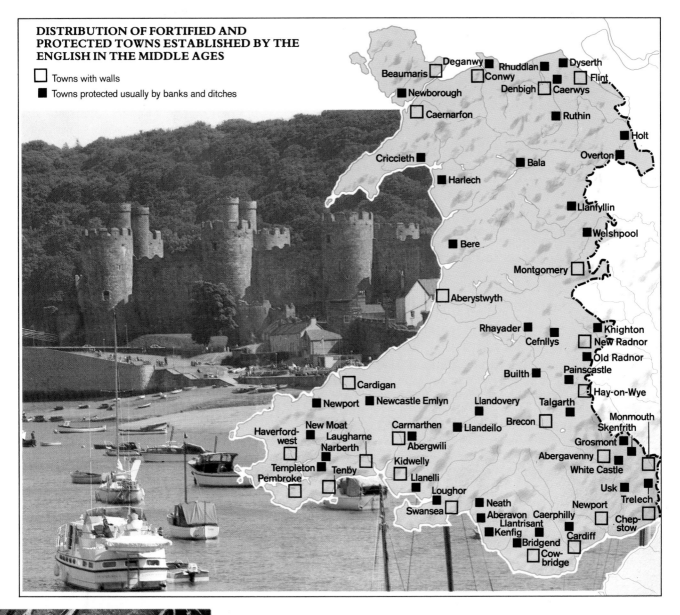

DISTRIBUTION OF FORTIFIED AND
PROTECTED TOWNS ESTABLISHED BY THE
ENGLISH IN THE MIDDLE AGES

☐ Towns with walls

■ Towns protected usually by banks and ditches

and tenants, holding his own court with powers of life and death, building castles, creating boroughs, levying taxes, minting coins, and even waging war on his enemies.

CAPUT, BOROUGH AND PRIORY

Each lordship had its own caput (Latin for 'head') or capital, where its chief castle was sited. That castle served a variety of indispensable functions. It was the strongpoint which housed the lord's troops and horses and protected him against his enemies. It became the headquarters of his administration, justice and police-system, and also served as a safe place for keeping goods, revenues, possessions and prisoners. Finally, even in its most primitive form, it was home for its owner and his family.

To provide for the needs of the caput and to foster trade within one lordship, it was usually necessary to encourage a community of traders and craftsmen to settle in the shadow of the castle's protection. Drawn from a non-Welsh population, this group was given a charter conferring on them borough status, ie, exclusive trading rights, and limited powers to establish their own town government and courts of justice.

Rhuddlan, as early as 1086 according to Domesday Book, boasted its borough rights and had a mint whose silver coins still survive in museums. Many other Welsh boroughs owe their origins to a similar process – Chepstow, Abergavenny, Monmouth, Cardiff, Brecon, Neath, Swansea, Haverfordwest and Pembroke, to name but a few. Even today, in every such ancient borough its Norman castle stands near the old centre of the town. Very often, too, a priory of Norman or English monks was introduced to strengthen the incomers' control of the Church.

ENGLISHRY AND WELSHRY

Most Norman lordships were divided into the two parts of Englishry and
Welshry. The former covered the favoured lowland areas lying below
600ft or even 400ft. Most of it was divided up among the lord's vassals in
return for their loyal services. For their own security they built lesser
castles or fortified houses, many of which still stand in lowland Gwent,
Glamorgan, Gower, Brecknock and Pembroke. They organized the land
into manors, farming them in open fields with serf labour.

The Welshry, by contrast, lay in the uplands of a lordship. There,
traditional Welsh pastoral farming continued, as did the native Welsh law
associated with the name of a 10th-century king, Hywel Dda ('the Good').
Welsh chieftains still ruled, owing hardly more than nominal allegiance to
Norman authority. Deeply devoted to their own language and customs,
they viewed their alien lord with smouldering resentment.

That hatred occasionally flared up into open opposition. Owain,
Prince of Powys, fell in love with Gerald of Windsor's wife, Nest, 'the
Helen of Wales'. Such was his ardour that he attacked the castle of Cenarth
Bychan (possibly Cilgerran), abducted Nest, set the castle on fire and all
Wales aflame. In an act of no less daring, Ifor Bach ('the Little'), scaled the
huge motte of Cardiff Castle by night and kidnapped Earl William, his
wife and son.

Owain Gwynedd's Coat of Arms. Owain, a native Welsh prince (d1170), ruled Gwynedd, North Wales

EARLY STONE CASTLES

Valuable though wooden castles had been, their weakness was that they
did not last. Timber rotted in time, and was anyway highly vulnerable to
fire. Stone structures, though requiring greater skill and more expense in
their building, were much more durable. The Normans had known their
value from the outset. As early as 1067–71, William FitzOsbern had built in
stone at strategically-important Chepstow. His oblong stone tower of two
storeys and part of the curtain wall are still visible there.

FitzOsbern's work was exceptional at the time, but from the 12th
century onwards, more stonework gradually appeared, though this
process was gradual and haphazard. Manorbier Castle in around 1130 had a
stone hall and gate-tower but timber defences; not until a century later
were those defences built in stone. At Rhuddlan in 1241–42 parts of the
fortifications were still made of wood, as they were at Raglan until as late
as 1400. The majority of lesser castles were never rebuilt in stone because
of the cost involved.

Even so, some examples of both basic types of early castle – those with
a great tower and those without – were reconstructed. Where a castle had a
great tower this was usually strengthened first. A powerful rectangular
stone tower (known in later centuries as a 'keep'), with its entrance at first-
floor level, replaced the wooden tower. Because of its weight it was not
usually built on the motte but at ground level nearby. It usually contained
the lord's residence, though some of the smaller ones hardly seem to have
been large enough for the purpose.

The ruins of some of these 12th-century towers still exist. Ogmore has
one that may go back to the age of its founder, William de Londres (died
c1126). Two neighbouring castles, Coity and New Castle (both at
Bridgend), each have a square keep and a curtain wall of the 12th century.

A more common way of refortifying a castle was to put up a 'shell-
keep' – a misleading term, since no keep or tower was involved. This
technique meant replacing the wooden palisade around the top of the
motte with a circular or polygonal wall. The bailey stockade might also
have been rebuilt in stone and carried up both sides of the motte to join the
shell-keep. Excellent examples can be seen at Cardiff and Tretower.

Medieval warfare – scaling the castle walls with a belfrey, or siege-tower

WELSH PRINCES REGROUP

Stronger castles would be needed as Welsh princes, no less than Norman
lords, became better organized. Though often divided amongst themselves, the Welsh were ever watchful of any chance to press their advantage
against the Normans. England's difficulty could be their opportunity.
Thus they were able to turn to good account English weakness during the
anarchy of Stephen's reign (1135–54), or the conflict between Henry II and
Becket (1162–70), or Richard I's absence on Crusade (1189–99).

During the long reign of Henry II (1154–89), Welsh princes came to an

LLYWELYN AB IORWERTH
(Llywelyn the Great) 1173–1240

Llywelyn the Great was one of the crucial figures in 13th-century Welsh history. He was reputedly born at Dolwyddelan, near the head of the Conwy valley, in 1173. His father, who held this part of North Wales, was to die soon afterwards, Llywelyn spending much of his youth in England. Yet by his early teens, the young Llywelyn was claiming his rights to parts of Snowdonia (Gwynedd); and in 1194, at the age of 21, he obtained the throne of Gwynedd.

A forceful and ambitious character, he was assisted in his rise to power by his early exposure to England and English ways. He married Joan, daughter of King John, and over the next few years became the master of northern Wales.

Ambition aside, Llywelyn's rise to even greater things was based partly on his vision of Wales, one he shared with Giraldus Cambrensis (see page 123), as a country weakened by disunity. He proceeded to impose a degree of cohesion – simultaneously strengthening his own position – through annexing neighbouring lands by force of treaty.

Although this policy inevitably made him enemies within Wales, the Welsh princes joined with Llywelyn when John attempted to subdue the whole of Wales by direct conquest. Llywelyn, always the opportunist and as skilful a politician as he was a fighter, used his powers of leadership to secure autonomy for Wales.

Thereafter, he kept the English in check by flexibility, cunning and statecraft, with brief raids balanced by tactical submission once the object had been achieved. Within Wales, his reforms were far-reaching. He introduced a revolutionary – for Wales – theory of government based upon centralized authority. He tried to remove divisive old customs. He reformed the Welsh church and its systems of law. He brought improvements to agriculture and administration.

But this all happened at a time when the English monarchy was weak, a situation that Llywelyn exploited to the full. His vision of a totally independent country was ultimately unrealistic, though he did impose a degree of unity previously unthought of.

Llywelyn, the great leader, died in Aberconwy in 1240, exhausted and crippled by his long efforts. Remembered, perhaps ambitiously, by a Cistercian annalist as 'that great Achilles the Second', Llywelyn certainly deserved the title Prince of Wales. Yet he never claimed it, limiting himself to the honours Prince of Aberffraw and Lord of Snowdon. This very modesty was a key to his character.

uneasy understanding with him. They recognized him as overlord and, in return, were given virtual freedom to rule their own lands unhindered. Amid the mountains of Gwynedd in the north west, Owain Gwynedd (1137–70) built up his own power, as did Rhys ap Gruffudd, The Lord Rhys (c1155–97) in the south-western hills of Deheubarth. It was there in Deheubarth that the old Welshman made his famous prophecy to Henry II that despite the harassment the Welsh had undergone, no other nation nor any other language but Welsh should 'before the Supreme Judge answer for this corner of the earth' on the Day of Judgement.

In defence of that independence the Welsh learnt many lessons from their enemies. Always masters of guerilla warfare, they now came to appreciate the importance of having castles of their own and of acquiring the tactics and the implements needed to reduce those of their opponents. They also perceived how to win and use the support of the Church and its clergy. Nor did they overlook the importance to their cause of the patriotic fervour of the poets or the value of their propaganda.

Hywel Dda, Howell the Good, the 10th-century Welsh ruler

13TH-CENTURY CASTLES

From about 1200 striking improvements in castle design were introduced, borrowed as a result of crusading experience in Greek and Arab lands and warfare in France. Basically they were intended to remedy the deficiencies of the rectangular tower. Any such keeps were bound to be weak at their angles, which were always in danger of being mined, and inevitably created 'blind spots', which defenders could not command except from directly above. To overcome these difficulties, free-standing circular towers, with the entrance still at first-floor, were built.

Most of the Welsh examples are to be found in West Wales, around Brecon, Gwent and just over the Herefordshire border. Incomparably the finest specimen is the tower, with walls 78ft high and 15ft thick, built c1200 by William Marshall within Pembroke Castle – at this time a base of exceptional importance for the conquest of Ireland. Smaller but excellent instances of the same design exist at Skenfrith, Tretower, Dinefwr, Bronllys and Caldicot.

Two particularly interesting examples, showing what apt pupils in the art of castle-building the Welsh had become, are to be seen at Ewloe and Dolbadarn. Ewloe has a fine D-shaped keep, probably built at the orders of Llywelyn ab Iorwerth (Llywelyn the Great). At Dolbadarn stands a round keep of about 20ft in diameter, rising to 40ft in height, leaving us in no doubt of the building skills which the Welsh had now acquired.

CURTAIN WALLS AND GATEHOUSES

During the 13th century, however, emphasis was placed increasingly not on strengthening the keep but the bailey or curtain wall. A particular feature was the development of the rounded tower at a number of separate points along the curtain wall. Each tower was one of a series of self-contained strongholds which enabled the defenders to cover the outer face and base of the wall while themselves remaining protected. Every tower also commanded the summit of the wall and divided it into sections, thus preventing a single break-in from endangering the whole castle.

At Chepstow, as at Pembroke, William Marshall brought the defences up to date c1190. He built the curtain wall between the middle and lower bailey with its gateway and towers, providing the castle with one of the earliest instances of rounded wall-towers with true shooting-slits. At Cilgerran, Marshall's son built two round towers astride the curtain wall.

The best impression of early castles which used rounded towers to strengthen the curtain wall may be gained from Grosmont and Skenfrith. Both are thought to have been rebuilt c1228–32 by Justiciar Hubert de Burgh, into whose hands they passed between 1219 and 1239.

Rounded towers in themselves were not always enough. It was also essential to ensure the security of the entrance – always potentially the weakest point of the defence. This was done by building a powerful gatehouse. In its earliest form it consisted of twin towers, usually D-shaped, on either side of the entrance. Admission to it across the ditch was gained via a drawbridge.

The gate-passage was formidably strengthened by a series of defences, including a gate and portcullis. In the vault above were 'murder holes', through which boiling liquids could be poured down and other weapons discharged. Furthermore, the defenders could fire arrows into the gate-passage through slits from the chambers on either side.

An early gatehouse still stands at White Castle, and another, partly ruined, at Montgomery, burnt by Llywelyn the Great in 1228.

WELSH STATE-BUILDING IN GWYNEDD

Mention of Llywelyn the Great draws our attention to the outstanding Welsh renaissance taking place in the Principality of Gwynedd during the 13th century. This was inspired by the two most gifted of all the Welsh princes: Llywelyn ab Iorwerth ('the Great', 1173–1240) and Llywelyn ap Gruffudd ('the Last', who ruled c1247–1282).

These princes managed to build up their own authority by exploiting to their own advantage those conflicts in which English kings found themselves entangled with France, the popes and even their own barons. Both rulers also successfully applied to Wales the most effectual methods of contemporary politics, diplomacy and warfare. Finding allies among English barons, they extended their territories outward from their north-western heartland of Gwynedd. They asserted their influence over lesser Welsh rulers and manipulated Welsh law in their own favour.

As the population of Wales, like that of the rest of Europe, was growing fast, the Llywelyns encouraged a more productive pattern of agriculture and settlement. To foster trade and exchange, they established little boroughs at places like Caernarfon and Pwllheli. The increased wealth thus created enabled them to finance their expensive aspirations.

Among their cherished projects were a number of castles capable of withstanding siege warfare. Nor were those castles built at Dolwyddelan, Dolforwyn or Castell-y-Bere mere copies of Marcher examples. They have been shown to have their own distinctive mode and style. Other Welsh princes, too, were active in castle-building at places like Dinefwr or Dryslwyn, and above all at Dinas Brân near Llangollen.

To defend these castles and to provide themselves with their armies, the Llywelyns organized a kind of native feudal aristocracy among their trusted followers. These clients were given lands on condition that they provided their princes with military backing. Other leading servants and diplomats were drawn from the highly-educated Welsh clerics belonging to monastic orders.

The high-water mark of the state-building policies of Gwynedd was reached at the Treaty of Montgomery of 1267. This agreement, reached between Henry III and Llywelyn ap Gruffudd, bestowed on the latter the

William Marshall's Coat of Arms. William, Earl of Pembroke, was one of the early Norman barons in Wales

Castle defences – archers and a stone thrower direct their missiles at attackers

proud title of Prince of Wales. Moreover, it recognized him as the overlord of the greater part of Wales. It was as near to a position of legal independence as ruler of Wales as he could realistically ever hope to come.

THE COMING OF THE CONCENTRIC CASTLE

The English response to the rise of Gwynedd is seen in the castle-building of the later 13th century. It also reflects the concentration of power in fewer but stronger hands. A smaller number of more powerful Marcher lords, backed by Edward I (king from 1272–1307), one of the strongest monarchs

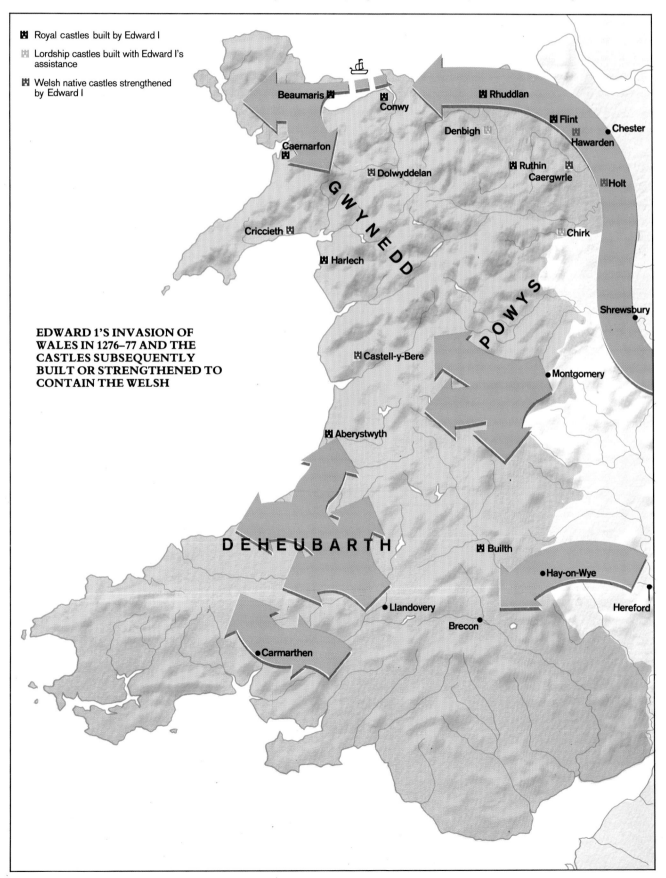

Royal castles built by Edward I

Lordship castles built with Edward I's assistance

Welsh native castles strengthened by Edward I

EDWARD 1'S INVASION OF WALES IN 1276–77 AND THE CASTLES SUBSEQUENTLY BUILT OR STRENGTHENED TO CONTAIN THE WELSH

ever to wear the English Crown, confronted the rising star of Gwynedd. The king and his lords had realized that all but the mightiest of castles were in danger from the Welsh; it was therefore no coincidence that around this time major works should have been undertaken on some of the most notable surviving castles. White Castle was heavily refortified by the king's agents in the 1260s or 1270s. The inner ward at Kidwelly was built by Payn de Chaworth c1275. Caerphilly, most significant of all the Marcher castles, was begun perhaps as early as 1268.

Caerphilly and Kidwelly were examples of the supreme achievement of medieval military architecture – the concentric castle. Such castles were provided with two sets of defences, one placed inside the other and each complete in itself. On the inside came the four-sided inner ward, with its walls taken up to an immense height and protected at each corner by a drum tower. The entrance(s) were sited between the towers and guarded by massive and elaborate gatehouses and sometimes by barbicans as well. Surrounding this inner ward, only a matter of yards away, was the outer ward. It, too, boasted a stout but lower curtain wall and round towers.

Kidwelly is one of the most pleasing of all Welsh castles in conception. So great was the natural strength of the site that when the outer ward and its formidable gatehouse were built, its curtain wall needed only to be a semi-circle and did not have to be taken round that part of the inner ward perched dramatically on a steep ravine.

Caerphilly, covering an area of around 30 acres, is, with Dover and possibly Windsor, one of the biggest castles in England and Wales. At its heart is the inner ward, an irregular quadrangle of huge curtain walls. Around it lies the outer ward with its lower battlemented walls designed to give a free field of fire from the inner ward. These two wards form only a part of its fortifications, however. Caerphilly is further protected by inner and outer moats, lakes, earthworks, and outer defensive platforms.

The man who built Caerphilly, Gilbert de Clare, Earl of Gloucester and Lord of Glamorgan, enjoyed an income about double that of the Prince of Gwynedd. But even his spending was quite overshadowed by that of Edward I, who, from 1276 onwards, embarked on a programme of castle-building unparalleled in scale and grandeur. Both Edward and de Clare intended that their castles should serve as a clear warning to the designs being nurtured by Llywelyn ap Gruffudd.

LLYWELYN AP GRUFFUDD (Llywelyn the Last) d1282

Llywelyn the Great, grandfather of Llywelyn the Last, had prospered during a time of English weakness. Although the latter Llywelyn was to achieve considerable distinction, an opposite scenario would ultimately apply as he – and all of Wales – suffered under a strong English king.

Llywelyn came to power at a time when King Henry III was in difficulty with his barons. Playing the game so familiar to his auspicious grandfather, Llywelyn exploited this weakness, forcing Henry to recognize him officially in the Treaty of Montgomery 1267 as Prince of Wales (a title that Llywelyn the Great had never, officially at any rate, been granted).

Llywelyn's distinction as Wales's first native prince contained the seeds of his own destruction. The rapidity of his rise to power matched its decline, largely brought about by England's new ruler, Edward I. Edward, unlike his predecessors, was a powerful, capable monarch. Llywelyn, misreading all the signs, refused to pay homage to the new king on his succession to the throne in 1272. Conflict became inevitable.

Edward had clearly expected the usual fealty from Llywelyn together with an acknowledgement of English overlordship over Wales. When Llywelyn refused, Edward attacked, and the Welsh prince was forced to make a humiliating peace under Edward's terms, as set out by the treaty of Aberconwy in 1277.

Llywelyn hung on to his title as Prince of Wales but suffered the indignity of a trip to London to pay homage. Whether or not the visit left any burning resentment and motive for revenge is debatable, though it is recorded that the Welsh party 'were much displeased at a new manner of living' and were mocked for their 'uncouth garb and appearance'.

However, Llywelyn was still a respected man, and his marriage to Eleanor de Montfort had English approval. Her death in childbirth a few years later was a portent of worse things to come.

In 1282 the Welsh rose in revolt and Llywelyn joined in protest against the insensitive behaviour of royal agents in Wales. Edward's second campaign against the Welsh was decisive. The Welsh forces were not organized for pitched battles, and Llywelyn was separated from his men near Builth Castle, recently rebuilt by Edward.

In one of those strange, accidental encounters that often crop up on the pages of history, Llywelyn was run through by a lance, killed during an unceremonious skirmish with an English trooper completely unaware of his opponent's princely identity. A monument beside the A483 at Cilmeri now marks this spot. Llywelyn's death was a shattering blow from which the Welsh never recovered. 'Oh God! That the sea might engulf the land!' cried the bards in despair. 'Why are we left to our long drawn weariness?'

Less poetically, it can be said that with the death of Llywelyn died all hopes of Welsh independence.

EDWARD I 1239–1307

Although he is generally remembered as the 'Hammer of the Scots', it is within Wales that King Edward I has most forcibly and yet so magnificently left his imprint.

Born in 1239, young Edward made an early start to his adventurous career by entering public life at the age of 12 and, at 14, marrying Eleanor of Castile, sister to the King of Spain. The chronicler, Nicholas Trevet, describes him as handsome, though having a slight droop of the left eyelid, with silvery hair that turned very dark in manhood and white as a swan in old age. His stature earned him the nickname 'Longshanks' for, in a common crowd, he stood head and shoulders above the rest. Devoting himself, in youth, to the practice of arms, these long limbs won him a reputation as a swordsman.

As to his character, he was a sincerely religious man, going early to the Crusade and, in later life, spending great sums of money on the Church. But he also had a streak of meanness that made him unready either to forgive or to forget. He was, however, very loyal to those he loved. Asked after King Henry's death why he had grieved more than for the death of his own small son, he answered that a son could be replaced, while a father could not.

Edward became king in 1272 at the age of 33, soon becoming a formidable ruler and a particularly able administrator and legislator. His insistently legalistic turn of mind was to colour all his actions at home and abroad and it accounted, in large part, for his wars in Wales, Gascony and Scotland.

Edward, with Llywelyn of Wales and Alexander of Scotland

Within the Welsh context, he is remembered for his conflicts with Llywelyn the Last and the magnificent chain of medieval castles that bear the Edwardian name.

On 28 November 1290, his beloved Queen Eleanor died suddenly near Lincoln. All the way back to London, the grieving king erected a beautiful stone cross at each of the twelve resting places along the journey.

Edward never returned to the Crusade, neither did he succeed in resolving matters in Scotland, dying on his way there in 1307 to conduct yet another campaign.

LLYWELYN AND EDWARD – ROUND ONE

The position conferred upon Llywelyn by the Treaty of Montgomery in 1267 was a temporary taste of power, lasting only ten years. In building it up he had already awakened opposition in more than one quarter. His situation was, at the best, one that would need careful nursing and yet Llywelyn seemed to be almost courting Edward's anger. He was reluctant to yield the homage and the money payments owing to the king, and he also arranged to marry Eleanor, the daughter of Edward's former arch-enemy, Simon de Montfort.

Just why Llywelyn misread the political signs of the times – whether he had been over-confident of his own strength or under-estimated his enemy's resources – we cannot be sure. What we do know is that his miscalculation, whatever the cause, brought down on his head severe retribution. By 1276–77 Edward had decided to settle accounts with Llywelyn. Acting as his own commander-in-chief he deployed the royal troops from the three bases of Chester, Montgomery and Carmarthen so as to coop the Welsh up within Gwynedd. By the summer of 1277 he used his fleet to cut them off from their corn-supply in Anglesey.

Llywelyn, confronted by such vastly superior odds, had no choice but to negotiate from a position of weakness. Humiliation predictably followed. The Treaty of Aberconwy (1277) stripped Llywelyn of the overlordship which he had won ten years earlier and deprived him of most of the territory he had won outside Gwynedd. All that was left to him was the devalued title of Prince of Wales, now almost empty of meaning.

THE EARLIEST EDWARDIAN CASTLES

Edward was determined that his victory should forever confine the lion of Gwynedd within his ancestral mountain lair. To hold him fast, the king had already begun the process of building powerful new castles at the critical forward bases of Flint, Rhuddlan, Aberystwyth and Builth. A huge labour force was recruited for the purpose which included at least 1,845 diggers, 790 carpenters and 320 masons.

When Edward started on these operations he was already a seasoned warrior and strategist who had experienced the rigours of war in France and the Holy Land as well as Britain. As a result he was familiar with the latest developments in the techniques of castle-building in all these lands. He was also well-acquainted with the nature of the planned fortress-towns of southern France, the 'bastides', and had a lively appreciation of the part they could play in holding down conquered territory.

The seal of Gilbert de Clare, the Norman lord who built mighty Caerphilly Castle

Furthermore, he took into his service one of the supreme military architects of the age, Master James of St George. This master builder was able to incorporate into the castles of North Wales the perfected refinements of medieval fortress-building. His outstanding legacy at Flint Castle is the great tower known as the 'donjon', whilst alongside the castle was built a new town in the pattern of a French 'bastide'.

Rhuddlan, too, received a new castle of concentric design and a new town girdled with earthworks. Here, a uniquely ambitious engineering task was undertaken, when the course of the River Clwyd was diverted and canalized for some two or three miles to give access to the sea.

Work on these first Edwardian castles went on from 1277 to the eve of the great Welsh revolt of March 1282. The very timing of that revolt itself can probably be explained in terms of Welsh alarm at the progress being made on the castles. There seems no doubt that the Welsh struck when the intensive summer season of building was about to begin.

THE FINAL CRISIS OF WELSH INDEPENDENCE

The sight of these towering Edwardian fortresses rising on the land and the oppressive rule of English officials provoked a great deal of justifiable Welsh discontent. Yet Llywelyn himself refused to be provoked. Ironically enough, it was not he who first rose in revolt but his younger brother, Dafydd, who had actually been Edward's ally in 1277. Once the Welsh banner had been raised in defiance, however, all Llywelyn's previous instincts and experience impelled him to place himself at the head of his people's cause.

This time it was a fight to the finish and as such was more bitter and protracted than the campaign of 1276–77. Edward's strategy was again

Methods of attack – the covered battering ram and trebuchet, or stone thrower (see also pages 18, 20)

The map shows Welsh fortune at a high point prior to the invasions of Edward I

WALES IN 1267
THE TREATY OF MONTGOMERY

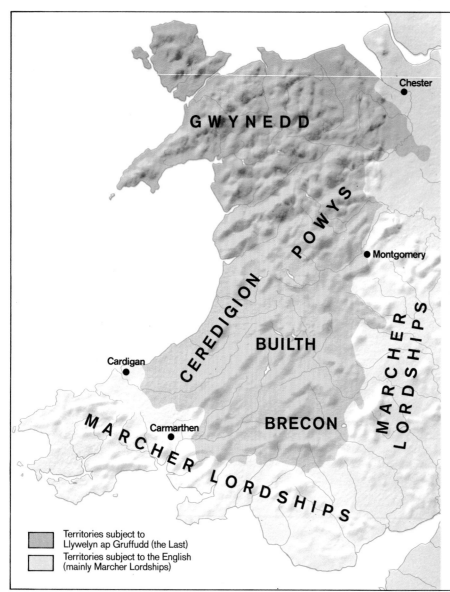

Territories subject to Llywelyn ap Gruffudd (the Last)

Territories subject to the English (mainly Marcher Lordships)

GWYNEDD

Chester

POWYS

CEREDIGION

Montgomery

Cardigan

BUILTH

MARCHER LORDSHIPS

Carmarthen

BRECON

MARCHER LORDSHIPS

much the same as before. He put pressure on the Welsh by land in West Wales and the Marches, and in North Wales despatched a sea-borne expedition to occupy Anglesey, while he sent an army along the coast to Conwy. Llywelyn attempted to break out to the south, lured perhaps by a report of possible new allies. In December 1282, cut off from his own men, he was struck down and killed, in one of those random incidents of war, without at first being recognized. A monument to Llywelyn still stands at Cilmeri, near Builth Wells, marking the place of his death.

Even before Llywelyn the Last's death, Edward had already determined to do something unprecedented in Wales – to fight a winter campaign, whatever the difficulties. His tenacity was rewarded. In January 1283 he captured Dolwyddelan Castle, focal point of Snowdonia's communications, and so opened the road to all parts of Gwynedd. Two other major Welsh strongpoints, Dolbadarn and Castell-y-Bere, were later overcome. Llywelyn's brother, Dafydd, was captured and executed.

For two centuries the Welsh had fought with the utmost bravery but the odds against them had finally been too great. Gwynedd had at last been crushed by the might of Edward I and its princes killed. With them died the political independence of Wales.

Edward had won a more complete victory over the Welsh in battle than any previous English king. But he was realist enough to know that Welsh princes had been beaten before, only to reappear or be replaced disconcertingly quickly. This time he intended that the defeat should be final. No Welsh successor to Llywelyn would be recognized; Gwynedd, always a prime source of trouble, would be brought under direct royal rule. An unprecedented programme of castle-building would ensure its permanent subordination to alien English authority.

The map shows Wales after Edward I's successful campaigns against her in 1276–77 and 1283–84

WALES IN 1284
THE STATUTE OF RHUDDLAN

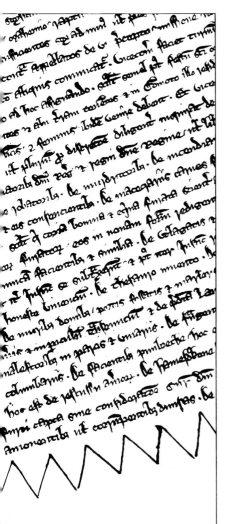

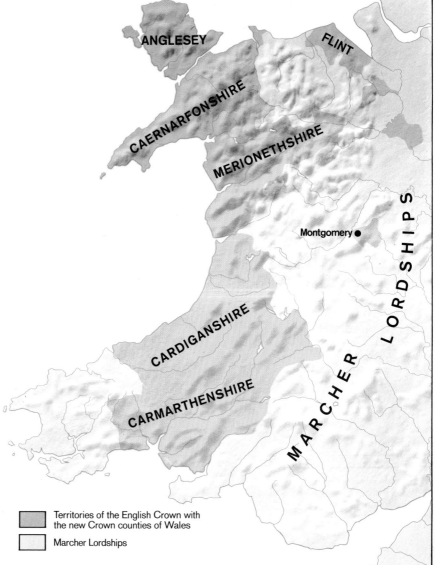

ANGLESEY

FLINT

CAERNARFONSHIRE

MERIONETHSHIRE

MARCHER LORDSHIPS

Montgomery ●

CARDIGANSHIRE

CARMARTHENSHIRE

Territories of the English Crown with the new Crown counties of Wales

Marcher Lordships

THE EDWARDIAN CASTLES OF NORTH WALES

In the 20 years between 1276 and 1296 Edward I built, or inspired the building of, no fewer than 17 castles in Wales. Three were remodelled from earlier Welsh ones – Criccieth, Dolwyddelan and Castell-y-Bere. Four more, Hawarden, Denbigh, Holt and Chirk, were put up by his trusted lieutenants at his instigation along the lines of his own castles. The finest of them, Denbigh, was built by Henry de Lacy, Earl of Lincoln, who began work in 1282. Though it is now in ruins, enough remains to show what an impressive building it was, with its immensely strong three-towered gatehouse modelled on that of Caernarfon.

The remaining ten castles (Flint, Rhuddlan, Aberystwyth, Builth, Ruthin, Caergwrle, Conwy, Caernarfon, Harlech and Beaumaris) were new ones of the first rank, some of the finest ever built. Included among them are Edward's four best castles – Conwy, Caernarfon, Harlech and Beaumaris. The first three were begun in 1283 and Beaumaris in 1295, after the dangerous rising of Madog ap Llywelyn. All were built near the sea, so

Coat of Arms of de Lacy of Denbigh, Earl of Lincoln

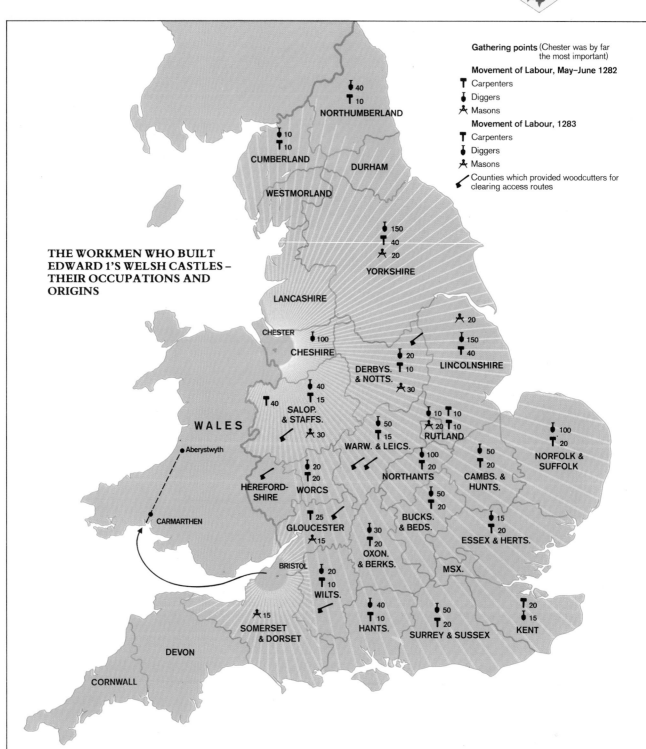

THE WORKMEN WHO BUILT EDWARD 1'S WELSH CASTLES – THEIR OCCUPATIONS AND ORIGINS

HARRI TUDUR
(Henry VII) 1457–1509

Harri, or Henry, embodies the fickle, ironic, unpredictable, often perverse shift of history. Just as Wales was at its lowest ebb soon after Owain Glyndwr's disastrous uprising, and suffering the miseries of the Wars of the Roses, the unthinkable happened – a Welshman acceded to the English throne.

When Henry VII became King of England in 1485, the days of an entirely separate Wales were numbered. By 1536 the Act of Union between England and Wales inextricably linked the two countries, so that Welshmen could perform the 'kind of public and necessary functions as well as Englishmen'.

Forgetting for the moment his influence on Welsh fortunes, Henry is, of course, an important national character as the initiator of the Tudor dynasty. The medieval genealogy is typically tortuous, but of one thing we can be sure: the Tudor line originated in Wales. Henry was born on 28 January 1457 in Pembroke Castle of an Anglesey family.

The young Henry became, during the long-running Wars of the Roses, the Lancastrian claimant to the throne. The rest is well-known. After a stirring march through Wales he defeated Richard III at Bosworth, thus ending the war and introducing a new period in Welsh history.

So what kind of man was Henry? He was conscious of his Welsh roots, and enjoyed many of the things Welshmen are famous for – music, poetry, literature and sport. He never forgot his Welsh heritage, after his accession employing heralds to trace his ancestry, rewarding Welshmen with important government and ecclesiastic posts, and flying the Red Dragon flag.

Although he was a wise and tolerant man, his popularity was not widespread. Within Wales, though, his position was secure. The bards saw him in almost mythological terms as a saviour figure, a new Messiah, the legendary Arthurian deliverer of Wales. Whilst in reality not scaling such heights, Henry was a very gifted leader, and his rise to power did undoubtedly bring a much-needed sense of purpose and self-confidence to a badly-shaken country.

Coat of Arms of Edward of Caernarfon, the Prince of Wales and son of Edward I

that they could be supplied by water without needing perilous expeditions by land to bring food or reinforcements. Huge though they were, they only needed a garrison of 30 to man them. All four are largely intact and constitute one of the most remarkable groups of medieval monuments to be seen anywhere. Their beauty, seen against the North Wales landscape of sea and mountain, is as memorable as their power.

Caernarfon, intended to be the centre of royal government and a palace for the king's eldest son, the Prince of Wales, is a castle of matchless architectural splendour and imperial allusion. With its polygonal towers and decorative horizontal layers of pink stone, it may well have been modelled on the imperial style of Constantinople's Theodosian Wall.

Harlech and Beaumaris are superb examples of the mature concentric castle. Harlech, perched proud and lofty above the waves of Tremadog Bay, with its breathtaking backcloth of windswept hills and rocky crags, must surely occupy one of the most romantic and photogenic of all castle sites. Beaumaris, though never quite completed, dominates the north bank of the Menai Strait and remains one of the most perfect instances of the concentrated might of the concentric castles.

Still surviving, too, are some of the fortified town walls built to defend the boroughs created alongside these castles. High above 'old Conwy's foaming flood' stand not only the magnificent castle but also some of the best-preserved medieval town walls in Europe. They were themselves an extension of the castle's own defences. Nothing could illustrate more perfectly the interlocking roles envisaged for castle and borough in safeguarding security, commerce and conquest.

The cost of this building programme was cripplingly high and may even have been so vast as to slow down drastically Edward's plans for conquering Scotland. Some £95–100,000 was spent on Edward's Welsh castles between 1277 and 1330, more than 80 per cent of it before 1301. Caernarfon Castle, town walls, quay and other buildings alone cost £27,000. Conwy and Beaumaris accounted for £14–15,000 apiece, and Rhuddlan for about £9,200. In so far as an equivalent sum in modern money can be given, this investment represented about £15 million.

A painting by G Childs of the Dowlais Ironworks, Merthyr Tydfil in 1840

Cyfarthfa Castle was built with the wealth of the Industrial Revolution

A Victorian genius. William Burges, the mastermind behind the reconstruction of Cardiff Castle

At Raglan, the Third Earl of Worcester (1548–89) began work on the splendid hall and long gallery. His son, the Fourth Earl (1589–1628) added summer-houses and garden walks set with statues. The Stradling family remodelled St Donat's Castle in the Vale of Glamorgan into a charming and attractive country house. In Gower Sir Rhys Mansel raised the four-storeyed building at Oxwich Castle with its large and airy mullioned windows. At Carew Castle in West Wales Sir John Perrott refashioned the medieval barracks into a palatial and peaceful mansion.

Up in North Wales the Middleton family acquired the former Edwardian stronghold at Chirk, where generations of them have lived as country gentlemen until our own day. Powis Castle, Welshpool, was bought in 1587 by the Herbert family, who then began the long process of turning it into one of the most sumptuous of the stately homes of Wales.

THE TRUMPET OF WAR SOUNDS AGAIN

In spite of all the peaceful advances of the Tudor era, the military significance of the castle had not entirely vanished. Not even the greater internal stability, nor the development of artillery had finally rendered them superfluous. When relations between King and Parliament deteriorated to the point of Civil War in 1642, many castles became major military bases once more.

Conwy was 'repaired, revictualled and supplied with ammunition' for the king by one of the borough's own sons, John Williams, Archbishop of York. Caernarfon, three times closely besieged by the Parliamentarians, successfully withstood their attacks, as did Harlech. Montgomery also attracted powerful forces to its defence and attack, and was the scene of fierce fighting before being won by Parliamentarian forces in 1644.

Raglan endured one of the most hotly-contested and best-recorded sieges of the war in the summer of 1646. Headquarters of the Earl of Worcester, one of Charles I's wealthiest and most loyal supporters, it was finally besieged by 3,500 men under Sir Thomas Fairfax. Its surrender on 19 August 1646 virtually brought the first Civil War to an end.

In the second Civil War of 1648, at Pembroke Castle it took the all-conquering Oliver Cromwell himself to bring the garrison to its knees. Neither here nor at Raglan had the use of gunpowder made a decisive difference, so strongly constructed were the old stone defences.

CASTLES OF THE INDUSTRIAL ERA

From the end of the 18th century onwards the Industrial Revolution completely changed the life of Wales. The population of the country, flocking into the teeming new industrial districts, increased beyond measure. Industries like iron, copper, coal and slate boomed prodigiously, and ports, canals, roads and railways flourished as never before. Huge fortunes were made by energetic entrepreneurs, a few of whom used their money to build, extend or re-fashion castles. Even in the modern age of manufacture there were those who saw the castle as the symbol par excellence of wealth and status.

One of the earliest was William Crawshay, the 'iron king' of Merthyr Tydfil, then the world's greatest centre of iron making. In 1825 he built Cyfarthfa Castle in its park of 600 acres overlooking his successful works. It proclaimed the arrival of the new barons of industry.

Some years later, between 1827 and 1837, the slate magnate GH Douglas-Pennant and his architect, Hopper, went even further. At an astronomical cost of £500,000 he erected Penrhyn Castle on the site of an ancient castle near Bangor to a design which adapted Norman architecture to the needs of the industrial world.

But the most remarkable of all was the Third Marquess of Bute, who succeeded his father, the creator of modern Cardiff, in 1848. Together with his architect, William Burges, he rebuilt in unique style both Cardiff Castle and also the unbelievably picturesque Castell Coch near Taff's Well. Between them they were responsible for redecorating many of Cardiff's principal rooms in a delightful if over-romanticized vein in what they believed to be an appropriately medieval style. They linked the oldest building in Wales's 20th-century capital not only with its medieval past but with its still more ancient Roman fort. What could better exemplify the continuity of history?

THE CASTLES
A to Z

A–Z CASTLE GAZETTEER

The following section of the book lists, in alphabetical order, 82 Welsh castles. They have been chosen because of their interest to the visitor, their historic significance to the reader, or a combination of both.

This is not, of course, a comprehensive list. The gazetteer concentrates on Wales's significant *stone* castles. Motte and bailey earthwork sites (see page 73) are not included here. Neither are sites which may be in a poor or overgrown state, with little or no upstanding remains.

Special features describing historic figures and themes appear throughout the gazetteer. Wherever possible, each one is placed close to the castle(s) with which it is particularly associated.

Please remember the following points when planning any visit:

OPENING TIMES A convenient system of standard hours applies to many castles in the care of the Welsh Office. Some of the sites listed, by

12	*Gatehouse*
13	*Great tower*
14	*Hall*
15	*Hoards*
16	*Hornwork*
17	*Inner ward*
18	*Keep*
19	*Lancet windows*
20	*Machicolations*
21	*Merlons*
22	*Moat*
23	*Outer ward*
24	*Pentise*
25	*Portcullis*
26	*Postern*
27	*Solar*
28	*Turret*

nature of their remains and locations, are freely accessible at all times. In many cases, we recommend that you make enquiries beforehand to avoid disappointment – this is a good general rule, since all opening arrangements are subject to change (please contact local Wales Tourist Board Tourist Information Centres). A small number of sites are closed to the public, though may usually be viewed from the surrounding area. Please respect all opening and viewing arrangements.

CHARGES Entry to many castles is completely free. Entry fees, when applicable, will vary site-to-site.

MAP REFERENCES These relate to the maps on pages 180 to 190. More detailed booklets are available from many of the listed sites, especially those in the care of the Welsh Office.

ARCHITECTURE EXPLAINED
Throughout the gazetteer, terms which may be unfamiliar are used to describe various features of castle architecture. Each term is explained below on an amalgamated castle, where all the architectural features of Welsh castles have been incorporated.

ABERGAVENNY CASTLE

The ruins of the castle where a Norman lord treacherously murdered his Welsh guests now stand in a peaceful public park in Gwent.

Hamelin de Ballon built an earthwork castle here, which was to be the head of his newly conquered lordship, on the site of the Roman fort of Gobannium. The castle was later strengthened through stone additions, and in the 19th century a folly was built on top of the motte. (An adjacent house now contains an attractive local museum.)

It was in this castle, in 1175 that William de Braose invited the local Welsh leaders to a feast and then murdered them. The Welsh later sacked the castle in retaliation and de Braose fell out with the equally ruthless King John who stripped him of his lands and castles and starved his wife and children to death in Windsor Castle. De Braose died in beggary in France.

Virtually all the surviving stonework is late 13th or early 14th century. Access to the castle is through a gatehouse and long gate passage projecting out from the curtain wall. To the right, the curtain wall runs down to a large multi-angular tower. Between gate and tower are traces of a probable hall.

In the Civil War, Abergavenny was garrisoned for the king, but in July 1645 the habitable parts were burnt and the garrison 'drawn out and quitted', though Charles I was there again in September in a last desperate effort to get the Monmouthshire gentry to support his failing cause.

IN CARE OF local authority

OPEN dawn to dusk

ADMISSION free

LOCATION south of the town centre

MAP REFERENCE 5 SO3014

COUNTY Gwent

Abergavenny Castle – within whose walls the Welsh Lords of Dyfnwal were murdered

Gilbert of Clare built a castle near the mouth of the River Ystwyth in 1110. Its banks and ditches can still be seen on a hill just over a mile south of the modern town. It was abandoned after being burnt down and rebuilt several times. A stone castle was built on another site and yet another during Edward's first campaign in Wales in 1277, still called Aberystwyth Castle although built on a new site on the sea-coast.

Edmund of Lancaster, the king's brother, took charge of operations. English workmen from the West Country were brought in by sea from Bristol. The goods of condemned Jews in that city provided some of the funds for building materials. By 1297 there were over 1,300 at work on the castle and town wall. Standards seem to have been poor, however, and the Welsh destroyed the unfinished works. Ten years later rebuilding was complete, at a cost of £4,300.

Aberystwyth's storm-torn tower, which is one of the earliest Edward I built in Wales

BARRY CASTLE

The ruins of Barry Castle are 13th and 14th century now consolidated by the local authority. From the earlier Norman earthwork castle on this site came the family of Giraldus Cambrensis.

The medieval chronicler Giraldus Cambrensis proudly told his readers how Barry had once belonged and given its name to his ancestors, the de Barri family. His father, William de Barri of Manorbier in Pembrokeshire, came from a family which had moved westwards from Glamorgan.

Early maps suggest that the present ruins may stand on the site of an earlier Norman earthwork castle which was the ancestral home of the de Barri family. Standing beside a road on the crest of a hill within the modern town, they consist of an L-shaped block of the 13th and 14th centuries, which seems to have occupied two sides of a squarish enclosure surrounded by a ditch.

The earliest part of the masonry castle is the eastern block, at right angles to the road. This contained a large hall with a solar

Scant remains of Barry Castle

block, originally two storeys in height and containing the castle's private apartments. In the 14th century a second two-storey wing was added at right angles to it, with a gatehouse, which forms the most interesting part of the present remains, tucked into the angle with the earlier hall. The gatehouse has a portcullis groove and traces of a chapel on its upper floor. Some time before 1622 a cottage, known later as 'Castle House', was inserted into the south wing.

IN CARE OF local authority

OPEN at all times

ADMISSION free

LOCATION In SW end of town

MAP REFERENCE 4 ST1067

COUNTY Dyfed

ABERYSTWYTH CASTLE

Several towers remain of Edward I's first castle in Wales, which took twelve years to build. After withstanding several sieges it was finally blown up by the Roundheads.

The site used is the promontory where the River Rheidol flows into the sea. Aberystwyth's plan is like two diamonds, one inside the other (the castle at Rhuddlan, built at nearly the same time, has a similar plan). Originally, there were round towers at all the corners, but the highest tower now left is a wall-tower, solid except for a passage leading through an outer gate to the outer ward (where the War Memorial now stands). On the opposite side, facing the town, are the remains of the twin-towered Great Gatehouse, with a smaller and lower outer gate in front of it, like Harlech. The square mound in front of the gate was a

stone barbican which cost £50 to build.

In 1294 the English custodian of the castle was murdered, but his widow defended the castle for six months until a seaborne relief expedition arrived. Garrison numbers were steadily reduced during the 14th century, however, and Owain Glyndwr captured the castle in 1404, sealing his treaty with Charles VI of France here. Prince Henry (later King Henry V) had to bring up a train of artillery to recapture it. Aberystwyth was strong enough to stand a siege in the Civil War but eventually, after the garrison had surrendered, the castle was blown up to end its life as a fortification, like many others.

IN CARE OF local authority

OPEN all reasonable times

ADMISSION free

LOCATION in public park on seafront

MAP REFERENCE 6 SN5882

COUNTY Dyfed

BEAUMARIS

Beaumaris, begun in 1295, was the last and largest castle to be built in Wales by Edward I. Here, his architect Master James of St George has perfected the ultimate in symmetrical concentric design, surrounded by a water-filled moat with its own protected access to the sea. Though planned to have lavish accommodation, the money dried up before it could be completed and it never reached its full height. However, Beaumaris remains the best example of a concentric castle in Britain with fine views across the Menai Strait.

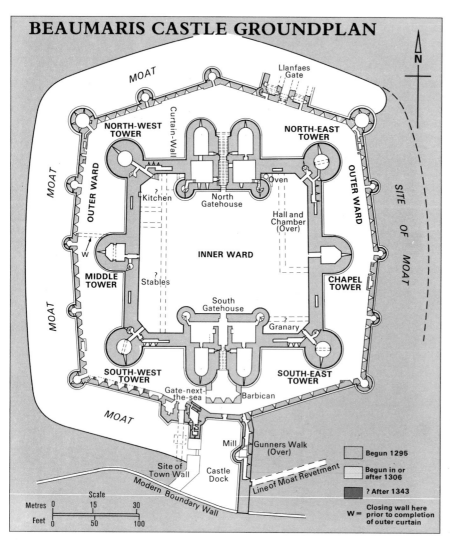

BEAUMARIS CASTLE GROUNDPLAN

N

MOAT

Llanfaes Gate

NORTH-WEST TOWER

Curtain-Wall

NORTH-EAST TOWER

MOAT

OUTER WARD

Kitchen

North Gatehouse

Oven

OUTER WARD

SITE OF MOAT

Hall and Chamber (Over)

INNER WARD

W

MIDDLE TOWER

Stables

CHAPEL TOWER

MOAT

South Gatehouse

SOUTH-WEST TOWER

Granary

SOUTH-EAST TOWER

Gate-next-the-sea

Barbican

MOAT

Mill

Gunners Walk (Over)

Begun 1295

Site of Town Wall

Castle Dock

Line of Moat Revetment

Begun in or after 1306

Modern Boundary Wall

? After 1343

Scale

Metres 0   15   30

Feet 0   50   100

W = Closing wall here prior to completion of outer curtain

The ground plan of Beaumaris clearly shows the oblique turn made necessary to reach the gatehouse once the outer gates were broached, thus putting the enemy at a distinct disadvantage

A drawbridge gave access to the 'Gate next the Sea', one of the 14 obstacles an attacker had to negotiate before reaching the inner ward

Although King Edward I of England might well have considered Beaumaris to be his finest creation after Caernarfon, today this castle is perhaps the least known and least visited of that mighty group of fortresses constructed after his second campaign against Wales in 1282. Those other castles, at Conwy, Caernarfon and Harlech, seem to clamour stridently for attention, each advancing its own undeniable claim of power, dominance or location. Beaumaris, on the other hand, has an altogether lower profile. It is not blessed with the impact of situation which the others all possess. Neither has it been, in recent times, along any major route, so it has not received the recognition that it unquestionably deserves.

The coast road running north east from Menai Bridge passes under an umbrella of trees on its way to Beaumaris, an unexpectedly English looking town with its clustered Georgian façades lining the seafront. Only at the far end of the main street does the castle, quite unannounced, come suddenly into view, its low, squat walls and close-set drum towers neatly reflected in the waters of its moat. Even at this distance it belies its proportions. But in walking around the moat, or entering through the outer gate into the inner ward, the sheer size of the immense castle soon becomes apparent. An enormous square of open, grass-covered courtyard unrolls beyond the narrow confines of the gatehouse. Here, inside its walls until not so many years ago, lay four good-size tennis courts, with plenty of room to spare.

MADOG'S REVOLT

It is across the water of the Menai Strait, to Caernarfon, that we must look first for events that were directly responsible for the creation of Beaumaris. At the end of September 1294, the Welsh in the north rose unexpectedly, under their leader Madog ap Llywelyn, spurred on by the threat of compulsory enlistment for a war in Gascony. They directed their main efforts at the unfinished defences of Caernarfon, which they took, killing

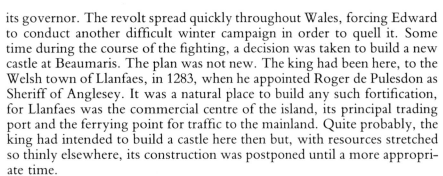

The castle as seen by an 18th-century engraver

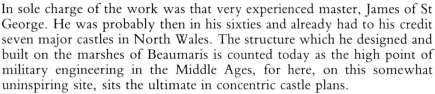

its governor. The revolt spread quickly throughout Wales, forcing Edward to conduct another difficult winter campaign in order to quell it. Some time during the course of the fighting, a decision was taken to build a new castle at Beaumaris. The plan was not new. The king had been here, to the Welsh town of Llanfaes, in 1283, when he appointed Roger de Pulesdon as Sheriff of Anglesey. It was a natural place to build any such fortification, for Llanfaes was the commercial centre of the island, its principal trading port and the ferrying point for traffic to the mainland. Quite probably, the king had intended to build a castle here then but, with resources stretched so thinly elsewhere, its construction was postponed until a more appropriate time.

On 10 April 1295, that time arrived. The English pioneer corps threw a pontoon bridge across the Menai Strait near Bangor and the whole army, together with a huge labour force, crossed over to the island and set up headquarters at Llanfaes. The entire Welsh population of the town was summarily evicted some twelve miles away to Newborough. Near to the old town was a 'fair marsh,' far more extensive than now and covered in bulrushes. On this unpromising ground building of the new castle of Beaumaris was begun.

ARCHITECT AND PLAN

In sole charge of the work was that very experienced master, James of St George. He was probably then in his sixties and already had to his credit seven major castles in North Wales. The structure which he designed and built on the marshes of Beaumaris is counted today as the high point of military engineering in the Middle Ages, for here, on this somewhat uninspiring site, sits the ultimate in concentric castle plans.

The idea of the concentric castle, with one high ring of defence inside a lower one, had gradually been growing since the late 1260's, when it was first perfected at Caerphilly in South Wales. It had great advantages of economy, unity and compactness over the older keep and bailey system, but its major asset was the tremendous increase in firepower which it provided. Defenders on the great inner walls could fire their missiles with ease over the heads of their fellows on the outside. Wherever possible, this approach had been adopted, in one form or another, at most of Edward I's Welsh castles. But only at the last of them, here in Beaumaris, does the system demonstrate its advantages with such force and yet such elegance.

In modern terminology, Beaumaris was a greenfield site. Unlike so many other places, it did not have an earlier existing fortification upon which to build. Nor was there any convenient natural feature of geography that could be exploited. With only the flat marsh and the sea at its disposal, the new castle would have to rely exclusively upon its own man-made defences.

Their first line is a wet moat of 18ft width which once encircled the whole castle but today it is no longer quite complete. At its southern end there stood a tidal dock for shipping, connected by a short channel to the sea. Here, ships of 40 tons laden weight could sail right up to the castle, tie up at the iron ring which still projects from its walls and unload their cargo straight into the outer ward through the door in its northern side. The dock was protected by the shooting deck on Gunners' Walk and here too lay the sluice gates, to control water levels, and a corn mill, which utilized the flow.

ACCESS DIFFICULTIES

Immediately across the moat is the low, eight-sided curtain wall of the outer ward. The battlements have nearly gone, but the circuit is complete enough to see that this curtain, together with its 16 towers, must have provided something like 300 firing positions at two or three levels. To enter the castle in the 13th century, one would have had to negotiate no less than 14 separate obstacles. Across the moat, a drawbridge gave access to the outer ward, through the Gate Next the Sea, with its murder holes and its stout wooden doors. Once through here, a cunningly devised oblique right turn gives access to the barbican and its gate while, inside the main inner gatehouse passage, there were two sets of wooden doors, an arrangement of spyholes, three portcullises and three groups of murder holes to negotiate before the inner ward was gained.

The medieval advantages of Beaumaris's concentric plan can still be appreciated for this castle approaches the ultimate goal of defence: it would have been virtually impossible to take by storm and, with its protected dock giving access to the sea, could not have been starved into surrender. The elegance of Master James's design can best be appreciated from the air, for Beaumaris is quite regular and symmetrical, combining with great skill and virtuosity the twin requirements of defence and accommodation.

An engraving showing the north entrance to Beaumaris

LAVISH ACCOMMODATION

It is to that accommodation we turn next, for here the intention seems to have been particularly generous. Both gatehouses of the inner ward were to have had grand suites of state rooms at their rear, much as at Harlech. The north gate, on the far side of the inner ward, was only completed as far as the Great Hall to its first floor level and the projected second storey was never built. Even as it stands today, with its five blank and gaping windows, it dominates the courtyard. Had it been finished, it would have towered to twice its present height. Another block of equal size was planned for the south gate, but this was never to rise further than its footings. The courtyard itself was originally lined, to east and west, by building ranges – stables and kitchens on one side, a further vast hall block on the other leading to the chapel – although here again we cannot be sure that they were ever built to full height. The six towers of the inner ward also had their chambers and all were interconnected by wall passages, so familiar to visitors to Caernarfon.

As at Caernarfon, one is left wondering who all this lavish accommodation was designed for. The answer may simply be that, in 1295, such luxury was thought to be a necessary requirement for the twin households of a king and, if he should marry again, his queen. At this time, the Prince of Wales was fast approaching marriageable age and, when that day arrived, might also need to put up at Beaumaris. There were also various royal officers to consider, from the constable and sheriff downwards, who would occupy the less grand quarters.

Master James of St George's great castle at Beaumaris was never finished. Events outside of Wales were to overtake its construction. The enormous injection of £6,736, which had supported 2,600 labourers in that first year of 1295, dwindled all too soon, with campaign demands from Gascony and Scotland. By 1298, the money dried up altogether. Despite minor building works in later times, it was never completed as originally intended and so it sits to this day, the proud blueprint never quite realized.

IN CARE OF Welsh Office

OPEN all reasonable times (standard hours)

ADMISSION some charge

LOCATION eastern end of town

MAP REFERENCE 10 SH6176

COUNTY Gwynedd

MASTER JAMES OF ST GEORGE

One can hardly read the accounts of the great castles of King Edward I without noting the constant references to James of St George, master mason. Who was this ubiquitous character and what exactly did he do?

A medieval master mason was, like a modern architect, responsible both for planning a building and superintending its construction. As for Master James, the records tell us very little about him personally, but his life history can be read between the lines.

Probably born c 1230, he is first mentioned in Savoy (on the French-Swiss-Italian border) working at the castle of Yverdon with his father, Master John, in 1261. Later, he worked at another great castle in Savoy, St Georges d'Espéranche (from which he took his name) and it was here, on a visit in June 1273, that Edward I must have encountered him.

Evidently James impressed the king for, in April 1278, he turned up in England, on his way to Wales 'to ordain the works of the castles there'. He was paid the high daily wage of two shillings (a weekly amount for an ordinary mason) and, on 20 October 1284, was granted three shillings a day for life, with a pension of 1s 6d for his wife, Ambrosia, if she should survive him. This was a high reward indeed, unequalled throughout the medieval period and it was further enhanced by his three-year appointment, in 1290, as Constable of Harlech Castle, which carried a yearly salary of 100 marks.

Although from 1298–1305 he worked in Scotland, it is in Wales that his services are most apparent, for he was directly responsible for at least 12 castles there. He was granted a life

pension in 1295, together with the manor of Mostyn in North East Wales, and he died sometime between his last mentions in the records, in September 1307, and May 1309.

BEAUPRE CASTLE

Located deep in the Vale of Glamorgan, Beaupre (also know as Old Beaupre) was the home of the Bassets. It is part medieval, part Elizabethan manor house. The richly-carved gate and decorated porch are its special splendour.

Beaupre, pronounced locally as 'Bewper', lies in seclusion amid the unspoilt countryside of the Vale of Glamorgan, through which runs the River Thaw

Beaupre, in its secluded setting in the pastoral Vale of Glamorgan was the home of the Bassets, one of the major gentry families of Glamorgan. Medieval Bassets built the earliest hall, with a defensible tower block at one end. But it was the Basset family of the Elizabethan period who built most of what we now see, including Richard Basset's gate and porch, both of fine Wiltshire or Somerset freestone in an Elizabethan version of classical Roman architecture. The outer gate bears the initials of Richard and of his first wife Catherine Mansel, with the date 1586 and their motto (in Welsh) 'Better Death than Shame'.

In the courtyard through the gate stands, on the left, a tall gabled block which began life as a medieval tower house. Richard Basset's Inner Porch, straight ahead, has been added to the (much altered) medieval hall. The courtyard itself is also an Elizabethan addition and the buildings around it have large mullioned windows. The central shield above the doorway of the porch carries Richard's arms quartered with those of his third wife, Katherine Johns.

One of the four small decorations set around the shield is a concealed peep hole. Below, an inscription on three small panels tells how Richard and Katherine built the porch 'with the tonnes', a reference to chimneys which have now vanished. At the sides, each of the three orders of classical architecture appears in its correct place – Doric below, Ionic beside the shield and Corinthian flanking the window above. The

room above the porch was quite evidently the haunt of some early 17th-century schoolboys, for its plaster carries a collection of graffiti, including a series of ships, one a pinnace of about 200 tons with a row of eight guns and flying the flag of St George. There are also ranks of pikes and muskets which seem to represent the tertias (companies) of a regiment in battle array, together with the names of Thomas and Rob Williams and the date 1632.

Ten years later the Civil War broke out and the boys may have experienced the reality of warfare. Sir Thomas Basset, an active Royalist, was captured by Parliament when Hereford fell to them, and lost most of his money in the war. His son, William Basset, dissipated much of what was left at the court of Charles II. By the end of the century, Bassets no longer lived at Beaupre, though the south range remained in use as a farmhouse and is still lived in.

IN CARE OF Welsh Office

OPEN at all times

ADMISSION free

LOCATION 1m SW of St Hilary, nr Cowbridge

MAP REFERENCE 4 ST0172

COUNTY South Glamorgan

Brecon Castle is cleft in two by a road. The ruin shown above, now in a hotel garden, is the medieval hall block

Castle of medieval bishops, Llawhaden

BISHOP OF ST DAVID'S CASTLE

A great fortified palace at Llawhaden, built and finally dismantled by the bishops of St David's. Enough remains to show the lifestyle and organization of an important medieval household.

When the medieval chronicler Giraldus Cambrensis visited the palace of his uncle, Bishop David FitzGerald of St David's at Llawhaden, he described it as a castle. The moat of that time survives, but the bank and palisade within have been levelled and covered by a palace built by David Martyn, bishop from 1293 to 1328. Martyn's palace consists of a series of buildings set out around a five-sided courtyard, strengthened with angle towers.

The front of the gatehouse stands to its full height, but is so thin that it looks like stage scenery. It was built as an extension to provide extra rooms to Martyn's Gate, which is the square block on the right of the passageway leading into the courtyard. Once inside, the Great Hall faces you: to your left are the bakehouse and barracks, to your right the visitors' lodgings and chapel.

In its day, the hall on the first floor, reached by a great staircase covered by a wooden porch, must have been imposing. The vaulted rooms below provided storage. To the right of the hall were the bishop's private rooms in a wing at the dais (upper) end. At the other (service) end of the hall was the buttery and pantry, for the preparation of drink and food respectively. Beyond lay the kitchen proper (notice the kitchen sink drain running through the castle wall). Further to the left is a large bakehouse (note the ovens) next to the well which is over 100ft deep.

A palace-castle like this probably only had a small permanent garrison of mercenaries, but they needed separate accommodation from the bishop and his guests. The two-storey block between bakehouse and gatehouse provided a small barracks and kitchen, for sleeping and eating in the same room was quite common in the Middle Ages.

Visitors would have stayed in apartments on the other side of the entrance. There are four sets in all, two on each floor, each with a large room plus a bedchamber (with latrine) in an angle tower. Such two-roomed apartments are commonly found in castles meant to receive important guests from time to time.

The Chapel of the Blessed Virgin stands between the hall and the lodgings, with rooms for the priest in the angle tower. Another tower contains the stair (note the carved heads at the entrance) to both the chapel and the bishop's finance office.

After more than 250 years of use, the castle was dismantled and lead stripped from the roof by Bishop Barlow, either because he wanted to remove his see to Carmarthen, or because he needed the money for his daughter's dowry!

IN CARE OF Welsh Office

OPEN all reasonable times (standard hours)

ADMISSION some charge

LOCATION 3m NW of Narberth at Llawhaden

MAP REFERENCE 2 SN0717

COUNTY Dyfed

BRECON CASTLE

Humphrey de Bohun's Great Hall is an impressive reminder of the medieval lordship of Brecon. Its shell now houses a hotel.

After Bernard of Neufmarché had defeated and killed the Welsh King of Brycheiniog, he built a motte and bailey castle on a low hill at the confluence of the Usk and Honddu rivers. This became the caput (head) of his new lordship, though centuries later the principal castle of Brycheiniog was unceremoniously cut in half by a modern road. To one side, in the garden of the Bishop of Swansea and Brecon, is Bernard's motte, with the remains of the Ely Tower, a 12th-century polygonal shell keep rather like that at nearby Tretower, on its top. On the opposite side of the road, behind the Castle of Brecon Hotel, is Humphrey de Bohun's hall block of about 1280, built soon after he had recovered Brecon from Llywelyn ap Gruffudd ('the Last').

The pillars of its vaulted ground floor survive in an inner courtyard of the hotel. The Great Hall, on the first floor, once had a magnificent timber roof and a polygonal latrine turret was added about 1300 to serve the numerous household. The hall was evidently much admired, for it was copied locally both at Crickhowell and Bronllys. Later, Brecon belonged to the Dukes of Buckingham, but Henry VIII's suspicions of his grandeur cost the last Duke his head and in 1521 Brecon finally passed to the Crown.

Documents and early pictures reveal a stone curtain wall with three towers, a western Great Gatehouse, a small postern gate on the line of the road leading up from the bridge and a chapel of St Nicholas within the castle. All are now gone.

IN CARE OF private owner

OPEN viewing from surrounding area only

LOCATION on hill above town

MAP REFERENCE 4 SO0429

COUNTY Powys

Bronllys Castle, a stone keep upon an early Norman motte boasting fine views

BRONLLYS CASTLE

The round keep of Bronllys was built to guard its mountainous border territory against the Welsh, but was re-modelled by a Welshman who had managed to become a Marcher lord. A well-preserved site.

Among the knights who aided Bernard of Neufmarché in his conquest of Brycheiniog from the Welsh was Richard FitzPons of Clifford in western Herefordshire. As a reward he was granted a tract of mountainous territory known as Cantref Selyf. To protect his newly-won territory he built a motte and bailey castle at the junction of the Llynfi and the Dulais rivers. This was of the usual Norman pattern, with a timber tower and surrounding palisade on top of the motte, with the hall and other buildings in the bailey at the foot of the mound. There was also a large rectangular outer ward where troops on campaign could safely encamp overnight in this dangerous border country.

It was probably FitzPons's great grandson, Walter de Clifford III, who added the round stone keep on top of the motte. Such towers were a simple and effective way of bringing a timber castle up to date in the 13th century, when wooden defences were becoming obsolete. The mound provided protection against siege engines, whilst on top of the tower there would have been a projecting circular wooden gallery from which archers would have had a lethal 360° field of fire.

Clifford had served in war against the Welsh with Hubert de Burgh, the builder of Skenfrith, and was one of the small, closely-knit group of Marcher lords responsible for many of the dozen or so round keeps built on the southern March. His tower has the battering base with moulding above which is almost a trademark of the group. It was originally one storey lower and in a good light one can see where the masonry of the original keep joins that of the added upper floor.

The visitor climbs the motte and enters the tower by a wooden stair probably similar to its medieval original. The house and gardens (privately owned and not open to the public) cover the bailey and a print of 1741 shows a large hall block where the stable now stands. The modern floor of the tower covers a basement whose stone vaulted roof is part of an internal re-modelling apparent throughout the tower, probably the work of Rhys ap Howel, a Welshman loyal to Edward I who acquired the lordship when the Cliffords became extinct in 1311. The simple pointed windows on the floor above were replaced by fashionable 14th-century cinquefoil heads and an upper floor added. By 1521 however, Bronllys was 'beyond repair'.

IN CARE OF Welsh Office

OPEN at all times

ADMISSION free

LOCATION 9m NE of Brecon on the A479

MAP REFERENCE 7 SO1535

COUNTY Powys

BRYN BRAS CASTLE

A sham castle of 1829–35, built at Llanrug for a local, landed attorney at law, Thomas Williams. It was designed, like Penrhyn, largely in the mock-Norman style. Today, it is still a furnished family home surrounded by superb gardens in the County of Gwynedd.

Bryn Brâs, like nearby Penrhyn just outside Bangor, is really a sham castle. It dates not from the strife and turmoil of the Middle Ages, but from the more settled and prosperous period of the 1830s. Its stucco-covered battlements and turrets are barely visible from the main Caernarfon-Llanberis road. However, they soon swing into view along the minor road to the castle which nestles half hidden in the lea of a wooded hillside, well sheltered from seaborne weather.

Today, Bryn Brâs presents a picture of domesticity that is nurtured by its present owners. It is still very much a home, its rooms and furniture continuously in use by the family. In this respect, it makes a pleasant change from the roofless medieval ruins

Beautiful stained glass and richly-carved furniture characterise Bryn Brâs

and bare furnishings at other castles.

Although the place is almost exactly contemporary with Penrhyn, there are only very scanty records of its building and it is not even known for certain who designed it. However, it does exhibit many of Penrhyn's features and the general style of the Norman revival is much in evidence, with its round arched openings and its chevron, billet and cable decoration. The fireplaces too, particularly in the entrance hall and in the sitting room, are almost exact copies of those at Penrhyn, although the glossy marble effect of their slate surfaces is now long since covered by paint.

Perhaps the most striking resemblance to its larger neighbour is the entrance hall itself – pure mock-Norman, with two large stained glass windows of the 1920s. Although its heavily-moulded decoration is now gaily painted, it conveys a similar,

though inevitably far less grand, impression to that of Penrhyn's Great Hall, designed by Thomas Hopper. Despite a lack of any supporting evidence, it seems likely, therefore, that Hopper also had a hand in the blueprints for Bryn Brâs.

Built between 1829 and 1835 for Thomas Williams, an attorney at law who had acquired his estates through marriage, Bryn Brâs Castle has been much embellished and added-to by subsequent owners, particularly in the 1920s. Today, its buildings and extensive, well-tended gardens have more of a comfortable and gracious atmosphere, far-removed from the stern necessities of life behind those medieval battlements which they strive so hard to emulate.

IN CARE OF private owner

OPEN at regular times, in spring, summer and early autumn. Please check in advance

ADMISSION some charge

LOCATION ½m off Caernarfon-Llanberis A4086 at Llanrug

MAP REFERENCE 10 SH5462

COUNTY Gwynedd

Despite the lavish décor the rooms at Bryn Brâs still retain a 'lived-in' quality

BUILTH CASTLE

Scant remains of a historically significant site. Llywelyn, the last native Prince of Wales, was killed in 1282 in an expedition against this castle fortified by Edward I.

The formidable earthworks of Builth Castle stand behind the main street of Builth Wells at its lower end. They occupy the end of a ridge which has been shaped into a large and high motte and a pair of baileys. Medieval documents and traces on the site show that there was once a substantial stone castle here, but all meaningful traces of masonry have disappeared, leaving only the earthworks.

The castle already existed by the mid 12th century. From 1229 onwards it changed hands several times between the English and the rulers of independent Wales, finally falling into English hands in King Edward I's campaign of 1277. The castle may have had masonry defences since the 1240's, but accounts listing the money spent by Edward on building work reveal an impressive amount of stonework, not all of it perhaps new. There are traces of buried masonry on the motte top, possibly from the 'Great Tower' listed in the accounts, which may have been a round keep like those at Bronllys and Tretower. This would have been surrounded by a stone wall with six turrets, a twin-towered gatehouse and stone walls to the inner and outer baileys.

In December 1282, Llywelyn ap Gruffudd ('the Last'), was killed in a skirmish at Cilmeri just west of Builth whilst attempting to recover northern Brycheiniog from the English.

IN CARE OF private owner

OPEN at all times

ADMISSION free

LOCATION follow footpath from Lion Hotel

MAP REFERENCE 7 SO0451

COUNTY Powys

At Builth Castle it is claimed that Llywelyn the Last was betrayed

CAERGWRLE CASTLE

Half hidden on its hilltop, Caergwrle Castle was built in 1277 by Dafydd ap Gruffud and displays hybrid features of design. Though captured and repaired by Edward I, it was soon accidentally burnt down.

A heap of masonry on a prominent site is all that remains of Caergwrle Castle

Caergwrle, or Hope Castle as it is often known, is very much a border fortress. Situated on an isolated hilltop, overlooking the adjoining villages of Hope and Caergwrle, it almost straddles the line of Wat's Dyke, an ancient earthwork running parallel to better-known Offa's Dyke in its northern section. The castle is not just a border fortress in geographical terms; its architecture and planning also reflect twin traditions, for it embodies elements of both English and native Welsh styles.

The builder of Caergwrle was Dafydd, the brother of the last native Prince of Wales, Llywelyn ap Gruffud. How he came to build here, in what was then the kingdom of Powys, is an interesting tale. Ousted by his brother from his rightful inheritance in Gwynedd, Dafydd travelled across the border to curry favour at the English court. Returning to Wales again, he became involved in an abortive plot to murder his brother. The plot was discovered and, once again, he was forced to flee to England, eventually fighting against his own countrymen with Edward I during the king's first campaign in Wales. After the war he was rewarded with two areas of land in Powys and Dafydd seems to have begun building this castle for himself in 1277, or very soon after.

Although obscured from below by trees and somewhat overgrown, the castle is an easy climb from the village. In plan, its strong curtain wall describes a rough arc, taking full advantage of the powerful natural defences of this former hillfort site. The remains of three towers straddle the curtain but, whilst these are of general English style, their siting, with almost no flanking field of fire, is very far from English. It is much more reminiscent of native Welsh defences, possibly because North Walians were generally spearmen, not archers, with correspondingly different methods of defence. Dafydd, with his cosmopolitan background, would quite likely draw on both traditions.

It was from Hope, on Palm Sunday 1282, that Dafydd launched his night raid on Hawarden which began the ill-fated second Welsh war. The castle was therefore a primary target for Edward I's troops, quite unnecessarily as it turned out, for the Welsh had already destroyed it. The king spent £300 on refurbishment and then granted it to Queen Eleanor. Unfortunately, on 27 August 1283, the whole castle was destroyed by an accidental fire, which endangered the lives of both the king and queen who were staying there at the time. It seems unlikely that it was ever repaired.

IN CARE OF local authority

OPEN at all times

ADMISSION free

LOCATION on hill above town

MAP REFERENCE 12 SJ3157

COUNTY Clwyd

CAERNARFON

Last great castle of King Edward I's second Welsh campaign of 1282–83, Caernarfon is both fortress and palace. Designed as the new seat of government for North Wales, it was the birthplace, in 1284, of its new English Prince, the ill-fated Edward II. Though sacked by the Welsh in 1294, it withstood all assaults by Owain Glyndwr and was never again surrendered until the Civil War. Extensively restored in Victorian and later times, it has, this century, seen two ceremonial Investitures of latter-day Princes of Wales. One of Britain's best known historic sites.

'If it be well manned, victualled and ammunitioned, it is invincible.'

So wrote John Taylor of Caernarfon Castle in the middle of the 17th century. It is easy enough for us, following in his footsteps today, to echo these sentiments on entering this great castle for the very first time. Climb the modern stone steps up from the road towards the King's Gate and look carefully about. Then, with the help of a little imagination, try to visualize the daunting task facing a would-be 13th- or 14th-century intruder.

The obstacles would have begun with a drawbridge, spanning the deep outer ditch which was twice as wide as now, taking up the whole width of the modern roadway. Whilst negotiating the bridge, our intruder might be prey to unseen archers, hidden behind the arrow-loops that pierce the gatehouse walls – two or even three times as many of them as he would expect, for these loops are cunningly designed with multiple embrasures on the inner face which more than doubled their firepower. (Firepower, in the end was what the castles of Edward I were all about.) Having, for the moment, overcome this hurdle, he would then be faced with an impenetrable series of stout wooden doors and iron-shod portcullises, five of the one and no less than six of the other, each and every stage flanked by yet more arrowloops whilst, all the time, danger lurked overhead from the aptly-named murder holes in the roof of the gate-passage. Small wonder, then, that the King's Gate at Caernarfon has been described as the mightiest in the land.

Although the castle has undergone successive alterations and repairs throughout its life, evidence of long-vanished features of defence still exists: the carved stone bearings that took the pivots for the drawbridge, the rebates and drawbar holes which show the position and thickness of the doors, and also the grooves down which once slid the weighty portcullis grilles. Two of these portcullises would have had to rise right through the floor of a chapel located directly above the gate passage – not an uncommon arrangement in a medieval castle where religion may have had its place, but was often tempered by rules of the sternest practicality and common sense.

Exhibits from the Royal Welch Fusiliers Museum in Queen's Tower

A PALATIAL RESIDENCE

Caernarfon Castle was designed to fulfil two functions. Self-evident is its role as a fortress, but it was also intended to be a great official residence and seat of government for King Edward's newly-created shire counties of North Wales. Indeed, it is the nearest building Wales has to a royal palace, having been owned continuously by the Crown ever since Edward I founded it in the summer of 1283. Its planning is unusual, being shaped rather like an hour glass which was originally divided by a cross wall, at the narrowest point, into two wards. Occupying most of the upper ward was the great earthen mound of an earlier Norman motte and bailey castle, thrown up around 1090 by Earl Hugh of Chester, during an early successful foray into North Wales. More recently, this has been levelled, but it still accounts for the difference in heights between the two wards.

In the 14th century, the lower ward would have been lined by timber-framed buildings though only foundations remain. To the south was a 100ft long Great Hall. Halls were often the most important single building

ROYAL INVESTITURES
For the investiture of Prince Edward in 1911, much restoration work was done to both Caernarfon town and castle. Upon his arrival Edward, then only 17, was escorted to his place by David Lloyd George, Constable of the Castle. Winston Churchill read the Letters Patent as George V invested his son. For the investiture of Prince Charles in 1969 the presence of TV cameras meant that millions could witness the Queen invest Charles with the insignia of the Principality of Wales and the Earldom of Chester; a sword, a coronet, a gold ring and a gold rod. The Prince paid homage to the Queen with these words: 'I, Charles, Prince of Wales, do become your liege man of life and limb and earthly worship, and faith and truth I will bear unto you to live and die against all manner of folks'.

Floodlit Caernarfon Castle, one of Britain's finest medieval fortresses

in a medieval castle. Visitors were received and daily business transacted in them, and all the occupants of the castle would eat there.

Normally, they had a service end, with pantry for dry goods and buttery for drink hidden by an elaborate carved wooden screen. The kitchen was usually located in a separate building, often some distance away, because of the high fire risk from the open cooking hearths, an eminently sensible arrangement which unfortunately resulted in the serving of luke-warm food. In Caernarfon's case, the kitchens were on the opposite side of the courtyard to the hall. One or two of their fixtures survive, such as the stone trough for the piped water supply.

Well-endowed though the public and service areas of the castle are, Caernarfon's private accommodation is outstanding. Most imposing, and commanding attention from everywhere within the enclosure, is the solid mass of the Eagle Tower, crowned by its triple cluster of turrets. Here, in the 13th century, lay the quarters of the castle's constable or governor, the King's lieutenant and first Justiciar of North Wales, Sir Otto de Grandson. Everything about it is on the grand scale, from its basement access to the water gate (more recently used by Her Majesty the Queen to enter the castle, when she invested her eldest son Prince of Wales in July 1969) to its imposing upper rooms and even the carved eagles, one of which originally crested each turret. Next in order of merit comes the Queen's Tower, almost as spacious, but having only three floors and, like all the other towers, one turret. The accommodation did not stop here: there was plentiful, if slightly less grand, space in the Chamberlain, Black, Cistern, North East and Granary Towers, to say nothing of what must have been meticulously planned and yet never built over the Queen's Gate and of a second Great Hall.

Why was there a need for all these private quarters when the castle's permanent garrison was normally a mere 30 men? The answer must be sought in its role in the newly created and annexed Principality of Wales. Not only was Caernarfon the official residence of the King's chief administrator and legal officer; it was also the birthplace of the country's new prince whom, so tradition has it, was presented to the Welsh nobles as a babe in arms. Caernarfon, with its capacity to take an entire royal household, council and guests, was undoubtedly designed as a base from which this Prince of Wales could rule his new dominion.

The groundplan of Caernarfon Castle

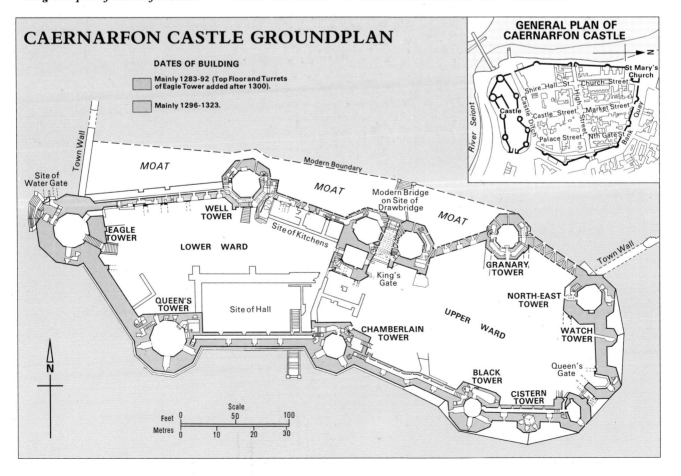

CAERNARFON CASTLE GROUNDPLAN

DATES OF BUILDING

Mainly 1283-92 (Top Floor and Turrets of Eagle Tower added after 1300).

Mainly 1296-1323.

GENERAL PLAN OF CAERNARFON CASTLE

AN IMPERIAL TOUCH

Though built at a time when the concentric idea of walls within walls prevailed, Caernarfon, as we have seen, had but a single curtain wall, albeit a massively powerful one. To make up for its lack of outer defences, the curtain was honeycombed by continuous defended wall passages at two separate levels. It is, however, the angular towers that lend that touch of architectural distinction not found to the same extent at Edward I's other castles. The majestic aspect is further enhanced by the many bands of coloured red sandstone that embellish its outward façade. To find a parallel to this, we must travel to the very gateway of Asia and Istanbul, once the great imperial city of Constantinople. Edward must have drawn inspiration from Constantinople's massive 5th-century walls – among the wonders of the Middle Ages – with their angular towers and alternating bands of Roman tile and masonry.

Caernarfon had its own links with the Roman Empire. Its Roman fort of Segontium, just above the modern town, was inseparably linked, in legend at least, with the emperors Constantine and Magnus Maximus. The latter, in particular, caught the imagination of the ancient Welsh story-tellers, becoming the central figure in one of the tales of the *Mabinogion*, a group of early Welsh romances. When Edward came to build at Caernarfon his own fortress palace, he seems to have made a deliberate attempt to recreate in stone some of the *Mabinogion's* spectacular descriptions of a great city with towers of many colours and eagles fashioned out of gold. Where better to turn, when casting around for a model, than to the fabled walls of Constantinople itself?

POMP AND CEREMONY

Throughout the Middle Ages, history largely passed Caernarfon by, the castle never fulfilling the role Edward I had evidently envisaged. The timber-framed apartments, so hurriedly rushed up in the spring of 1284 to accommodate the king and queen while awaiting the birth of their new son, lasted barely ten years. They were swept away in the Madog rebellion of 1294, when both castle and fortified town were captured and sacked. Prince Edward, indeed, never again set foot in Caernarfon. Created Prince of Wales in 1301, at a great ceremony farther down the coast at Nefyn, he spent the remainder of his life in England or France, only rarely visiting his lands of Wales.

A century later Caernarfon saw almost its last action, when its 28-strong garrison managed successfully to fend off the spirited assaults of Owain Glyndwr in 1403 and 1404. Surrendered finally in the Civil War to the Parliamentary forces under General Mytton, Caernarfon then suffered the fate of most of the castles in Wales. Neglect and cruel weather soon took their toll and within a short space of time the place was roofless.

An engraving made in about 1770 shows how little the castle has changed

The view across the outer and inner wards from the castle's ramparts

IN CARE OF Welsh Office

OPEN all reasonable times (standard hours)

ADMISSION some charge

LOCATION western end of town

MAP REFERENCE 10 SH4763

COUNTY Gwynedd

SPECIAL FEATURES Eagle Tower – exhibition and audio visual programme, Queen's Tower – Royal Welch Fusiliers Museum; North East Tower – 'Princes of Wales' exhibition; Chamberlain Tower – arms exhibition

The great revival in Caernarfon's fortune came in the 1840's when the eminent architect, Anthony Salvin, was commissioned to restore the ruined stonework. This renovation was carried on throughout the century, later under the direction of the castle's deputy constable, Sir Llewellyn Turner. So it was that by the early years of the present century David Lloyd George was able to suggest that the young Edward should be invested as Prince of Wales in an open-air ceremony at Caernarfon Castle. It was the first time that a Prince of Wales had been invested in his principality since those far off days of 1301 and no effort was spared to ensure the success of the event. Finishing touches were made to defective battlements, many of the towers were given new roofs and floors of Quebec oak, and decorative wrought ironwork was used to complete the fixtures and fittings.

Since Edward's investiture in July 1911, Caernarfon Castle has become an almost obligatory venue for any Royal Tour of Wales. Over the years, it has received King George VI and Queen Elizabeth (the present Queen Mother) after the Coronation in 1937, Her Majesty Queen Elizabeth II in 1953, after her own Coronation, and, more recently, the Prince and Princess of Wales on their first joint tour in 1981.

Caernarfon is probably best known though as the majestic setting for the last ceremonial Investiture of Prince Charles as Prince of Wales in July 1969. Watched by an estimated worldwide television audience of 500 million, the Prince swore fealty to his Sovereign. Caernarfon Castle had at last come into its own.

CAERPHILLY

'Giant Caerffili' as a medieval Welsh poet termed it, its towers and curtain walls rising from the waters of its lakes, is one of the great surviving fortresses of the medieval western world. This huge, 30-acre site in Mid Glamorgan is equalled in size among British castles only at Dover and perhaps Windsor. With its massive gatehouse, water defences and concentric lines of defence, Caerphilly represents a high point of medieval military architecture. Only recently has its stature as one of Britain's great castles been generally recognized.

The site chosen in 1267 by the Norman lord Gilbert de Clare for his castle had been, 1,200 years earlier, occupied by a Roman fort whose remains were found unexpectedly during excavation in 1963. It would have held a battalion of 500 infantry, stationed here to pacify the surrounding hill country. The Romans arrived in the time of the Emperor Vespasian (about AD 75) but about 50 years later conditions were sufficently peaceful for them to be moved to northern Britain by Hadrian.

When the Normans conquered South Wales, they concentrated on the fertile coastal plains. The mountain uplands, devoid of good ploughland, difficult to capture and hard to retain, were left to the Welsh. So, from the initial conquest of Glamorgan by FitzHamon to the time of Gilbert de Clare 200 years later, the boundary between Normans and Welsh hereabouts lay on Caerphilly mountain, a moorland massif that is still a geographical barrier between Cardiff and Caerphilly.

THE EARLY CASTLE

This period of virtual truce ended when, due to the embroilments of national politics, the minor Welsh lords of upland Glamorgan found themselves caught between the ambitions of the last native Prince of Wales, Llywelyn ap Gruffudd, in the north and Gilbert de Clare to the

Caerphilly Castle boasts a tower that out-leans Pisa and has fine defences

south. Llywelyn wanted to unite all Welsh-controlled territory under his rule and in 1262 he seized Breconshire. Only the small Welsh lordships in areas close to Caerphilly such as the Rhondda, Machen and Senghenydd stood between the two mighty opposites.

Five years later, when Llywelyn had been politically weakened by the defeat of his English ally Simon de Montfort, Gilbert de Clare struck. He strengthened his northern frontier by seizing Gruffudd ap Rhys, ruler of Senghenydd and imprisoning him in Kilkenny in Ireland. He then began building his new castle, probably initially a rapidly-built wooden structure of palisades and towers which could gradually be replaced in stone.

In the previous year, Gilbert had been present at the siege of Kenilworth Castle, where the surviving supporters of Simon de Montfort had been starved out after a long and bitter struggle. Kenilworth was surrounded by wide lakes which had greatly helped the defenders, and memories of these water defences must have been very much in Gilbert de Clare's mind as he planned Caerphilly. It is doubtful, however, that he had any conception of how large and elaborate the finished work would be when he began building here on 11 April 1268.

SITING AND STRENGTH

The strategic importance of the site is best appreciated by approaching Caerphilly on the A469 north from Cardiff. As the road crests Caerphilly mountain, there is a panoramic view of the town below.

The castle itself was built to a concentric design with successive lines of defence set one inside the other, so that when the attacker stormed one line he would then find himself face to face with a second; moreover, this second wall would usually stand higher than the first, the unfortunate attacker becoming a nicely-positioned target for the archers on the wall top. This is the system of defence which is also seen at its fullest development in Edward I's great North Wales castles.

WATER AND STONE

Although the moat is obviously wide and wet enough, and the walls intimidating enough, the defensive principles applied at Caerphilly can only be understood, in their totality, from the air. A seemingly impregnable series of concentric stone and water defences radiates, in a succession of larger and larger circles, from a central inner ward.

The first line of defence against any attack consisted of the outer moat spanned by two drawbridges backed by a huge curtain wall and gatehouse (through which one enters the castle today). The lakes made it almost impossible to use many of the normal methods of siege warfare. Stone-firing catapults could not be brought within range of most of the perimeter; siege ladders were useless (save from boats) and it was impossible to tunnel under the waters of the lake to undermine the walls. In addition, a large number of besiegers would be needed to picket the perimeter of the lakes to prevent supplies reaching the garrison.

The inner moat and the gatehouses of the outer ward were the second line of defence. Finally, there stands the very core of the castle, its inner ward. This is a large quadrangle enclosed by four curtain walls, with massive round towers at each corner (one of them is the celebrated leaning tower which out-leans even Pisa) and yet more gatehouses on the east and west sides. These gatehouses protect the points of entry and could be shut off and held separately should the rest of the castle fall.

DE CLARE AND DESPENSER

Work on these formidable defences had scarcely begun before they were seized by Llywelyn in October 1270. King Henry arranged for them to be held by a neutral force pending negotiation, but in the following February, de Clare's constable of Cardiff Castle arrived at the gates and asked to be allowed to check the armoury. Once inside, he let in armed men who recaptured Caerphilly for de Clare, who was never again parted from his castle. Building probably continued until his death in 1295 and his son, another Gilbert de Clare, may have completed his father's work before his death in battle at Bannockburn in 1314, the last of his line.

Caerphilly passed to his sister Eleanor and her husband Hugh le Despenser the younger, the beloved favourite of Edward II. Despenser

Line drawing of Caerphilly c1770

earned the hatred of the Welsh by putting to death in 1318, the native chieftain Llywelyn Bran, who had been imprisoned after leading a rising against the harsh rule of the royal administrator of Glamorgan after de Clare's death. As was the style of medieval politics, within a few years Despenser, along with his king, suffered the same fate.

THE GREAT HALL

Before his demise, however, Despenser rebuilt the Great Hall of Caerphilly in magnificent style. The timbers of its roof rested on carved capitals with portrait busts which probably represent King Edward II, his Queen Isabella and the young Prince, the future Edward III. The tall windows are decorated with the fashionable 'Ball-flower' ornament of the period and two of the king's leading craftsmen, the carpenter William Hurley and the mason Thomas of Battle were employed on the work. This cavernous hall, now used frequently for banquets and other social functions, is one of the most striking features within the castle. The present roof dates from about 1870 and the windows have recently been re-glazed and partly restored.

DECAY AND RESTORATION

With the threat of an independent Wales removed, and with the main seat of the lordship of Glamorgan over the hill at Cardiff, Caerphilly Castle gradually fell into decay. In Elizabethan times, its stone was robbed to build a house for a local family of gentry. It may have been then that the leaning tower shifted, perhaps as a result of the marshy soil, for the wall of the north platform also leans, though not so dramatically.

In the 19th century, the ruins were restored, and in places rebuilt, by Lord Bute. The extent of his work can be seen from photographs of the castle before and after restoration in the exhibition in the outer gatehouse. This tells the story of Caerphilly Castle and the surrounding area in detail. Models, many illustrations and an audio visual programme on the tragedies of Llywelyn Bran and Edward II are also included.

Caerphilly is an unexpected site, standing as it does in the middle of an unpretentious South Wales valley town. Possibly because of the prejudice surrounding its location, only now is the castle's true stature as a fortress of tremendous power and dignity becoming generally appreciated. Experts may quibble about Caerphilly's precise placing in the ranking order of medieval castles. Indisputably, it is near the top.

This 14th-century bronze tankard was found at Caerphilly Castle

IN CARE OF Welsh Office

OPEN all reasonable times (standard hours)

ADMISSION some charge

LOCATION in town centre

MAP REFERENCE 5 ST1581

COUNTY Mid Glamorgan

SPECIAL FEATURE exhibition in outer gatehouse

Caerphilly's groundplan shows its concentric design and water defences

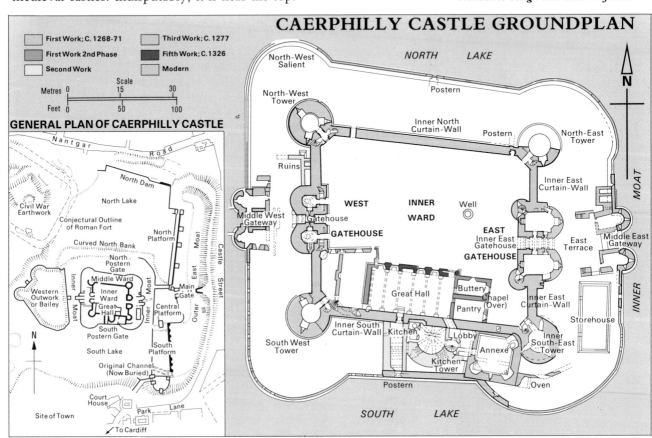

WILLIAM MARSHALL (A Norman Baron) c1146–1219

In the summer of 1189, the sons of Henry II were in revolt against their father. All his friends, except a loyal handful, had deserted the dying old king. One of them, a landless knight, the younger son of John Marshall, unhorsed the king's son, Richard 'Lionheart', in a skirmish and, had he wished, could have killed him. When he became king, Richard, remembering and respecting the knight's loyalty and prowess, gave him in marriage to Isabel de Clare, daughter of Strongbow and heiress to wide estates in England, Wales and Ireland. The penniless knight became William Marshall, Earl of Pembroke.

Marshall played an influential role in Wales in the unstable early period of Norman invasion and domination. His monuments – the castles at Chepstow, Pembroke and Usk – are still with us. So is a verse biography in Norman-French, *Historie de Guillaume le Maréchal* (edited by Paul Meyer, Paris 1891–1901 – no English translation, alas), written by one of his household.

As a young man, Marshall took part in tournaments. Far removed from the romantic, chivalrous re-creations we often see on our screens, these were dangerous and disreputable events which attracted many wild young men. Prizes were not lady's favours, but the horses and armour of defeated opponents. It was a tough school for the profession of arms, but one that could be profitable for a poor knight.

One final scene: In spring 1219, Marshall lay dying. Easter was near, a time of year when he customarily gave fine new clothes to all his knights. His money chest was brought to his bed. The clergy urged him to spend the money for the good of his soul, on masses and gifts to the Church. But, as ever, he was loyal to his own ideals. For the last time, William Marshall gave his knights their Easter robes.

The effigy of William Marshall (left) lies next to that of the second Earl of Pembroke

CALDICOT CASTLE

Caldicot, an impressive castle, is perhaps less celebrated than it deserves. Its round keep and fine 14th-century gatehouse reward close examination. It was still largely intact when restored in the last century by J R Cobb, castle-renovator extraordinary.

'Durand the Viscount', says the Domesday Book, 'holds of the King one dwelling called Caldecote'. The Normans were here by 1086, and the motte on which the present round keep stands and the other substantial earthworks which underlie the stone castle may well derive from that period. The earliest stonework on the site is the round keep, faced with squared blocks of local gritstone.

This keep has architectural features (a battered back base with bold roll-moulding) characteristic of a local group of round keeps (cf Bronllys, Skenfrith). Inside is a deep basement, above which are well-equipped domestic rooms with windows seats and fireplaces, signs that its occupants were of fairly high status. The semi-circular external projection, again typical of this local group of keeps, houses a latrine.

DE BOHUN'S INHERITANCE

Caldicot formed a small separate lordship, an independent 'island' within the area of the lordship of Chepstow. The keep was probably built by Humphrey de Bohun, the 'Good Earl' of Hereford who inherited the lordship in 1221. There was a succession of de Bohuns, all confusingly named Humphrey, until the death of the last in 1373.

The curtain wall is later than the keep, and its rougher masonry is built against it, obstructing an arrow-slit. The curtain then runs down to the curious West Postern Tower, sometimes called the 'De Bohun Gateway' (the name is no doubt a quite recent invention). This has the very unusual feature of a doorway in the side of the tower giving access outside the castle. There is a similar tower-gate at Pembroke; it has recently been suggested that William Marshall the Elder may have brought the idea back with him from the Holy Land (where similar gates are known) to Pembroke, after which it was copied by Humphrey de Bohun. If so, we have that rare feature in British castles, something which can be shown to have been influenced by the Crusades.

We know that building work was going on at Caldicot in the 1340s and the Great Hall, next to the Great Gatehouse, belongs to about this time. It was once an extremely fine building, but only one face now remains, forming the outer wall of the castle.

On a site of great antiquity stands Caldicot Castle, two miles from the sea and on a Roman road once known as Via Julia

THOMAS OF WOODSTOCK TAKES OVER

Eleanor de Bohun, daughter of the last Earl Humphrey, married Thomas of Woodstock, sixth son of King Edward III. Thomas spent large amounts of money on the castle in 1384–89. The Woodstock Tower, the smaller of the two gatehouses, is certainly his work for he had built into it two stone blocks bearing his name and that of his wife – 'Thomas' and 'Eleanor'. The interior of the Woodstock Tower, which has been lived in until very recently, is quite plain, but the Great Gatehouse is magnificently appointed, a suitable residence for a son of the King. The hall on the first floor is particularly fine and now provides a splendid setting for medieval banquets which help to pay for the maintenance of the castle.

A BLOODY ANCESTRY

Thomas of Woodstock, Duke of Gloucester, was murdered in 1397. His daughter Anne married Edmund, Earl of Stratford. Their son Humphrey became first Duke of Buckingham who was killed at the Battle of Northampton at the beginning of the War of the Roses. Caldicot passed to the king, but was later returned to the Staffords until Edward, the third Duke, fell foul of the suspicions of Henry VIII in 1521 and was beheaded. Caldicot returned to the Crown and became part of the Estates of the Duchy of Lancaster. If nothing else, the castle's frequent changes of ownership demonstrate that in the 14th and 15th centuries, nobility was a dangerous trade.

The visitor will notice a number of fireplaces from vanished buildings against the inner face of the curtain wall. The castle walls would have been lined with two-storey timber-framed buildings providing lodgings for minor members of the ducal household (a certain amount of such build-

Caldicot's pretty gardens delight visitors

ings can still be seen on the back of the Great Gatehouse).

In the late 19th century, Caldicot was purchased by J R Cobb, a wealthy antiquary who bought and restored a number of Welsh castles, including Pembroke and Manorbier. It now belongs to the local authority and is the appropriate setting for regular medieval

Caldicot's tower was probably built by Humphrey de Bohun in the late 12th century, when the castle was surrounded by a moat

banquets. Caldicot also houses a museum in which the figurehead of one of Nelson's flagships, the *Foudroyant*, is a prized exhibit.

IN CARE OF local authority

OPEN at regular times, check in advance

ADMISSION some charge

LOCATION 5m SW of Chepstow off the M4 at Junction 22

MAP REFERENCE 5 ST4888

COUNTY Gwent

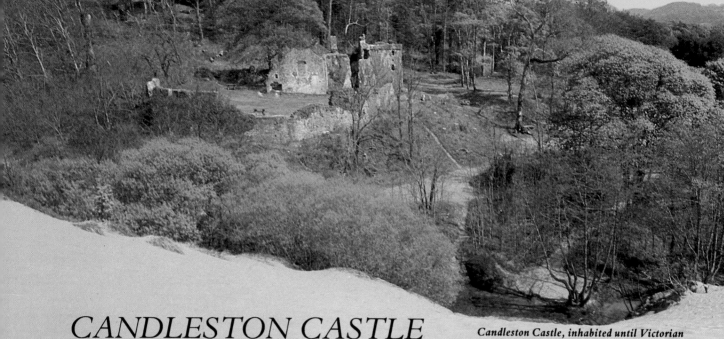

CANDLESTON CASTLE

This castle, on the edge of wide sand dunes, near Bridgend, preserves the name of the de Cantelupes, an early Norman family of Glamorgan.

The situation of Candleston, in a wooded valley on the edge of the sand dunes of Merthyr Mawr Warren, is picturesque and memorable. The castle consists of a 15th-century rectangular tower with a later hall adjoining it and a bailey with a battlemented curtain wall. This bailey is roughly circular and the curtain wall curves round at the top of a slope which probably represents the bank of an earlier Norman earthwork castle.

Many of the smaller Anglo-Norman settlements in South Wales have names which derive from that of an early settler plus the suffix – ston ('ton' being a manor or farm).

Thus Gileston is Giles's manor or farm. Candleston was once Cantelupe's ton, commemorating the family of William de Cantelupe.

William came to South Wales in 1128 and Cantelupes lived here until the late Middle Ages, when their line died out. Their arms were once displayed above the splendid 15th-century fireplace in the hall. After their time, Candleston passed through various hands (this historic site was a farmhouse within living memory).

The tower is of two storeys, the lower being a vaulted basement, whilst the upper was the solar or private room of the family.

Candleston Castle, inhabited until Victorian times, is now a sad ruin

The hall has a fine and elaborate 15th-century fireplace, with curved decoration, but the panel bearing the arms of the Cantelupes was stolen from it some years ago. There are also some scant remains of farm buildings.

IN CARE OF private owner

OPEN at all times

ADMISSION free

LOCATION On minor road near Merthyr Mawr, 2m SW of Bridgend

MAP REFERENCE 4 SS8878

COUNTY Mid Glamorgan

CARDIFF CASTLE

In the centre of Wales's capital city stands a tremendous 'three-in-one' castle – Roman, Norman and Victorian. Reconstructed walls of a Roman fort enclose a medieval shell keep, extensive lawns and the Victorian fantasies of William Burges. Today's castle is a product of a remarkable partnership between this unique architect and one of the world's richest men, John Patrick Crichton Stuart, Third Marquess of Bute.

Standing tall in the busy city centre, next to modern shopping precincts and Victorian arcades, Cardiff Castle at first sight looks like a purpose-built Hollywood recreation, a too-good-to-be-true version of a medieval fortress; which it almost is, for the present ornate structure is the work of that Victorian genius, architect William Burges, who reconstructed the castle for the 19th-century coal and shipping magnate, the Third Marquess of Bute.

But first appearances can be deceptive. Cardiff is a site of great antiquity, with sufficient medieval and Roman associations to satisfy even the most dedicated historic purist. Through the main entrance, which leads into spacious, grass-covered grounds, stands a magnificently-preserved Norman keep, built in medieval times when the castle was a power base for the invading Normans. Cardiff's past can be traced even further, for the crumbling brickwork at the base of the curtain wall is nearly 2,000 years old, a reminder that this site was chosen as a fort by those early empire builders, the Romans, during their occupation of Britain from the 1st century AD.

IN THE BEGINNING

Prior to the arrival of the Romans around AD 75, there was probably no settlement here at all. The Romans immediately recognised the strategic advantages of the site, constructing an eight-acre fort on the banks of the River Taff where the military road from Caerleon to Carmarthen crossed the tidal estuary, a natural junction and good outlet to the sea.

Initially, a wooden stronghold was constructed, later to be replaced by a stone fortress, similar to the 'Saxon shore' forts of southern and eastern England. Parts of this are still visible, forming the outside wall of Cardiff Castle. They were excavated and restored early this century in such a way that carefully distinguishes old from new. The Roman work, in white lias stone, is separated from the modern by a band of reddish stone. Particularly impressive is the North Gate, which can be viewed from within the castle lawns or from neighbouring Bute Park.

The Norman motte and keep at Cardiff, one of the best-preserved in Britain

THE NORMANS ARRIVE

Before the coming of the Normans, this part of Wales was ruled by a native Welsh ruler, Morgan Mwynfawr, a 10th-century king from whom Glamorgan's name is derived. As part of the Norman Conquest, William I gave his comrade-in-arms, Robert Fitz-Hamon, carte blanche in the borderlands and the south with the promise that he could keep what he captured. FitzHamon established a Norman lordship here by defeating the last ruler of Glamorgan, Iestyn ap Gwrgan.

Initially, a timbered palisade was built on the moated hillock within the decayed walls of the old Roman fort. This sustained attacks from some of the more wilful natives and was replaced, by the end of the 12th century, by a stone structure, the twelve-sided shell keep which still stands today. By the end of the 13th century, further reconstruction and strengthening were necessary, at which time the castle's total weekly upkeep amounted to 23s 3d. Later additions to the shell keep include a 15th-century gatehouse and stairs.

By the 18th century, the castle land passed, by marriage, to the Marquess of Bute. The first Marquess re-modelled the house and grounds using the architect Henry Holland and the landscape specialist 'Capability' Brown. But by Victorian times, their efforts were regarded as old-fashioned and dull. When the Third Marquess came of age in 1868, he set to work to remedy this.

A CASTLE RECREATED

Today, Cardiff stands as a unique monument to the self-confidence and prosperity of the Victorian age. Its ornate, extravagant interior and exterior celebrate the wealth and personality of the Third Marquess, the man at the centre of Cardiff's boom-town bonanza period as a coal-exporting port. Bute, a remarkable man, had sought refuge from an unhappy childhood in books and in dreams of an idealised medieval past. He was naturally drawn to the equally remarkable William Burges, medievalist, architect and creator of a world of romantic fantasy inspired, at times, by the influence of the opium pipe.

The Marquess, reputedly the richest man in Britain with an annual income of over £300,000, gave Burges the chance of a

Victorian reconstruction – the medieval fantasy of the Octagonal Tower

lifetime by devoting a not inconsiderable part of his fortune to the castle's wholesale reconstruction. Burges rose to the task, creating what can only be described as a fantasy palace.

Work began in 1868, continuing after Burges's death, in 1881, well into the present century. The Clocktower (1869–1873), stands at the corner of the castle, intended by Burges as a dominant vertical feature on an otherwise flat site. Outside are painted statues of the planets and bright heraldic shields under a complicated and satisfying roofline. Inside is a bachelor idyll, designed for Lord Bute in the years before his marriage, with summer and winter smoking rooms and a bachelor bedroom.

These rooms are rich with stained glass, painted sculpture, decorated tiles and elaborate symbolism – time is the theme of the winter smoking room, showing the days of the week, the zodiac months and the four seasons; gems and rocks are displayed in the bachelor bedroom; and the world with its continents, birds, beasts and starry sky is represented in the summer smoking room. The chimney pieces in the smoking rooms depict the pleasures of the seasons, especially love making – an occupation for both summer and winter.

THE BUTE TOWER
Bute married in 1872 and work on the castle continued. In 1873 construction began on the new Bute Tower, with a second suite of rooms – dining room, sitting room, bedroom and roof garden. The dining room has

a chimney piece with angels and the inscription (in Greek) 'Entertain Angels unawares'. The theme is Abraham and Sarah, and the stained glass has other episodes in the life of Abraham, beneath one of Burges's astonishing painted Arab ceilings.

And so the rooms continue – the Seven Deadly Sins and another astounding ceiling in the sitting room, the Seven Churches of the Book of Revelation in the bedroom. The bathroom has a rich variety of marbles and Turkish wooden grilles. A spiral staircase leads to the top of the tower and the roof garden, with cast bronze flower boxes, a bronze Madonna and child and cool tiled walls with illustrations of more Old Testament subjects. It was, thought Burges, like something from 12th-century Provence.

Inside the 16th-century Herbert tower, Burges added two further rooms, a study (for Lord Bute's librarian) and the Arab Room. This latter room is Burges at his most unique. It is at once the authentic Islamic art of Cairo and a stage set for a Victorian production of Aladdin. The soft-toned grey, blue and yellow marbles of the inlaid and lower walls together with openwork cedar window shutters and patches of bright tiling produce a harmony of light like a chord. This is a room for harps and guitars, for long comfortable robes, for strong coffee and tobacco. Only the arms of Lord Bute over the fireplace strike a slightly incongruous note. Burges was working on this room at the time of his death and the openwork panel of white marble over the fireplace bears an inscription put there by

The purely functional Norman keep contrasts strongly with the Victorian opulence opposite

Lord Bute to commemorate their partnership. Above is one of the most astonishing of Burges's gilded honeycomb ceilings with its groups of little jelly-mould domelets and a set of stained glass windows.

BURGES'S ALLEGORY
The Beauchamp Tower, built in the 15th century by the 'Kingmaker', Earl of Warwick, contains the overpoweringly rich Chaucer Room. It has much in common with the Drawing Room at Castell Coch (which Burges also rebuilt for the Marquess) – the same panelled walls with flower paintings, the same birds of the air disporting among trees and branches, even a balcony. High on a pinnacle above the fireplace, Geoffrey Chaucer presides over the room.

In the library is heavy Burgesian allegory. Above the door, two apes struggle for the Book of Knowledge. Around are prophets, apostles, kings, Greek authors, Roman emperors and Welsh princes. Above the fireplace, four of the five sculptured figures represent ancient alphabets – Greek, Assyrian, Hebrew and Egyptian. The fifth figure may be a Celtic monk, or it might be Lord Bute – or both!

The great Banqueting Hall is by far the largest of the rooms. High above is an oak hammer beam roof and a blaze of heraldic shields. On the walls are murals showing events in the Civil Wars. Robert Earl of

The extraordinary gilded Islamic ceiling in the Arab room of the Herbert Tower dates back to 1881

Gloucester appears on the great fireplace – a Burges *tour de force*. He rides out of the gates of Cardiff Castle, the battlements alive with ladies and trumpeters, whilst an unhappy Robert Duke of Normandy, the Crusader son of William the Conqueror who was imprisoned here for many years, peers sadly out from between the bars of his prison window.

The inscription below describes Robert Earl of Gloucester as Comes Glo. This is a perfectly good medieval abbreviation, but knowing Burges, one wonders whether it is merely coincidence that it can also be read – in a mixture of Welsh and Latin – as 'Lord Coal', not a bad description of Lord Bute. This Burgesian pun says much about his relationship with a patron who appreciated – and permitted – the joke.

CARDIFF'S LEGACY

Burges and Bute planned much more. A projected Grand Staircase was never completed and a Wagnerian plan to convert the medieval shell keep into a gigantic chapel never materialised. But work continued after Burges's death, and indeed after Lord Bute's. The animals of the animal wall, peering down from their battlements on the passing citizenry of Cardiff, date from the 1880s and the reconstruction of the Roman fort belongs to the 1920s, but Burges's architecture and Bute's riches have given Cardiff a unique legacy. Today, medieval banquets are held in part of the castle.

IN CARE OF local authority

OPEN all reasonable times

ADMISSION some charge

LOCATION city centre

MAP REFERENCE 5 ST1776

COUNTY South Glamorgan

SPECIAL FEATURES museum of the Welsh Regiment; medieval banquets

CARDIGAN CASTLE

After changing hands frequently, the castle became the centre for administering Edward I's new county of Cardigan.

After the death of Rhys ap Tewdwr, lord of much of South-West Wales, Roger, Earl of Montgomery built a castle here in 1093. Old Castle Farm, about a mile down the Teifi from the town, probably marks the site of this first castle. But Norman occupation was short-lived and the castle changed hands more than 15 times in the next century and a half, being sold to King John by Maelgwyn ap Rhys and then destroyed by Llywelyn ab Iorwerth ('the Great') in 1231.

At some unknown time, its location also changed to a site within the town. William Marshall began rebuilding the castle, and a new keep and town walls were added in 1250. King Edward I made it the new administrative headquarters for his new shire of Cardigan (1279), although subsequently the castle was badly neglected until after the suppresssion of Owain Glyndwr's revolt, when new buildings were put up to house the constable.

The present castle is on the hill within the town, overlooking the bridge. It is strictly private, but some of the outer walls, with two small round towers, can be seen from the public streets at Castle Green.

Little remains of Cardigan Castle, where it is said the first National Eisteddfod was held in 1177

IN CARE OF private owner

OPEN viewing from surrounding area only. Old Castle Farm site not accessible to the public

LOCATION on hill within the town

MAP REFERENCE 2 SN1846

COUNTY Dyfed

THE ORIGIN OF THE CASTLE

Man has needed protection ever since he made his first enemy. But early fortifications were for the protection of large communities – Iron Age hillforts, Roman camps, Anglo-Saxon burghs. By contrast, the castle is a private fortification, the fortified residence of a lord.

The idea seems to have arisen in 9th-century western Europe, with the break-up of the Western Roman Empire after the death of Charlemagne. New local lords, struggling to survive, needed to fortify their bases either by making their homes out of strong towers or by putting separate defences around their places of residence. Stone defensive towers built about AD 1000 can still be seen in the Loire valley, France.

THE CASTLE COMES TO WALES

The Normans' success in expanding their influence in Europe is due mainly to their use of cavalry operating from such fortified bases. When Edward the Confessor returned to England in 1051 after his temporary exile, he brought with him some Norman supporters, who settled around Hereford and built three or four castles (including Hereford itself) in the next few years before their expulsion.

Soon after the Norman Conquest of England, these Herefordshire castles were rebuilt and many others were built on the Welsh March. The Norman penetration of Wales along the coastal plains and up the Severn valley is marked by a series of earthwork castles reaching as far as Anglesey in the north-east and St David's in the west by the 1080s. Naturally enough, the Welsh themselves built castles in response, and the fluctuating fortunes of war meant that some lords, both English and Welsh, found it necessary to rebuild their castle elsewhere from time to time.

THE CASTLES OF WALES – THEIR IMPORTANCE

The majority of the Norman castles in Wales were built of timber and have long-since rotted away. There are no great stone keeps like the Tower of London, although at Chepstow there is the earliest complete stone castle hall in Britain.

The 13th-century castles of Wales, on the other hand, are quite superb. This is especially true of the remarkable, unparalleled series built by King Edward I, each different yet part of one overall grand design. Although the Edwardian castles tend to dominate, the stone castles built by the Welsh themselves must not be overlooked (Edward found they had little need for improvement when they fell into his hands). The same can be said of those built by the English baronage, which often contained ideas well ahead of their time. Caerphilly and Pembroke, for example, must appear on any list of the world's great castles.

To end on a less military note, no traveller in the peaceful Usk valley should fail to visit the complete fortified manor-house at Tretower and the palatial (but wrecked) Raglan Castle, to understand how the low and the high Welsh lords lived in the later Middle Ages.

This detail from the Bayeux Tapestry, created in the 11th century, shows the building of a castle

64

CAREW CASTLE

Gerald of Windsor's private castle, Carew, has been altered several times. It contains unique medieval 'maisonettes' for the constable and chaplain of the garrison; also two successive Tudor wings of palatial grandeur, all standing two or three storeys high.

From the roadside, Carew is something of a disappointment, since this side was thrown down by a mine sprung underneath it at the time of the Civil War, and only the angle towers give a hint of the exciting remains. By the entrance gates is a Celtic cross erected about 1035 in memory of Mareddud who ruled Deheubarth (South West Wales). Nearby is a watermill of an unusual type, worked by the tide ebbing and flowing in Milford Haven.

This tidal creek determined the site of the castle, making it accessible to sea-going vessels. The ridge on which the castle stands was also of strategic importance near to the lowest point at which the creek could be forded at low tide. Unfortunately the ridge was waterless, and supplies had to be piped in from a distance away.

FROM RHYS AP TEWDWR TO ELIZABETH TUDOR

Tradition has it that Carew was founded by Gerald of Windsor, Constable of Pembroke Castle, who married Nest, daughter of Rhys ap Tewdwr. Nest, a figure of romance and intrigue, is said to have had a son by King Henry I whilst hostage. After Gerald's death, she married the Constable of Cardigan Castle and had a third family. All three families took part in the Norman conquest of Ireland. In Wales, Nest is best remembered as the grandmother of Giraldus Cambrensis.

Nothing remains of Gerald's original castle, but the 'Old Tower' (see below) may have been part of the 'house of Carrio' which King John seized in 1210 whilst passing through Pembroke on his way to Ireland.

Most of the medieval parts of the castle were built between about 1280 and 1310 for Sir Nicholas de Carew, a monumental effigy to whom can still be seen in the Carew Parish Church.

Renowned for its beautiful setting, Carew Castle towers above the tidal waters of the Carew River

Sir Nicholas's grandson sold Carew to Sir Rhys ap Thomas, who joined Henry of Richmond (Harri Tudur) immediately upon his landing at Dale nearby, and accompanied him to the Battle of Bosworth (1485) where Henry defeated King Richard III, thus becoming Henry VII, first of the Tudor monarchs.

Rhys turned Carew into a comfortable residence; with Pembroke so near, he had little need of major defence. In 1507 he held a great tournament here in celebration of the Tudors, but 25 years later his grandson was beheaded and the castle seized by King Henry VIII. First Queen Mary, and later Queen Elizabeth I, gave Carew to Sir John Perrott, who was said to have been a natural son of Henry VIII. Perrott built a new wing on to the castle but he in turn fell from favour and died in the Tower of London, before he could be beheaded.

AFTER THE TUDORS

According to a bizarre local legend, Sir Roland Rhys, a tenant of the castle in Jacobean days, set his tame ape on a local Flemish merchant whose daughter had eloped with his son. Later, this unreliable animal attacked its owner, and the castle was set on fire. But most of the damage seems to have been caused by a mineshaft dug under one side of the castle at the time of the Civil War in order to make such a strong place untenable.

DEFENCES AND FORTIFICATIONS

As you approach the castle along the ridge, look out for the ruined wall on each side of the path running back in the form of a V, with a platform for guns on the left. This is a ravelin, a cheap and common form of defence during the Civil War, designed to break up a frontal assault on a stronghold.

The next line of defence, on this one side only, is a plain wall enclosing the original castle ditch. The original doorway is concealed behind a Tudor gate. Notice the size of the holes on each side, nearly a foot square, for the bars which closed the door (there are similar barholes on the inner door). This middle ward between the two doors was protected by the large tower on the left, which seems to have been the lavatory block for the whole castle, and is perfect right up to its battlements. To the right is the half-octagonal tower containing the chapel (see below).

The original entrance to the inner ward was through the 'Old Tower' of King John's time, just to the right of the present entrance, but this passage was blocked up in the 13th century. Notice the murder holes in the vault above the present passage, and the vertical grooves at the far end to take the portcullis. Boiling oil was far too expensive to pour through murder holes: rocks, wastewater and rubbish made far better and more cost-effective missiles.

A MEDIEVAL STRONGHOLD AND TUDOR PALACE

Carew is interesting not only for its fortifications. Architecturally, it bridges the gulf between the primarily military castles of the late 13th century and the more comfortable fortified manor houses of the 15th century. The 13th-century Great Hall in the inner ward is flanked by large round towers (on the far side) which rise from square bases. Sir Rhys ap Thomas altered all the medieval windows into a 'Tudor Gothic' style, adding an oriel window and a new staircase to the hall. The stair was housed in a three-storey porch, with heraldic shields carved below the upper windows – the coats of arms are Henry VII's, flanked by those of Arthur, Prince of Wales and of Catherine of Aragon. Taken together, this dates the porch to 1501 or 1502, just before the time of the great tournament.

The range on the right with rows of large rectangular windows, was built by Sir John Perrott later in the 16th century. Notice the great half-round oriels on the outside toward the water. This range consists of only five rooms, the top floor forming an Elizabethan 'long gallery' aptly named at over 50yd in length.

At the corner between the Elizabethan range and the entrance passageway is the residential block, a complicated set of buildings containing the unique medieval 'maisonettes'. The large rooms near the courtyard form another hall (over vaulted storage), backed by a separate suite of rooms adjoining the vaulted chapel, running up through three storeys. Sir Rhys altered these too, and put in the grand staircase.

IN CARE OF private owner

OPEN summer months, check in advance

ADMISSION some charge

LOCATION On A4075, 3m E of Pembroke

MAP REFERENCE 2 SN0403

COUNTY Dyfed

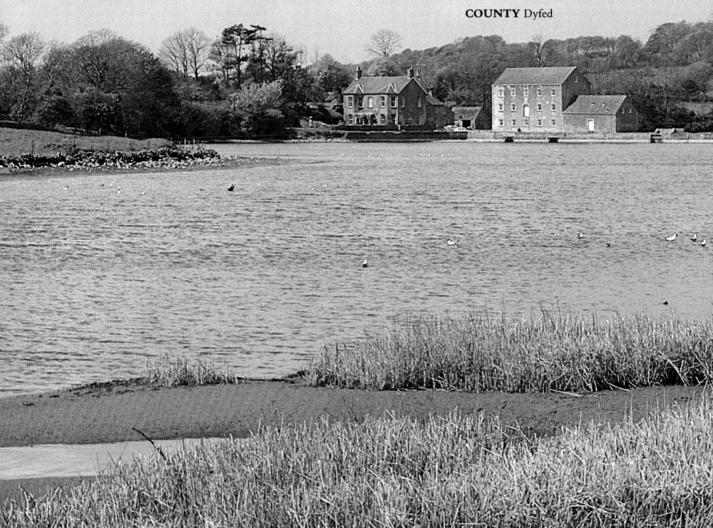

CARMARTHEN CASTLE

The Earl Marshal's 13th-century keep and gatehouse stand beside the site of the most westerly Roman fort and town in Wales.

William FitzBaldwin came by sea from Devon on the orders of King William II (Rufus) and built a castle at Carmarthen, probably on a site further down river, in 1093. It was soon abandoned, periodically being rebuilt and destroyed. It is not certain when the move was made to the present site, on the edge of the derelict Roman fort, but the position was probably chosen as overlooking a good crossing point of the River Tywi. In 1215 it took Llywelyn ab Iorwerth ('the Great') only four days to capture the castle and raze its defences to the ground.

Seized by the Earl Marshal from Llywelyn, the castle was rebuilt so strongly that it withstood a three-month siege. A detailed survey of the time mentions the great gate and keep with its five clustered turrets which can still be seen, together with a hall, stable, chapel and kitchen. Buildings for the royal administrators of South West Wales were

Carmarthen Castle's most significant remains are the motte and gatehouse flanked by impressive twin towers

added in the 14th century, and the whole castle was regularly repaired and whitewashed to protect the stonework. This whitening, a common practice in medieval times, is the source of the familiar names of White Castle (near Abergavenny) and the White Tower of London.

The castle had to be considerably repaired after being sacked by Owain Glyndwr, supported by a French force of 800 men-at-arms, 600 crossbowmen and 1,200 infantry. Amongst the new fittings was a Flemish painting of St Mary and St John, on a wooden panel, for the reconsecrated castle chapel.

IN CARE OF local authority

OPEN at all times

ADMISSION free

LOCATION town centre

MAP REFERENCE 3 SN4120

COUNTY Dyfed

CARREG CENNEN CASTLE

An 'eagle's nest' on a spectacular site near Llandeilo, the castle is still much as it was when built 700 years ago, with complicated defences including a genuine underground passage. A romantic, beautiful site.

Alan Sorrell captured the timeless atmosphere of Carreg Cennen Castle in his romantic reconstruction

Roman coins have been found on the summit of this lofty castle crag, which rises 300ft above the Tywi valley. Such a site must have been used as a fortress from early times, but it first appears in written history in the 13th century. Captured from the Welsh by Payn de Chaworth, Lord of Kidwelly, it was surprised and retaken by Llywelyn ap Gruffud's brother and dismantled in 1282. Patched up by the Earl of Gloucester, the castle held out even though its garrison had been badly cut up in a Welsh ambush. A local Welsh rising took place in 1287, when Rhys ap Maredudd captured both Carreg Cennen and Dryslwyn in one day. The existing castle was built about this

time by John Giffard, Lord of Brimpsfield in Gloucestershire.

A century later, John Skidmore held the castle against Owain Glyndwr for over a year, but eventually surrendered it. Some of the walls were demolished then, but the castle was finally garrisoned by Sir Richard Herbert of Raglan and Sir Roger Vaughan of Tretower to prevent it from falling into the hands of brigands and robbers. Eventually 500 men with picks and crowbars were dispatched to make Carreg Cennen unin-

habitable. It was repaired in the 19th century, though it still retains the air of a romantic ruin.

A NATURAL STRONGHOLD

The fortifications do not cover the whole hilltop, but they do block access from the only easy approach. The rest of the site is well protected by formidable natural defences in the shape of sheer limestone cliffs and steep-sided slopes. Entry is through the outer ward, whose wall has small solid round watchtowers at the corners as well as on each side of the gate. To the left is the base of a large medieval limekiln, burning material dug from the limestone quarry ditch alongside.

A long, stepped ramp formed the approach to the inner ward. It had three gates, each with a pair of deep pits crossed by wooden bridges which could be removed in time of danger. The inner ward was protected by a ditch cut in the rock, a defensive structure which also served as a medieval reservoir, for part of it was lined with clay to collect rainwater. The decorated holes draining the castle roofs into the reservoir can still be seen in the curtain wall.

INNER WARD

The corner towers now rise only a little above the curtain walls, giving the castle a very squat – and solid – appearance. Some of the towers are square in plan (with the corners cut off) but the oldest is the round tower to the right of the gatehouse. The evolution of weaponry has left its mark here, where an arrowslit has been opened up to make it suitable for the insertion of an early musket. Above the entrance are traces of an open arch for a murder hole, and the grooves for a portcullis can be seen at each end of the passage – so the gatehouse, with its arrowslits at all levels, could be held against attack whether from within or without the inner ward; there are even watercisterns attached to the towers. Galleries at first-floor level lead into the curtain walls on each side, with upper doorways giving access to the battlements.

A magnificent vista across the Brecon Beacons National Park and the Black Mountain from Carreg Cennen Castle

Acres of picturesque farmland surround the limestone crag where Carreg Cennen Castle sits, above the Tywi Valley

To the left of the gatehouse is the main residential block. Notice the size of the kitchen fireplaces and the remains of the Great Hall with its chapel in a projecting tower.

UNDERGROUND PASSAGES

One of the castle's most interesting and dramatic features can be found in the far left-hand corner of the inner ward. Here, steps lead down to a postern (or sallyport) from which a narrow vaulted passage runs along the edge of the cliff to the entrance to a cave. The cave itself runs back from the cliff under the outer ward. We know that it was occupied in prehistoric times, since four skeletons were found here under a stalagmite layer, one with a pendant made from a horse's tooth.

The entrance to the cave is partly walled up (the pigeonholes in it suggest that it served as a dovecot to improve the food supply). At the far end is a natural basin into which water percolating through the rock drips slowly. This supply would have been quite insufficient for any sizeable garrison, so we can assume that the passageway and wall were constructed simply to prevent attackers from establishing themselves here under cover.

IN CARE OF Welsh Office

OPEN all reasonable times (standard hours)

ADMISSION some charge

LOCATION 4½m SE of Llandeilo on minor road. Access by 2–300yd uphill footpath from car park

MAP REFERENCE 3 SN6619

COUNTY Dyfed

CASTELL COCH

Castell Coch is a Victorian fantasy and pure fairytale. Its grey needle-sharp spires and rosy-brown towers rising out of green beech-woods on a hill slope north of Cardiff are one of the most unexpected sights in Wales. It was the creation of Lord Bute and the architect William Burges. Their love of the Middle Ages was matched with erudite knowledge and the result is unique; like something from a Hans Christian Andersen fairy story.

John Patrick Crichton Stuart, 3rd Marquess of Bute, was responsible for Castell Coch, a Victorian extravagance

Driving north on the A470 out of Cardiff, past the suburbs, golf courses and motorway flyovers, the first-time visitor often blinks twice at what seems a medieval mirage amongst the modern predictability at the fringes of the city. Above the dual carriageway, on a rocky slope in thick woods, stands a vision of Camelot, a Sleeping Beauty's castle, a refugee from Disneyland. Castell Coch, a few miles north of the city centre, is no phantom. It is real enough, though without the historic pedigree of a genuine medieval fortress. Inevitably, Castell Coch is another of architect William Burges's 19th-century romantic, fantastic re-creations.

Its Welsh name means 'The Red Castle', a reference to the unfaced red sandstone used in the construction of a much earlier stronghold here: Castell Coch, for all its Victorian whimsy, is a site of great antiquity. In the late 13th century, the new Lord of Glamorgan, Gilbert de Clare, built a castle here in the Taff gorge, protecting Cardiff from the north. Its small circular ward and projecting round towers, perhaps on the site of an earlier earthwork castle, recall Neath. By the 19th century it was a picturesque ruin, half buried in its own debris. Castell Coch's rebirth as a Victorian phoenix was due to the two men, Burges and Bute, who were concurrently performing a similar rescue mission at Cardiff Castle.

BURGES'S PLAN

In 1871, the Marquess of Bute asked his architect, William Burges, to report on what should be done with Castell Coch. Burges prepared a richly-illustrated report, a work of art in its own right, recommending reconstruction. Work began in August 1875 and the structure of the castle was complete by the end of 1879. Burges died suddenly in April 1881 and the interior decoration and fittings were completed over the next ten years from Burges's drawings and models. J S Chappell's furniture in the style of Burges is a worthy tribute, but often the hand of the master is missing. Camelot remains a dream.

William Burges was a small, bearded man with an almost adolescent delight in dogs, parrots, practical jokes and medieval fantasies. He was also a highly professional architect, the son of a successful Victorian civil engineer. Burges's respect for sound construction and for the use of durable materials of good quality gave even his wildest dreams a structural integrity, keeping them firmly based in reality.

MEDIEVAL INFLUENCES

Burges also had a profound knowledge of medieval architecture, gained not only from books and from a formidable amount of travel in Europe and beyond, but from many cold and wet days, often spent perched upon scaffolding, measuring and drawing medieval buildings. Yet he was no mere antiquarian, faithfully reproducing the past. His variations on medieval themes are

highly original compositions.

Medieval architecture had a powerful appeal for many Victorians, who had seen England change from a land of villages ruled by landowning squires to one where wealth and influence came from smoke-grimed cities full of cotton mills, blast furnaces and cholera-ridden slums. Reaction against this took many forms. One was a craving for the medieval Catholic Church and its architecture (Lord Bute's own conversion to the Roman faith caused no little stir). This hankering after a medieval, feudal past is a thread that runs through much Victorian art and literature, from Tennyson's idylls of King Arthur to the Gothic splendours of the Houses of Parliament. Ironically, Lord Bute's evocation of his idealised past was created from iron and coal royalties as an industrial magnate.

The visitor approaches Castell Coch through beech-woods scented with wild garlic. Lord Bute had vineyards here, but the product never caught on, save as communion wine. At the top of the drive the towers and spires of the castle suddenly come into view. The lower parts of its walls are medieval, but all above is Victorian. Outstanding are the striking conical tower-tops, which taper to needle sharpness and lend the castle its romantic, fairytale air.

Across the bridge (which is a real working drawbridge) and under a gate with a portcullis, the visitor passes through into a small circular cobbled courtyard with a staircase up to an encircling gallery.

INSIDE THE CASTLE

The first of the decorated rooms is the banqueting hall, the most restrained of the rooms and something of a dry aperitif to the rich feast that is to follow. It has a religious theme. King Lucius, the mythical bringer of Christianity to Roman Wales, stands over the chimney piece and the walls are decorated with themes from some illustrated book of legends of saints and martyrs. This decoration, like the furniture, was carried out after Burges's death.

The drawing room next door is undiluted Burges, with rich colours, lofty ribbed dome and galleries to astonish the visitor. Burges originally intended this as two rooms, one above the other, but he later threw the two into one with magnificent effect. The lower part of the walls have wood panelling in dark green and gold inset with flower paintings. Above are murals of scenes from Aesop's fables, full of typical Burges touches. A frog holds a bottle of medicine for the frog in his throat and a monkey has Victorian side whiskers.

Portraits of members of the Bute family hang from painted ribbons with a background of cranes, foxes, cats, monkeys and flocks of wild birds set among golden apples and green foliage. Even the door surrounds have moulded caterpillars and snails. Over

Fantastic murals depicting Aesop's fables decorate the walls and ceiling

(above) The conical turrets of Castell Coch in true fairytale style

the fireplace the three Fates measure and divide the span of life in painted statues not to everyone's taste. Above is the gallery and the ribbed vault where Burges's beloved parrots and exotic birds fly amid the starry vault of heaven. The theme is the whole world of nature, and time, like an ever rolling stream, bearing all its sons away.

THE BEDROOMS

At another level, the room is something of an anthology of aspects of late Victorian romanticism. Its form appears to be a copy of the interior of a medieval castle in the south of France (the Tour de Constance at Aigues Mortes near Arles). In contrast to this opulence, Lord Bute's bedroom up the spiral staircase is of spartan austerity, with an uncomfortable-looking bed, a hip bath and sparse stencilled decoration. Even the delightful sculptured rabbits, hedgehogs and guinea pigs on the fireplace mantel have an air of the Victorian schoolboy.

Lady Bute's bedroom is at the top of the tower, with wide views over the landscape of the Taff valley. Its colours are deep reds, greens and golds, silhouetted against white. In the panels of the domed ceiling, monkeys and squirrels cavort among bunches of grapes and foliage. Around the room is an arcade of Gothic arches, on the capitals of which are birds with their nests and young.

In the centre of the room stands Lady Bute's bed flanked by two splendid but uncomfortable looking chairs. Burges once made it plain that he regarded medieval authenticity as far more important than mere comfort. The medieval-style painted cupboard and the celebrated castellated hand basin also add to the splendour, but all the furniture dates from after Burges's death and is really a tribute to his memory by his associates.

A READY-MADE FILM SET

Back in the open air, the gallery leads to the kitchen, equipped with furniture for formidable Victorian dinners and a baby's high chair – a suitable haunt for Alice in Wonderland's Cook/Duchess. Further on, past authentically recreated shutters to the battlements, and down a long and narrow flight of steps, is the dungeon. The only prisoner ever recorded to have languished here in chains was the film star Alan Ladd (not surprisingly, the castle is a favourite location for many film-makers). A small square opening high in the wall projects a suitably-dramatic pencil of light on the centre of the dungeon floor.

Castell Coch is a decorative extravaganza. As with Burges's work at Cardiff, words are ultimately not enough. His architecture, more than most, is a visual experience. It demands to be seen. The rooms within the castle draw the visitor into a closer and closer focus of attention, an initial jumble of shape and colour narrowing down to a

Close attention to detail for which William Burges was famous, extends even to the courtyard of Castell Coch

multitude of beautifully-executed points of individual detail. Always, there is something else to look at; usually, it is surprising, humorous or stimulating.

An exhibition in a room off the courtyard tells more of Lord Bute, of Burges and of other buildings created by him. Some of Burges's original drawings for Castell Coch are particularly worth seeing.

Castell Coch was never intended as a permanent habitation, but rather as a pleasure dome 'for occasional occupation in the summer', as Burges put it. The intended chapel was never completed. The castle's last brief occupant was King Edward VIII on a tour in the 1930s of the depressed industrial valleys, his last function before abdication.

IN CARE OF Welsh Office

OPEN all reasonable times (standard hours)

ADMISSION some charge

LOCATION Just off A470 at Tongwynlais, 5m NW of Cardiff

MAP REFERENCE 5 ST1383

COUNTY South Glamorgan

CASTELL DINAS BRÂN

Native Welsh castle of c1270, dramatically sited above Llangollen. Probably built by Madog, Prince of Powys, the castle encloses a large rectangular area. Little upstanding masonry. Superb views from summit.

Dominating the skyline from its position on a hillside above the Dee Valley, Castell Dinas Brân was well placed for defensive purposes

Travellers to Llangollen, along the London to Holyhead road, cannot fail to notice on its hill the ruins of Castell Dinas Brân, for it dominates the town and the whole valley of the Dee. The very essence of a romantic ruin, from a distance its stumpy walls look like a row of rotten teeth. Despite the formidable climb, it has long been popular with visitors; their feet have cleared the summit of its bracken so that the interior of the castle is carpeted in a rich velvety green sward that might be the envy of many a municipal groundsman.

The castle draws heavily upon its situation for, despite the somewhat meagre nature of its remains, it manages to lure visitors continually from the valley below. Though one can ride part of the way up from the town by car, the last and steepest part of the journey has to be made on foot. But the effort has its reward, especially on a fine day, in the stunning view from the summit.

'Dinas', in fact, refers to an Iron Age hillfort, which the medieval castle builders adapted to their own purpose. The Iron Age bank and ditch are clearly visible, encompassing the eastern part of the hill in a broad sweep. There is also a splendid rock-cut medieval ditch, 15–20ft deep, with sides that are still vertical in places. On reaching the castle, one is immediately struck by the unexpected size of the place. Rectangular in plan, it is about 300ft long and 130ft wide. At its eastern end are the remains of a small square keep, entered at first-floor level and possibly earlier in date than the main structure. At the north-eastern corner are the foundations of a narrow, elongated gatehouse of unusual design, with English-style twin towers, while, standing astride the southern curtain wall there is what seems to have been a 'D' shaped tower. The main upstanding masonry, so prominent from the valley, is all that survives of a hall block.

Dinas Brân was probably built just before 1270, by Madog of Bromfield, Prince of this part of Powys. The castle seems to have been constructed for prestige, rather than actual defence and, on that score, must have far outranked any other native Welsh castle. In the end, its garrison burnt it in 1277, in the face of the inexorable advance of the armies of King Edward I. The English commander, Henry de Lacy, suggested in a letter to the king that the castle be rebuilt 'for there is no stronger castle in Wales, nor has England a greater', but his proposal was never carried out and Dinas Brân was left to decay.

IN CARE OF local authority

OPEN at all times

ADMISSION free

LOCATION 1m NE of Llangollen. Cross Dee Bridge and canal and follow signposted footpath.

MAP REFERENCE 12 SJ2243

COUNTY Clwyd

CASTELL-Y-BERE

Native Welsh castle, founded in 1221 by Llywelyn the Great. Much ruined today, it draws great attraction from its lonely, peaceful setting below Cader Idris near Abergynolwyn. The triangular enclosure has D-shaped towers at either end, once embellished with decorative sculpture.

'1221, Llywelyn took from Gruffudd, his son, the cantref of Meirionnydd, of which he had gained possession, and the adjoining commote of Ardudwy. And he began to build a castle in it.'

So the Welsh chronicle of the princes refers to the foundation of Castell-y-Bere. It is our only surviving documentary record of the place until the Edwardian wars, more than 50 years later. Though undoubtedly a native Welsh castle, built by that renowned Prince of Gwynedd, Llywelyn ab Iorwerth ('the Great'), our knowledge of it is based solely upon the familiar accepted circumstances of history and on minor archaeological excavation.

LLYWELYN'S STRONGHOLD

Llywelyn the Great rose to power in Gwynedd around 1200 and spent the next two decades establishing his authority over the remaining parts of independent Wales. In 1216, he made a settlement at Aberdyfi, dividing the southern areas amongst his allies and this effectively secured most of the country under his leadership. After this, he began to style himself Prince of North Wales, but he evidently felt the need to provide some physical sign of his authority. The building of Castell-y-Bere in 1221 was presumably an attempt by Llywelyn to exert

This 14th-century bucket, found inside Castell-y-Bere, is now in a museum

his hold on the southern boundary of Gwynedd. Like many another native Welsh castle, its purpose was not so much to resist English infiltration as to secure internal borders against quarrelsome compatriots.

Today, Castell-y-Bere is a peaceful and atmospheric spot, nestling at the foot of Cader Idris, in the mountainous heart of Mid Wales. Although it can be reached easily by car, it is well off the beaten track and demands a certain degree of dedication on the part of prospective visitors. The effort is well rewarded, for its siting is certainly dramatic, with superb views all around.

After parking the car and on walking around the long spur of rock through the trees, with the castle walls above, the tranquillity of the place soon takes over. Suddenly, the entry comes into view, its most prominent feature now a flight of solid-looking oak steps that carry visitors past the site of drawbridge and portcullis and up into the main part of the castle. Within the inner courtyard, one invariably senses a reflective, almost melancholic atmosphere, for the ruins of Llywelyn's castle, perched forgotten

In the shadow of Cader Idris the ruins of Castle-y-Bere take on some of the serenity of the surrounding countryside, though this was once the scene of some of the bloodiest battles of the Middle Ages

amidst their rocky mountain fastness above the valley of the Dysynni, speak of a different, distant age. Once the fortress would have controlled traffic up the valley and over the mountains towards Dolgellau. Now it all passes either further south, through Abergynolwyn, or along the coast, so that even the original purpose of the castle is no longer evident.

DEFENCE AND DECORATION

In plan, the area enclosed forms an elongated triangle, following the shape of the rock. Towers command each angle, while a fourth tower, outside the enclosures, overlooks the approach from the valley below. The entrance is quite elaborate, defended by an outer barbican, with rock-cut ditches and drawbridges with at least one portcullis flanked, from above, by two towers. At either end of the castle are elongated 'D' shaped apsidal towers, which are quite a common feature in native Welsh castles. The southern one appears to have acted as a keep, which could have held out, as a last resort, if the courtyard should fall. Its counterpart to the north was evidently highly decorated on the inside, with fine quality sculpture (some of which is now on display in Criccieth Castle) and appears to have contained a chapel on its upper floor. The high standard of the carving bears eloquent testimony to the considerable wealth and prestige of its

builder, Llywelyn the Great.

Castell-y-Bere was probably in occupation throughout the middle years of the 13th century. With the conquest of Wales by Edward I, however, its fortune was to change considerably, for it was captured by English forces on 25 April 1283. After the army's departure, five masons and five carpenters remained behind 'to carry out various works'. What these were, we cannot be sure, except for the walls linking the south tower with the remainder of the enclosure, which probably belong to this period. As at many other castles, King Edward founded a new borough here, but it seems to have been short lived. Madog's rebels laid siege to the castle in 1294 and quite possibly burnt it. The garrison was withdrawn after this and, without English protection, the new town too was abandoned. After that, nothing further was heard of Castell-y-Bere.

IN CARE OF Welsh Office

OPEN at all times

ADMISSION free

LOCATION N of Abergynolwyn on minor road to Llanfihangel-y-pennant

MAP REFERENCE 8 SH6608

COUNTY Gwynedd

THE EARLY CASTLES

The early castles built by the Normans were, in comparison to the formidable stone structures of later times, rudimentary defences usually of earthwork and timber. Known as motte and bailey castles, they were primarily designed as cavalry bases. Such castles contained a hall and chapel, well and kitchen, sleeping quarters and stables, storerooms and workshops, all surrounded by a ditch with a bank on the inside, topped with a high wall. Entry would be by a bridge across the ditch to a gap in the bank. The enclosure was termed the bailey. A tower overlooked the bailey, both to control its operation and to act as a look-out point. Raising the tower on an earthen mound (the motte) gave it both extra security and a better view.

Most motte and bailey castles had only timber walls which have long since rotted away and allowed the earthworks to collapse. But large mottes are still visible all over Wales – for example inside the courtyard of Cardiff Castle, or between the Roman city of Caerleon and the River Usk. Practically every village in the old county of Montgomeryshire, Mid Wales, has a motte (or two), and a whole string of them can be spotted alongside the A5 between the towns of Llangollen and Betws-y-Coed.

BUILDING A MOTTE AND BAILEY

Although no Norman writer has described how castles were designed, painstaking excavation of some examples have given us the information. The actual layout depended on the site and resources available as well as on the needs of the lord and his men. Ditches would be dug to a V-shaped profile, unless they were to hold water, when the sides would be made as steep as possible.

The banks and mound might be faced with timber to make them unclimbable, or be finished with a crust of clay to prevent their erosion. Mottes often took advantage of a natural hill or rock or even an earlier man-made mound, such as the ancient tumulus in Rug Park, near Corwen. In some cases, the base of the tower might be incorporated into the motte as it rose.

Although timber was the building material of the time, the buildings themselves often stood on stone foundations to slow down rot. Owain Glyndwr's old-fashioned motte and bailey home at Sycharth (near Oswestry) illustrates this

Tomen y Rhodwydd, a few miles south east of Ruthin, is the site of an early motte and bailey castle

practice, even though it was built long after the early castle period. Excavation of the motte-top here revealed the base of Owain's medieval hall, burnt by Prince Henry in 1403.

VISITING THE EARLY CASTLES

Apart from a few in public parks, most motte and bailey castles are on private land. The owner's permission must be obtained before exploring them, although many can be easily seen from the road or a public footpath. Only a few can be mentioned here but hundreds exist; Tomen y Rhodwydd, in the Alun Valley near Ruthin; Pencader, near Carmarthen; Tomen y Mur near Trawsfynnyd; and Old and New Radnor.

At Bronllys, Llandovery, Skenfrith and Tretower Castles, the small motte carries a later round tower. In Powis Park, Welshpool, there are two motte castles as well as the stone one. Carew, Manorbier and Penhow Castles contain early defence towers built of stone. Other examples of early masonry include the Norman halls built by William the Conqueror's steward at Chepstow and Monmouth Castles, and a later example at Manorbier. All these are regularly open to visitors; see the gazetteer for details of admission fees (if any), opening times and map references.

The grassy mound of Tomen y Mur, near Ffestiniog

CHEPSTOW CASTLE

Chepstow is one of the most memorable of Welsh castles. Though it may not have the powerful unity of Edward I's fortresses in North Wales, it has majesty enough of its own. Probably the first stone castle in Britain, improved and added to right up to the Civil War and beyond, it is therefore one of the few sites which illustrates the different periods of castle building. It stands in a superb setting above the Wye river.

Set high on a river cliff near the mouth of the Wye, Chepstow guards the river crossing where the route along the coastal plain enters Wales. Within a few months of the Battle of Hastings in 1066, William the Conqueror established his companion-in-arms and boyhood friend William FitzOsbern as a palatine Earl of Hereford (with special powers normally reserved to the king). FitzOsbern's task was to pacify the Marches of South Wales and before he died in battle in Flanders in 1071 he had built castles at both Chepstow and Monmouth as bases for military operations. The Domesday Book tells how 'Earl William built the castle of Estrighoiel' (Chepstow). His rectangular hall-keep, the core of the later castle, still stands as the oldest dateable stone secular building in Britain.

This very early type of keep, a stone hall rather than a tower, is very similar to other 11th-century hall-keeps in the Loire Valley and in Normandy. Its bonding courses of red Roman tile, robbed from the Roman ruins of Caerleon or Caerwent, misled 18th-century antiquaries into thinking it a Roman building. William FitzOsbern's hall was on its upper floor above a ground floor basement. There was probably an arcade of wooden posts down its centre, supporting the floor of the hall above.

THE EVOLUTION OF THE KEEP

Entry to the hall was by way of a round-headed Norman doorway with a pattern of carved decorative stonework in its head. Inside the door, a tunnel-like stair in the thickness of the wall leads up to the hall. The

The soaring towers and Great Gatehouse of Chepstow Castle are an evocative reminder of Norman strength and power

hall interior was re-modelled later in the Middle Ages, but the original round-headed Norman arches, some of them later blocked, can easily be distinguished from the pointed 'Gothic' arches of the later work. In the late 13th century a second floor was added above the wall. Interestingly, no original Norman openings appear in the southern wall, away from the river, since this wall was part of the defensive exterior of the castle. Seen from outside, it appears as a blank cliff of stonework, relieved only by a series of shallow buttresses. This archaic feature reminds us that we are looking at an early stage in the development of the Norman keep.

Inside the hall, the upper end would have been partitioned off with a cross wall to form the private room of the lord of the castle. Status was an obsession even then, for round-headed arcades, with traces of their original decoration, suggest a room of some architectural elaboration, emphasising the rank of its occupant.

FitzOsbern's castle was protected on the north by high river cliffs and on the south by

a broad and steep valley. To the east and west, along the limestone ridge on which the castle is sited, were stone-walled baileys – the present upper and middle baileys – unusual for this date when most castle baileys were defended by palisades of wood. The present lower bailey and the barbican were added to the castle later.

WILLIAM MARSHALL'S REWARD

When Richard, before he became king, had been in rebellion against his father, Henry II, one of the few who loyally stood by the old king was a landless knight and mercenary soldier, William Marshall, who achieved the feat of unhorsing Richard 'Lionheart' in a skirmish. Richard recognized the value of Marshall's loyalty and rewarded it by marrying him to la pucelle d'Estriguil 'The maid of Chepstow', heiress to Chepstow Castle and to much else. Some time between his marriage in 1189 and his death in 1219 William strengthened the vulnerable eastern face of the castle with a stone curtain wall and two half-round towers. These are perhaps the earliest examples in Britain of the use of round towers projecting out from a curtain in the new defensive mode of the 13th century. The gateway is a simple arch in the thickness of the curtain, tucked in

between one of the round towers and the river cliff and not, as it would have been a generation later, a twin-towered gatehouse.

William Marshall's five sons continued their father's work, extending the castle by adding the lower bailey at the east end, where the visitor now enters the castle, and a barbican at the upper west end. This arrangement divided Chepstow into four separate wards in line east to west, with FitzOsbern's Great Tower in the middle. The Great Gatehouse on the east is theirs, though the rest of their work in the lower bailey has disappeared in later rebuilding. The tower in the middle ward is theirs also, though it is now called after a 17th-century bishop, author of Holy Living and Holy Dying, who was imprisoned here.

FAMILY MONUMENT

The younger Marshalls were all dead by 1245. Yet they left, in the barbican, a fine memorial, its tower and gateway deserving careful scrutiny. The square tower between the upper bailey and barbican contained rooms of high quality and may have been the camera (private suite) of the countess and her ladies. It still has traces of its original painted decoration under one window. A bridge crosses the ditch to the barbican and

The curtain wall at Chepstow is in fact two walls with an earthen filling; it runs from Marten's Tower to the corner tower of the middle bailey

the small postern gate in the ditch bottom would have enabled messengers or raiding parties to slip out unseen, particularly in time of siege.

The fourth and final major period of rebuilding at Chepstow was by Roger Bigod III, one of Edward I's greatest magnates. Bigod built a hall complex – the block of buildings on the visitor's right at the entrance to the castle – as accommodation for his large household and for guests. He evidently foresaw the possibility of having to entertain a visiting magnate, perhaps even the king himself, with a separate household. Two Great Halls are therefore provided, their service arrangements interlocking neatly in the central section. Across the ward was Marten's Tower, with a suite of private apartments for Bigod and his family.

THE HALL COMPLEX

Work on the hall complex began about 1278 and it was probably complete in time for a visit by Edward I (Bigod's foresight had been rewarded) in December 1285. Next to

Dwarfing nearby houses, Chepstow is equally impressive in a modern-day setting as it was in the Norman Conquest

the gatehouse is the Eastern Hall, with the camera of its lord on the upper floor. At the other, a large service hatch (now blocked) communicated with the cross passage which served as an arterial passageway for the servants supplying food and drink to the two halls. All necessary facilities were provided for them – a large vaulted cellar where wine and foodstuffs could be stored; a cupboard for linen or cutlery; and a double seater latrine perched out high above the river cliffs.

Each hall had a pair of small rooms at its lower end, a buttery for drink and a pantry for cutlery and dishes. The arrangements for these were particularly ingenious, for the Western Hall was at a higher level than the East Hall and was reached from the cross passage up a flight of steps. The pantry and buttery block was therefore on two storeys, with the ground floor serving the east and the first floor serving the west.

MARTEN'S TOWER

Across the courtyard is Marten's Tower, named after Henry Marten, an extreme Cromwellian republican, who signed Charles I's death warrant and was imprisoned here for many years after the Restoration. He might well have been quite comfortable, for his tower contains a series of spacious rooms with fireplaces and large windows and an elegant private chapel with a portcullis slot in the floor. On the roof, a series of stone figures surmount the battlements – a garrison in stone.

By Tudor times, Chepstow had come into the possession of the Herberts of Raglan. Large rectangular mullioned windows were inserted in various parts of the castle and lodgings built against the curtain walls to house servants and minor officials. Usually, only the fireplaces of these remain. At the outbreak of the Civil War, Henry Herbert, Marquess of Worcester, garrisoned Chepstow for the king. The area saw much action in the war, but the castle held out until October 1645, when it surrendered after a short siege.

CHEPSTOW IS CAPTURED

When fighting broke out again in 1648, a local gentleman, Sir Nicholas Kemeys, seized Chepstow for the king. Cromwell besieged it, but left Colonel Ewer to finish the job whilst he went to reduce Pembroke. With the walls breached by Ewer's artillery, most of the garrison surrendered, but Kemeys was killed in the assault, either fighting in the breach or summarily shot afterwards. After the Restoration, the castle remained garrisoned until 1690. The strengthening of the southern curtain wall (as a protection against artillery) and its loopholing for musketry may date from this time. Thereafter, the castle gradually became a picturesque ruin.

IN CARE OF Welsh Office

OPEN all reasonable times (standard hours)

ADMISSION some charge

LOCATION overlooking the River Wye N of the town centre

MAP REFERENCE 5 ST1383

COUNTY Gwent

CHIRK CASTLE

Chirk was originally a lordship castle of the time of Edward I. Built c1295–1310 by Roger Mortimer, it has been much altered by its many subsequent owners and is unique among Edwardian fortresses in having been occupied continuously to the present day. Contains fine state rooms of neo-Classical and 19th-century Gothic style.

*'A Castle fayre, appeered to sight of eye,
Whose walles were great, and towers both large and hye
On side of hill, it stands most trim to viewe
An old strong place, a Castle, nothing newe,'*

Detail from the 18th-century ornamental gates, entrance to Chirk's parkland

So wrote the soldier poet, Thomas Churchyard, of Chirk when he visited it in 1587. His words are as apt today for, alone of all the North Wales castles, Chirk has been continuously inhabited throughout its long and often chequered history. Although, inevitably, it has undergone a gradual transformation from austere defence to gracious home, from a distance its curtain walls and squat drum towers present a perfect picture of the strong, medieval border fortress which, in essence, it still is.

AN ORNATE ENTRANCE

Chirk lies in the romantic border country of the Marches, redolent with the memories of past struggles between Welsh and English forces. Today, the castle is well hidden from the casual notice of travellers on the A5 for it is located on a side road a short way westwards from the centre of the little town. Soon a magnificent pair of crested, wrought

iron gates loom into view, resplendent in ornamental black and gold. Made around 1719 by two local craftsmen of Bersham, Robert and John Davies, they are perhaps the most ornate examples of early 18th-century ironwork to be seen in the country.

Originally, these gates were made for the north side of the castle, enclosing an outer court, but later they were moved and have been in their present position since 1888, where they grandly announce entry to Chirk's 468 acres of parkland. On passing through the gates, there is still no sign of the castle. But gradually, on climbing the slope, it makes its appearance – an intriguing blend of medieval fortress and Jacobean, mullioned windows, in a splendid 18th-century landscape setting.

MEDIEVAL CHIRK

The story of Chirk really begins in 1282, when Edward I, having successfully embarked on the first stage of his campaign of conquest in Wales, granted the lordship to Roger Mortimer on 2 June. Whether or not Mortimer began building at that time is not known, but there must certainly have been some kind of administrative and military base here. At any rate, the serious revolt of Madog ap Llywelyn, in 1294, may have made necessary a change of plan for, on grounds of style, the present castle seems to date from after this time. Its plan and general character bear a striking resemblance to the inner ward at Beaumaris, begun in April 1295. Indeed it is not impossible that here, as at so many places elsewhere, the hand of the king's chief military architect, James of St George, may have been at work.

When first built, Chirk was rectangular and no doubt concentric in plan, with a now-vanished encircling outer wall. In conception, it was almost certainly larger than it is today, stretching on the south side to nearly twice its present length. Thus it

Many different styles of living are apparent at Chirk. It seems incongruous to see what was once a mighty fortress surrounded by landscaped gardens

would have had four corner towers, three centrally-placed curtain towers and, on the south side, presumably, the great twin-towered gatehouse that is now so obviously missing from its medieval layout. Whether or not these additional features were ever built, we cannot say. Neither can we be sure that the towers were ever taken to their full projected height, for they are certainly truncated, as they stand now, very much like those of unfinished Beaumaris. It may be that, when Roger Mortimer fell from grace in 1322 to be imprisoned and finally executed in the Tower of London, building work had simply not been completed.

LUCKLESS OWNERS

Unlike Beaumaris where there was only a single main period of building, Chirk had many subsequent owners who impressed their stamp on it. At least six of its medieval castellans were executed for treason and their estates seized by the Crown – after Mortimer came the Earl of Arundel, beheaded in 1326; Roger Mortimer IV, hanged in 1330; Arundel again, beheaded in 1397; the Duke of Somerset, beheaded in 1464; and, finally, Sir William Stanley, beheaded in 1495.

By the late 1530's, when Henry VIII's antiquary, John Leland, visited it, he spoke

of 'a mightly large and stronge castel, with dyvers towers, a late welle repayred by Syr Wylliam Standeley'. By this date, however, and almost certainly after the tenancy of Stanley, a good deal of rebuilding had been carried out, including the addition of the 'newe lodgynges' of the south range.

Substantial damage was done at the time of the Civil War and Sir Thomas Myddelton, to whom ownership had passed, was faced with an enormous bill for repairs and new work, which amounted to around £30,000. With the changed ideas of the following century, however, Chirk was considered old-fashioned. In 1756, Lord Lyttelton considered it to be 'the most disagreeable dwelling-house I ever saw: nor is there any magnificence to make amends for the want of convenience'.

CHIRK REBUILT

From the 1760's, therefore, an ambitious programme of modification was begun by the young Richard Myddelton. This resulted in the magnificent series of state rooms, in the north wing, designed in the neo-Classical style, which are the great glory of Chirk Castle today. Additional space was gained by scouring out the 15ft-thick walls of the medieval towers; indeed, the grand staircase itself is cunningly and

Extensive alterations have transformed Chirk into a stylish stately home

elegantly contrived within the confines of the north tower (you can still see the original wall thickness, if you look closely). The wheel came full circle in the 1840s, when fashions reverted to Gothic and the architect A W Pugin, designer of the Houses of Parliament, was chosen to make the rather unsatisfactory additions to the east range.

So today, Chirk stands proudly in its acquired parklands, its 13th-century exterior hiding an intriguing amalgam of later architectural styles. Only one tower now retains its medieval character to any substantial degree but, as an exercise in the adaptation of a great medieval fortress to the changing needs of later times, it is unique in Wales.

IN CARE OF National Trust

OPEN at regular times during spring, summer and autumn. Please check in advance

ADMISSION some charge

LOCATION 1m W of Chirk

MAP REFERENCE 12 SJ2738

COUNTY Clwyd

CILGERRAN CASTLE

Two powerful towers on a crag characterise this castle, which stands in a beautiful position overlooking a gorge of the River Teifi, where coracles (small wickerwork boats) still float from time to time.

William the Conqueror visited St David's and met Rhys ap Tewdwr, the ruler of Deheubarth, a kingdom which covered most of South West Wales. But not until after Rhys's death did the Normans really penetrate into the region. Cilgerran may have been the castle from which Nest, Rhys ap Tewdwr's daughter, was abducted by Owain, son of the Prince of Powys. Cilgerran Castle first appears in recorded history a century later when it was captured by William Marshall, Earl of Pembroke, in 1204. It is recorded that he spared the lives of the garrison, an event clearly uncommon enough to merit a mention.

THE NORMAN CASTLE
Cilgerran stands at the tidal limit of the Teifi, accessible to large ships and at the lowest crossing-place of the river at all states of the tide. Here the river runs through a gorge, and a stream (the Plysgog) falls into it from a side valley, so cutting off a rocky promontory. To the right of the modern entrance is a wide ditch, isolating the base of the promontory, with a precipice to the left. The slopes of the ditch can be seen in the gardens running down to the patch along the bottom of the ditch. Whether there was ever a motte – a Norman mound – at the far end of the castle is arguable: the castle is certainly strong enough without one.

Cilgerran and many other castles fell to Welsh assaults led by Llywelyn ab Iorwerth ('the Great'). William Marshall's son managed to recapture Cilgerran in 1223 and set about rebuilding it with a strongly-defended inner ward at the far end of the spur.

THE GREAT TOWERS OF CILGERRAN
William Marshall II made a five-sided inner ward by building two great round towers with short lengths of curtain wall between them and on either side, and cutting a ditch in the rock in front of the towers. Evidently, this work was hastily done – the ditch running across the front of the castle is not of uniform width, and the masonry consists of stones of all shapes and sizes.

Each round tower had four storeys, the wall facing an attacker being over three feet thicker than the rest. The upper floors were carried on wooden joists – the holes for them can be seen inside each tower – and were lit by windows facing the inner ward (and so protected from attack). Spiral stairs linked the upper floors, but the ground floor had a separate entrance for defensive reasons. In the 14th century the right-hand tower was partitioned to form a strong-room. The second floor of each tower had doors leading out on to the battlements of the curtain wall, and the top floors had fireplaces, whose chimney shafts and hoods are still in place.

Between the great towers is a small doorway through the curtain wall (here eight feet thick) protected by a portcullis worked from the battlements above. In front was the great ditch 40ft wide. This doorway would allow the defenders to sally out against the besiegers either directly or, by way of a narrow terrace, to another door in the wall crossing the end of the ditch. From there they could attack the besiegers from the rear.

INNER GATEHOUSE
This lies to the left of the great round towers. It was of three storeys, with a portcullis at each end of the passage and a vaulted room – perhaps a chapel – above. A wall-passage with arrowslits connected it to the nearer round tower, and there was an open parapet-walk above to complete the

The rugged castle of Cilgerran stands above a deep gorge overlooking the River Teifi, scene of the annual coracle festival held each August

defence on this side. On the other side the precipice was defence enough, but a square tower and thick curtain walls were later added – probably not much later, since the castle was derelict by 1275, the English having suffered a disastrous defeat in this area in 1258.

However, active service did not end for Cilgerran until much later. There was a short-lived revival of the castle in 1377, when Edward III ordered repairs to counter a threatened French invasion. A limekiln was built behind the gatehouse, and a quarter-round tower put up on the far side of the kitchen, looking downstream towards the sea. The refurbished castle must have been quite strong, for it held out during Owain Glyndwr's uprising in the early 15th century.

IN CARE OF Welsh Office

OPEN all reasonable times (standard hours)

ADMISSION some charge

LOCATION 3m S of Cardigan

MAP REFERENCE 2 SN1943

COUNTY Dyfed

The west walls of Coity (above) probably date from the 14th century, when the castle was almost completely rebuilt

COITY CASTLE

Coity, in the pastoral Vale of Glamorgan, was originally a Norman ringwork of earth and timber, later strengthened with a stone keep and curtain wall. These defences enabled it to stand siege by Owain Glyndwr, but Parliament was so worried that Henry IV mounted a special relief expedition to rescue the trapped Lord of Coity.

Coity takes us back to the days of the early Norman lordships. The castle was the head of the lordship of Coity, which in turn was a member of the greater lordship of Glamorgan. It was held by the Turbevilles, who, by conquest or marriage, had supplanted an earlier Welsh lord. Legend has it that Payn de Turbeville used the subtler means of marriage. 'Marry my daughter and you shall have all my lands without bloodshed', said Morgan, the Welsh ruler of the region.

De Turbeville, one of Robert FitzHamon's knights in the original conquest of Glamorgan, probably first built a castle here in the early years of the 12th century. It consisted of a Norman ringwork, a circular ditch surrounding an embanked area protected by a timber palisade and fighting platform. A gate tower mounted on solid wooden posts would have controlled access and inside would have been Payn de Turbeville's wooden hall. There may have been an outwork on the side now occupied by the outer ward, but if so it would have been levelled when the outer ward was built.

FROM WOOD TO STONE

Towards the end of the 12th century, Sir Gilbert de Turbeville was probably responsible for bringing the castle defences up to date by rebuilding them in stone with a square keep and curtain wall. The keep survives, much altered, as one of the twin towers of the middle gate, leading from the outer to the inner ward. The Norman curtain wall still encircles much of the perimeter of the inner ward, though several large sections of it have been taken down and replaced by later walling.

In the 13th century, the defences were again modernised. A circular tower was built against the south side of the curtain wall, projecting out into the ditch and containing arrow-slits which allowed protective fire for this sector of walling. There may also have been other towers along the curtain which have now vanished.

FOURTEENTH-CENTURY REBUILDING

Most of what we see today belongs to the 14th century, when the castle was extensive-ly rebuilt and re-modelled and a new outer ward was perhaps constructed, replacing an earlier version protected only by a palisade and ditch. The angles of the outer ward were protected by square towers (unfortunately, the one at the north-west angle has disappeared).

The east gate is flanked by two square towers. That on the north is the much-altered Norman keep, with medieval ribbed vaulting inserted into its interior and a small Tudor annexe on one side. The other gate tower, and the gate itself, are 14th century, as are the buildings inside the ward. They are perhaps the work of Sir Roger Berkerolles, who had inherited the lands of the Turbevilles by marriage. Also of this period is an east gate, with drawbridge and portcullis, leading out towards the church. The 14th-century buildings on the opposite side of the ward include a hall and chapel, both at first-floor level and reached from the courtyard by a circular stair.

GLYNDWR'S ASSAULT

The castle later passed to Sir William Gamage, who had probably completed its refurbishment before he was beseiged in it by the followers of Owain Glyndwr. In 1404 the House of Commons asked Henry IV to mount a relief expedition to rescue the

The 14th-century gatehouse (right) could possibly have been added to Coity Castle by Sir Roger Berkerolles, who inherited the land not by means of bloodshed, but by marriage

Lord of Coity 'who was and had long been besieged in his castle of Coity'. But it was too late in the year and the relief force became literally bogged down in the mud of the Glamorgan roads as the rains of a Welsh autumn set in. In the spring, Prince Henry (the future Henry V) launched a further offensive, which drove Glyndwr's forces out of Glamorgan.

Alterations and improvements were subsequently carried out, and another storey was added to the hall block, the gables of which can still be seen. But the end of the castle was in sight, for in 1584 Barbara, the daughter of the last of the male Gamages, married Sir Robert Sidney, later second Earl of Leicester. Thereafter, with no resident lord, the castle fell into decline.

IN CARE OF Welsh Office

OPEN all reasonable times (standard hours)

ADMISSION some charge

LOCATION Off A4061 2m NE of Bridgend

MAP REFERENCE 4 SS9281

COUNTY Mid Glamorgan

CONWY

Built by Edward I as part of his master plan to subdue the Welsh, Conwy was both fortress and garrison town. It still retains a complete ¾ mile circuit of town walls, much of it open to the public. The castle, dating from 1282, is one of Wales's finest, with eight massive round towers and barbicans at either end. Originally approached up an enormous stone ramp, which no longer survives, it is divided into two wards. Though now roofless, the great hall and royal apartments are still impressive. Fine views from the battlements.

The first view of Conwy Castle, on crossing the estuary from the Llandudno side, is almost guaranteed to quicken the pulse. In the distance, its towers rise majestically, even menacingly, as if standing guard over the trio of latter-day bridges which now speed the crossing from the gentler landscape of North East Wales into the foothills of Snowdonia.

The river crossing was once made only by ferry. Then came the great era of highway improvement and with it, in 1826, Thomas Telford's new suspension bridge, its castellated towers echoing those of the medieval fortress above it. Two decades later came the railway, forging across the Conwy river on its way towards Holyhead and the boat to Ireland; so, in 1848, the engineer Robert Stephenson built his own castellated bridge, its single span of tubular grey metal running side by side with Telford's elegant suspension cables. Stephenson's bridge still carries the railway but time and progress have overtaken its neighbour, for Telford's road bridge, now an historic monument in its own right, can be crossed only on foot. Today, the highway is carried across on a third bridge, built in 1958 to a functional design devoid of any mock battlements.

THE TOWN

From Telford's bridge, the skyline is dominated by towering castle walls. It soon becomes apparent, however, that here is not just a castle but a whole fortified town, protected by walls and regularly-spaced towers. From the castle, they run along the front of the little quay, then climb steadily up to a rocky brow above the town before descending, once again, to the castle on the other side. Of all King Edward I's foundations in North Wales, Conwy retains most authentically its historic status as a garrison town. Its complete circuit of town walls is still intact, over ¾ mile in length, with 22 towers and three original gateways. Walls and castle were all built during a frenzied period of activity between 1283 and 1287, a tremendous achievement which only amounted to about 36 months of continuous work all told. The final cost of the project to the Crown was around £15,000, equivalent today to something like £10 million.

Conwy's town walls may be the finest in North Wales, but they were by no means unique. All but three out of the 17 Edwardian castles here were built with defended town boroughs into which English merchants and traders were encouraged to come and settle, promoting their new way of life. Most of these boroughs had little more than earthworks to surround them, but Conwy and also Caernarfon were given elaborate fortified walls where, 700 years later, visitors can still walk along the battlements or wander the medieval streets. For all their grandeur, one of the most endearing features of the walls at Conwy is the neat row of 12 garderobes, latrines for the garrison, which project over the outside of the section beside the Mill Gate. Here, one can still catch a brief glimpse, across the centuries, of the stark yet ordered day to day life of a 13th-

(above left) Alan Sorrell's interpretation of the castle in its prime shows how little time has changed it

Conwy's groundplan (right) illustrates the architectural genius put to use in its building

century garrison soldier – not so different, in many respects, to that of his modern counterpart.

THE CASTLE

No visitor to Conwy should leave without walking at least part of the walls. The castle, by virtue of its pre-eminence, speaks for itself. First impressions are of tremendous military strength, dominating position and a unity and compactness of design. Its eight almost identical towers seem to spring from the living rock as if they had sprouted there; indeed it was the very formation of that rocky site which dictated the castle's eventual layout.

Unlike most of King Edward's other new fortresses in Wales, Conwy was built not to a concentric, but to a linear plan (so too is Caernarfon). Instead of an outer circuit of walls, it has two lower barbican outworks at each end and, instead, it was divided by a cross wall into two quite separate wards, so that either could hold out independently if the other should fall. In the Middle Ages, both the castle and the town walls would have looked startlingly different to our eyes for, instead of bare grey stonework, they would have had an overall white rendering, quite common in those days.

FORCING AN ENTRY

Today's way in, up the sloping concrete path that leads into the castle, imparts a mild sense of disappointment. Could this really have been the way the entrance looked in the 13th century? Where were all the gates and portcullises and where was the drawbridge? It is not, of course, the original arrangement, for the opening in the side of the gate passage is entirely modern. Once, a huge stepped ramp of masonry would have led up, from the site of the present day roadway, towards the entry. A drawbridge, guarded by a portcullis, would have dropped down onto it, crossing what must have been a very deep chasm. The grooves for the portcullis are still there, as are the pivot holes for the drawbridge axle and, in the far wall, the remains of the steps that led up to a room above the gate containing the winches and pulleys that controlled them. The outer gate passage was probably roofed over and would have led up towards the west barbican, where a stout wooden door barred the way. The barbican itself was quite open, so that any attackers who might reach it could be picked off with ease from the walltops of the castle above. In short, entry was no easy matter, whatever the modern arrangements might imply.

INSIDE THE WALLS

Once inside the inner ward, there is an impression of openness. But look at the foundations on the ground and you will see that, in fact, it would

Telford's graceful bridge, spanning the estuary, leads to Conwy's gatehouse

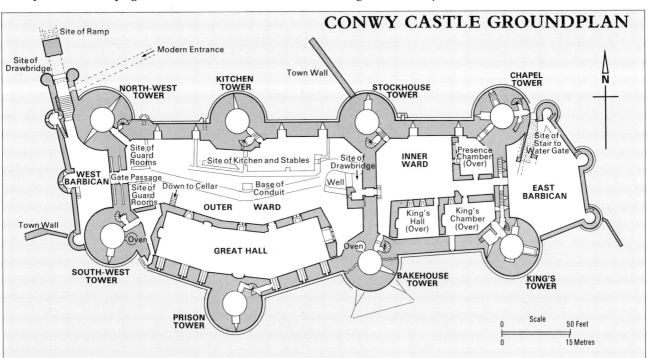

CONWY CASTLE GROUNDPLAN

Site of Ramp

Modern Entrance

Site of Drawbridge

Town Wall

NORTH-WEST TOWER

KITCHEN TOWER

STOCKHOUSE TOWER

CHAPEL TOWER

N

Site of Guard Rooms

Site of Kitchen and Stables

Site of Drawbridge

INNER WARD

Presence Chamber (Over)

Site of Stair to Water Gate

WEST BARBICAN

Gate Passage

Site of Guard Rooms

Down to Cellar

Base of Conduit

Well

EAST BARBICAN

Town Wall

Oven

OUTER WARD

King's Hall (Over)

King's Chamber (Over)

SOUTH-WEST TOWER

GREAT HALL

Oven

BAKEHOUSE TOWER

KING'S TOWER

PRISON TOWER

Scale

0   50 Feet

0   15 Metres

F

View over the Castle's ramparts and surrounding area from the Bakehouse Tower at Conwy Castle

originally have been rather cramped for space. Here, just inside the gate passage, would have stood the guardrooms, the stables and also the kitchens serving the Great Hall opposite. The Great Hall dominates the outer ward, 125ft in length and built to an unusual bowed plan to adapt to its rocky foundation. Though some of the tracery in the windows still survives to give an impression of its former grandeur, the uninitiated visitor might find the place bewildering, for it is now split longitudinally into two separate levels. Not surprisingly, it would never have looked like this; formerly there was a basement for storage and a grand first floor (the level one now comes in at). For the first few days in the year when the king, or some other important guest was in residence, Conwy's hall no doubt looked a fine sight – bustling with activity, its walls hung, perhaps, with fine tapestries and its tables glittering with silver plate. The rest of the time, it would have been quite a different story because, for most of the year, the castle would have been half empty, its occupants reduced to a governor and small resident garrison.

Leaving the hall, one passes beside the castle well and, over the site of a further drawbridge, through to the inner ward. Here lay the private quarters of the king and queen, installed at a cost of approximately £320 in 1283. When they were in residence, royal standards would have billowed from the tops of the turrets, which crown each tower of the inner ward. Sadly, these once sumptuous apartments have been reduced now to bare shells. One tower, however, still retains its beautiful little chapel which, even now, displays a quality of decoration in a state of preservation that is quite unmatched at any other Edwardian castle. This chapel has been re-floored and re-roofed to protect it from exposure.

A veritable armada of small boats bob lazily on the tide of the River Conwy's wide estuary

IN CARE OF Welsh Office

OPEN all reasonable times (standard hours)

ADMISSION some charge

LOCATION eastern part of town

MAP REFERENCE 11 SH7877

COUNTY Gwynedd

THE QUEEN'S GARDEN

In the east barbican, just outside the inner ward, there was originally a small garden. It was probably planted at the request of Edward I's wife, Queen Eleanor, who seems to have been a keen gardener. She had one outside Caernarfon Castle and another was planted outside her temporary quarters in Conwy town, during July 1283. Turf for the lawn was shipped specially from further up river and the plot was fenced with the staves from an empty barrel. Records tell us that on a warm evening in July, her squire, Roger le Fykeys, was paid three pence for attending to its first watering.

The east barbican had its own access to the river, through a small water gate in the gap beside the Chapel Tower, but the stepped ramp that once curved around and down to the river below has long since vanished. Despite this additional means of escape, King Edward I was actually besieged in Conwy by the rebel forces of Madog ap Llywelyn, during January 1295. Though food and drink were running dangerously low, the chroniclers of the time reported with astonishment that the king resolutely refused to take for himself the last remaining cask of wine but, instead, chose to drink the water and honey mixture with his men.

Afterwards, Conwy subsides almost into obscurity, a magnificent, forgotten relic. Its greatest battle proved to be the one against decay and, only a generation after its completion, it was in need of substantial repair. By 1627, a survey reported it dangerous to enter, 'the leads being decayed and broken above and almost all the floares fallen down'. It saw some action during the Civil War, but afterwards was left to the elements. Today, Conwy is one of Wales' most atmospheric sites, its jumble of walls, towers and masonry evoking an authentic medieval air.

BUILDING A MASONRY CASTLE

A motte and bailey castle could be built in a matter of weeks or months, using the labour and materials immediately to hand (see *The early castles* page 73). But to put up a stone castle was quite another matter, requiring considerable planning and organization over a period of years. Conwy Castle and town walls were constructed remarkably quickly, in about five years; Caernarfon dragged on for over 25, and was never finally completed as planned.

Often the lord did not even own the site of his proposed new castle, and had to compensate the landowner, if not his tenants. Thus King Edward I gave land to the monks of Strata Florida Abbey in exchange for the site on which he built the last Aberystwyth Castle.

MANPOWER

The lord required an 'engineer' or a military architect to translate his needs for buildings and defences into masonry by design and construction. Such experts were scarce, so Edward I brought a specialist designer all the way from Savoy to help design his new castles in Wales (see *Master James of St George*, page 41). A resident clerk of works was also needed, to oversee the work and administer its finances – a household knight, or the constable-to-be, might be appointed to do this job.

Specialist artisans – quarrymen and masons, woodcutters and carpenters, plumbers and smiths, miners and ditchers – were also required in numbers that the immediate locality could never provide. So, for Edward's work in North Wales, workmen were assembled by quota from nearly every shire in England. Around 3,000 men were engaged on the king's works during the building season – late spring, summer and autumn. If this does not sound very many today, remember that the population of England was only one-tenth of what it is now.

By any standards, the labour force was intelligent, trained, well educated and well travelled. The resulting work was sophisticated and highly skilled, with masonry constructed to finer tolerances than were used in iron by the early railway engineers of the 19th century.

WAGES

During the building of the North Wales castles, most of the workmen were on weekly rates ranging from four shillings for a master mason down to six pence for a woman labourer. Master James of St George was paid two shillings *a day* and his fee of 100 marks a year as constable of Harlech Castle brought this up to the equivalent of two pounds a week. To convert this into modern currency is dangerous, but James of St George was undoubtedly receiving an income comparable with the leading entrepreneurs of today. Even the unskilled labourers were getting two-thirds of skilled rates. Piecework did occur for special tasks (a dozen toilet cubicles at Conwy cost £15) and there was also sub-contracting (individual towers at Harlech, for instance).

MATERIALS

In Wales, building stone was often quarried from the site itself (in England it was often necessary to buy stone and carry it a distance). Much of the rough materials came as spoil from the cutting of the castle ditches by the miners. But for fine work – fireplaces and windows, for example – stone came from further afield. Red Cheshire sandstone was used in many North Wales castles for details, whereas the stone for the main walling came either from the underlying rock (as at Conwy and Harlech) or nearby; Beaumaris and Caernarfon were built from Anglesey stone. Local shore sand provided a good mortar aggregate in each case.

Timber – for scaffolding as well as for floors and roof frames and boards – often had to come from a distance ready-cut. Until the royal woodcutters arrived in the Conwy valley, much castle timber was shipped around from England. Iron came up from the Forest of Dean (Gloucestershire) and Chester, and lead from the Mendips as well as Derbyshire.

CONSTRUCTION

Most Welsh castles were founded on solid rock, which needed

Castle renovation goes on into the 20th century. Here, a new roof is constructed at Caerphilly

levelling to some extent. Caernarfon Castle, unusually, is founded on shale or compact gravel. In 1212, King John paid for smiths and iron hammers 'to break the rocks in the ditch of the castle of Yale'. Many hand tools in use today are little different from those used by the Romans, and there was little medieval building machinery, although a hand winch was bought for Caernarfon. In order to improve access to Rhuddlan Castle, the River Clwyd was diverted into a new three-mile channel cut by men from the Fens of East Anglia.

Walls were often built with good facing stone, with rubble and mortar poured into the space within. At Rhuddlan, the core has held together where the facing stone has been stripped away. When building stopped for the winter, walls would be covered with turf or thatch to stop frost from cracking them.

TOTAL COSTS

Caernarfon cost about £20,000 to erect, Beaumaris and Conwy £15,000 each and Rhuddlan and Harlech around £9,000. Altogether, nearly £100,000 was spent on Edward I's castle-building. This was more than could be raised in a year's taxes for all purposes of government, but of course the buildings took many years to put up. The castles were a relatively cheap insurance (or defence) policy: compare their cost to the £150,000 which Edward spent in one year's campaigning against the Welsh.

Edward I applied the maxim 'many hands make light work' to his building requirements, employing around 3,000 men in the building season

cc auoient sur eur les .iij. princes deuant no mes nemuoth jenam et sulen.

De la tour latel selon la bible. *pes aus gilbiti me fecit*

at cca mesrmes nos solan loo

In this detail from a 13th-century French illustration the King watches keenly as workmen build his castle

The examples quoted here have been selected from the royal records. No doubt the barons went about building their castles in much the same way, but few accounts survive. The money would come from local revenues (tolls, fines, feudal dues) in cash or kind, but ready cash to pay workmen and traders had to be carted up from the treasury. We hear of strikes and go-slows when the pay was slow in arriving.

ARCHITECTURAL STYLE

Castles in Wales followed the same broad pattern of development as those in England. However, border warfare and the 'Final Solution to the Welsh Problem' produced different needs and different approaches. The Norman rectangular keep is rare (and smaller) in Wales compared to England, but there are some unique versions (Bridgend, Tretower). The round keep is very common in Wales, particularly in the south, and a distinctively 'Welsh' type of elongated D-shaped tower has been identified.

At Pembroke we have not only the finest round tower but also what is probably the first twin-towered keep-gatehouse in Britain (at least since Roman times). Caerphilly, with its remarkable water defences, ushers in the great series of 'Edwardian' castles. There was little need thereafter for new castles – or the money to pay for them – and although a new palace was built at Llawhaden and a number of small fortified manors in Gwent and Glamorgan, only the nouveaux riche Herberts, with their palatial Raglan and its seigneurial Yellow Tower of Gwent survives from the late Middle Ages, before the Tudor ostentation of Carew and Oxwich.

CRICCIETH CASTLE

Standing high upon its rock, dominating the little seaside town, Criccieth is mainly a native Welsh castle of the two Llywelyns. Taken by Edward I in 1283 and refortified, it was eventually destroyed by Owain Glyndwr in 1404. The castle commands superb views over Tremadog Bay.

Most visitors go to Criccieth for the sea, not realizing that it has a castle at all until, on rounding the brow in the road from Porthmadog, the fortress comes into view, perched high above the town. With its pleasant seaside air, the resort of Criccieth is largely sheltered from severer forms of weather, tucked up safe beneath the crook of that long finger of land, the Lleyn Peninsula. Criccieth's benign location is best appreciated from the top of the castle hill. Here, on a fine day, the views are truly panoramic – westwards, out to the tip of Lleyn, north and east towards Snowdonia and southwards over the broad, majestic sweep of Cardigan Bay. A more splendid situation would be hard to imagine and its value as a military lookout is immediately evident.

OBSCURE ORIGINS

In origin, Criccieth is a native Welsh castle. It seems to be of three main building periods, none of them directly recorded and, unfortunately, scholars now disagree about who built what, so that it is impossible to be certain about its history. What we do know is that part was built by Llywelyn ab Iorwerth ('the Great'), part by his grandson, Llywelyn ap Gruffudd ('the Last') and part by King Edward I.

The castle is nearly concentric in plan, having an inner ring, with twin-towered

Criccieth Castle crowns a rocky promontory and commands sweeping views over Tremadog Bay (top left)

The crumbling north west side of Criccieth Castle (bottom left)

Good examples of arrow-slits can be seen within the walls of Criccieth (below)

gatehouse, curtain walls and a rectangular tower. To the north, east and south, there is the outer curtain wall with two further rectangular towers at either end and a small outer gateway.

THE GREAT GATEHOUSE

The inner ward, most likely the earliest part of the castle, is all of one build. It was probably built around 1220–30 by Llywelyn the Great. Most impressive today is the high, twin-towered gatehouse, with three outward facing arrow-loops to each tower and its lofty, defended gateway. Standing over twice the height of any other surviving parts, it is the main feature of the castle. Although ruined on the inner side, it still presents an imposing spectacle from without. This Great Gatehouse has no parallel at any of Llywelyn's other castles. Indeed, apart from Castell-y-Bere, most of them have no gatehouses at all. Interestingly, both gatehouse and the whole inner ward are close in style to the inner ward of Montgomery Castle, built by the young King Henry III, between 1223 and 1227.

On the outside of the gatehouse, at low level, are traces of the rendering which once covered all the rougher masonry of the castle. The entrance itself was protected by a portcullis and barred gate, with murder slots above while, from the battlements, regularly-spaced square holes indicate that there was provision for a timber fighting platform to overhang the gate. Later in its history, probably during the time of Edward II, the top stage of the gatehouse was heightened, as one can see from the tell-tale lines of the filled-in crenellations.

The next part of the castle to be built was probably the south western part of the outer ward, with its simple gateway and large,

rectangular tower. This most likely dates from the 1250s or '60s, during the time of Llywelyn the Last and may, at one stage, have joined the western angle of the inner ward, making an outer bailey extension.

THE ENGINE TOWER

Almost certainly, the latest addition is the Engine Tower at the north end of the castle. From recent research, we know that Edward I spent £353 on refortifying Criccieth in 1283 and most of it went, no doubt, on building this tower and its adjacent lengths of curtain walling. Two pairs of garderobe, or latrine shafts, on its seaward side show that it had at least two floors. The tower can be seen with siege engine installed, in the foreground of the painting by Alan Sorrell, depicting the castle as it would have looked in its prime.

During Madog's rebellion, both Criccieth and Harlech were victualled by ship from Ireland. Some of the supplies taken in were prodigious – 6,000 herrings, 24 salted pigs, 18 cheeses, 20 pounds of twine from crossbows, to say nothing of the 109 carcasses of mutton and 30 of beef already in store. Small wonder that the castle succeeded in holding out.

Under Edward the Black Prince, Criccieth had a distinguished Welsh constable, Sir Hywel ap Gruffydd ('Sir Howel of the Battle-axe') and, even well into the Elizabethan period, a daily dish of meat was served to the poor by the yeoman attendants in front of his axe.

Criccieth's end came abruptly in 1404, with its capture by Owain Glyndwr. The castle was sacked and burnt, never to rise again. The castle now houses an interesting exhibition on the theme of the native castles of the Welsh princes.

IN CARE OF Welsh Office

OPEN all reasonable times (standard hours)

ADMISSION some charge

LOCATION on hill overlooking town

MAP REFERENCE 10 SH4938

COUNTY Gwynedd

CRICKHOWELL CASTLE

The important, though little known, ruins of Crickhowell Castle lie behind a main street of a pleasant, small country town.

Along a pathway beside the town cricket field are the remains of one of the major castles of medieval Brycheiniog (later Breconshire, now in part of the 'new' county of Powys). On the right is the massive motte. Climbing to its top, one finds the grass-covered remains of a circular shell keep, a stone ring wall around the perimeter of the summit. Originally, this would probably have been like the one at nearby Tretower. Today it survives only as a series of intriguing humps and ridges in the turf.

At the bottom of the mound, a needle of masonry is all that is left from a twin-towered gatehouse which guarded the steps up the motte. The castle bailey forms a small playing field, presented to the town by a local man in memory of his son, killed at Loos in 1915. On one side is part of a large rectangular hall block with a pair of towers, one round, one square, copied from the similar pair on the hall at Brecon. They date from about 1300. An 18th-century print showing a length of curtain wall towards the river with small circular towers, gives us a clearer idea of how the castle would have looked.

This castle of the Turbevilles, and its associated small market town, seems to have had a fairly peaceful history. Crickhowell occurs rarely in the historical annals, though the townsfolk were given a royal grant towards walling their town in 1281 and orders were issued in 1403 to ensure that the castle was defensible against Glyndwr.

An interesting feature of Crickhowell Castle (below) is the large conical mound said by many to resemble Cardiff keep

IN CARE OF local authority
OPEN at all times
ADMISSION free
LOCATION in the town centre
MAP REFERENCE 5 SO2218
COUNTY Powys

DEGANWY CASTLE

Ancient fortified site, crowning twin hills, overlooking Conwy estuary. Little remains of either castle of Llywelyn the Great or Henry III. Destroyed 1263. Superb views of coast and mountains.

The castle of Deganwy, crowning the two prominent hilltops on the east side of the Conwy estuary, is a very ancient fortified site, dating back to the Roman period and possibly beyond. Today, however, practically nothing is left on either hill, save the stumpy remains of sundry walling and the shallow depressions of outer ditches.

This dearth of remains is compensated for by superb, all-round views of estuary, Conwy Castle and town, the mountains of Snowdonia and the Isle of Anglesey.

The site of Deganwy is of great importance strategically, geographically and also culturally, for the River Conwy forms a

Deganwy Castle stands on two volcanic outcrops overlooking the Conwy estuary

DENBIGH CASTLE

Hilltop castle with an almost complete circuit of town walls dominating the modern town. Denbigh was a lordship castle of Edward I's second campaign, built by Henry de Lacy in 1282.

The castle of Denbigh is an underrated and far too little-known site. It has the misfortune to lie midway between two main east–west routes; one carrying visitors each summer, in their thousands, through to Betws-y-Coed and the heartlands of Snowdonia, the other following the coast to resorts at Rhyl, Colwyn Bay and Llandudno. Denbigh town receives little of this passing traffic, its hilltop castle remaining comparatively undiscovered.

Approaching from the south, the castle ruins high above the town dominate the horizon. Below them, medieval town walls plunge precipitously down the rock towards a great angular tower at its foot, before sweeping upwards again on the other side.

Denbigh's very name provides a hint of underlying earlier Iron Age defences. There is not a trace of these today, however; nor of the residence of the native Welsh princes which we know stood here until 1282, for the castle works have obliterated all such remains. At one time, Llywelyn ap Gruffudd's brother, Dafydd, regarded this as his main stronghold. Here he had his court, containing a hall, private chamber, chapel, bakehouse and buttery. The defences of this native stronghold kept at bay the English army for almost a month in 1282.

Denbigh's castle walls sit like a hollow crown on the hill summit

FIRST BUILDING

On 16 October 1282, the king granted the lordship of Denbigh to Henry de Lacy, Earl of Lincoln. The royal records tell us that Edward I stayed here with de Lacey until the end of the month, putting his staff and his resources at the earl's disposal, to help with his new building operations; indeed, £22 was contributed to the work from the royal purse (more like £15,000, in today's terms). This is all the records have to tell us, for afterwards the castle works became de Lacy's responsibility, as with the other castles of Marcher lords – de Grey at Ruthin, de Warenne at Holt and de Mohaut at Hawarden. We do know, however, that the king's chief military architect, Master James of St George, was personally involved in the works at Denbigh and so a good deal of its layout and design may well be his work.

The castle encloses a large, roughly oval area, which encircles practically the entire hilltop. If there had been an Iron Age hillfort here, it is more than likely that it would have followed more or less the same line as de Lacy's later work, which perhaps explains why there is no longer any evidence of an early site. The defences were clearly built in two stages. As at other castle, the primary effort went into securing a strong, safe base for garrison and builders. Here, the southern and western sides were built first, along with part of the town walls. The enclosure was probably completed by the walls of the native princely stronghold that preceded it. This work is distinguished by thinner curtain walls and half round towers. By 1284,

great divide between Snowdonia's uplands and the gentler lands of the north east. This physical barrier corresponds also to a major cultural frontier – to the east are the much anglicized lands of the Four Cantrefs, overrun long ago by Norman and Saxon, to the west is Pura Wallia, Welsh Wales. The craggy hills of Deganwy, overlooking the Conwy, have thus acquired great historic military significance.

Llywelyn ab Iorwerth ('the Great') built a castle here in the early years of the 13th century and, for a while, it served as a prison for his rebellious son, Gruffudd. The one notable feature from Llywelyn's castle is a finely carved stone head, now in the National Museum of Wales, Cardiff. In 1241, Llywelyn's son Dafydd destroyed the castle in the face of an English advance and, that same year, King Henry III began to rebuild it. To his rebuilding can be attributed almost all the remains visible today. In 1263 this, in turn, was captured and thrown down by Llywelyn ap Gruffudd ('the Last') with such tremendous ferocity that barely one stone now remains upon another.

IN CARE OF private owner

LOCATION Right of public access via footpath leading from rear of housing estate just off B5115 near junction with A546

MAP REFERENCE 11 SH7879

COUNTY Gwynedd

the building was far enough advanced for de Lacy to think about stocking his deer park and, by 1290, he had granted the first borough charter to the Burgesses who were living in his new town. The first testing was not long in coming. During the rising of Madog ap Llywelyn in 1294, a Welsh force captured Denbigh Castle. De Lacy was beaten back in all his attempts to retake it, only succeeding after the revolt was finally crushed.

LATER BUILDING

The remainder of the defences seem to date from after this episode. This later work is readily recognizable by its different-coloured stone, thicker curtains and angular towers. Most impressive is the great gatehouse, with its three interlinked, octagonal towers. This is still by far the most striking single feature of the castle and was built to a very high quality, no doubt reflecting the power and prestige of its owner. The standard is plainly evident in the chequered limestone and sandstone work and in the decorative niche with its statue of King Edward I. Guarding the front of the gatehouse was a barbican, no longer to be seen today. The tower on the right was known as the Prison Tower where, in 1561, there was said to be a 'deape dongion'. On the other side was the Porter's Lodge Tower and, between them, one would have entered a great vaulted octagonal chamber. Above it lay a similar chamber with yet another storey planned, but perhaps never built, on top of it.

The remainder of the castle contained various buildings ranged around its walls, such as halls and chambers, but most of these are little higher than foundations today. The earlier defences, with their half round towers, were strengthened during the second phase of building by the addition of an outer wall, or mantlet, which is joined onto an elaborate sloping barbican, protecting the postern gate.

WALLS AND WELL

The town walls were also strengthened after Madog's revolt. The most important addition here was the heavily-defended section of wall which sweeps down the rock from the Countess Tower to encompass the Goblin Tower, with its deep well, before rejoining the main wall further up the hill. This stretch can still be walked by visitors and is a steep, but rewarding climb, with panoramic views out over the Clywdian Hills. Evidently the castle well proved to be insufficient to support the garrison and the supply from the deep well was provided in its stead. It is said that de Lacy's eldest son fell into the well and was drowned, as a result of which Henry never finished the castle.

In later times, the town was attacked frequently. In the 16th century it moved outside the walls onto the more level ground around the market place. The castle was refortified in the Civil War when King Charles I stayed here for a few days, but after a prolonged siege, it finally surrendered to Parliament and redundancy.

The dignified ruin of Denbigh Castle overlooks the town from Denbigh hill. Its gatehouse is its most impressive feature

IN CARE OF Welsh Office

OPEN all reasonable times (standard hours)

ADMISSION some charge

LOCATION on hill above town

MAP REFERENCE 11 SU0565

COUNTY Clwyd

SPECIAL FEATURES museum/exhibition inside castle; town walls (key available from castle); friary (at bottom of town)

RHYS AP GRUFFUDD (A Welsh Lord)

By the time The Lord Rhys came to power, the Normans had been in Wales for over one hundred years. So how did a bona fide Welshman (for Rhys was descended from a line of native Welsh princes) hold a position of such influence in a country that had ostensibly succumbed to the Norman Conquest?

Rhys is still something of a folk-hero within Wales, for he represents the spirit of resistance and independence which was by no means extinguished by the Normans. At times he fought against them. Mostly, he worked with them without compromising his native rights, epitomising the conviction held by the wise Giraldus Cambrensis (see page 123) that Englishman and Welshman should avoid a master/servant relationship.

In agreeing to represent the interests of the English King, Henry II, Rhys ruled in South Wales from his seat at Dinefwr Castle. His titles are many and various – The Lord Rhys, Lord of Ystrad Tywi, Ruler of Deheubarth, Prince of South Wales. Undoubtedly the most powerful Welsh ruler of the late 12th century, his life helps us better to understand the realities of the so-called 'Conquest'. History is rarely defined in black and white, a simple process of winners and losers; in this case, it would make a nonsense of Rhys's largely successful policy of living independent of and yet in harmony with England.

Rhys's strength came more from his adventurous and aggressive spirit than his wisdom. He was a formidable man, arrogant and restless, a born fighter with an appetite for both building and attacking castles. Yet he was also an early patron of the arts.

His contribution to Welsh culture is still with us, for in 1177 he called together at Cardigan Castle what is now recognized as Wales's first National Eisteddfod (today an important annual celebration of poetry and music).

An early patron of the Arts, Rhys ap Gruffud founded the National Eisteddfod in 1177. Today this yearly cultural festival attracts thousands to its 'meeting of the bards'

Rhys ap Gruffudd is thought to have died about 1197 and is buried in staunchly-Welsh hill country at Strata Florida Abbey near Tregaron, a Cistercian abbey he founded on the 'Vale of Flowers' in the upper valley of the Teifi. An appropriate resting place for a native who refused to be intimidated by the Norman invaders.

DINEFWR CASTLE

Welsh princely castle with a dramatic silhouette, on a river cliff above the Tywi at Llandeilo. It was the seat of The Lord Rhys and the site of one of Llywelyn ap Gruffud's greatest triumphs.

Situated in a private park just outside Llandeilo, the old castle is best viewed from the secondary road (B 4300) which runs along the Vale of Tywi towards Dryslwyn Castle. Dinefwr (or Dynevor) was the old capital of South Wales, and had been the home of the family of Hywel Dda ('the Good') long before the castle was erected.

Dinefwr Castle consists of two wards side by side along the edge of the river cliff. The inner ward is protected by a curtain wall flanked by towers inside a rock-cut ditch, whereas the outer ward has only an earth bank and ditch defence visible among the undergrowth. There is a large round keep inside the inner ward, probably dating from the early 13th century except for its top storey, which is smaller in diameter and was added about 1660 as a summerhouse. On the side away from the cliff the curtain wall has been knocked down and a 15th-century hall and solar built in its place.

Dinefwr was the seat of the powerful Lord Rhys, one of the most influential Welsh rulers at the time of Henry II (see above). Subsequent ownership of the castle was frequently contested between Rhys's descendants. It was dismantled in 1220 by Rhys Grug in order to prevent Llywelyn ab Iorwerth ('the Great') from having it. Llywelyn ap Gruffudd ('the Last') raised an English siege of the castle in 1257 and cut to pieces the sizeable army attacking it. After it had been finally surrendered to King Edward I it was seized by another Welshman, Rhys ap Maredudd, who considered he had the best claim to it as a supporter of Edward. The Earl of Cornwall thereupon recommenced a siege by cutting trenches, and the garrison fled during the night.

The castle ditches were then cleaned out and extended, some buildings repaired and others added. Granted to Hugh le Despenser, the castle was seized and wrecked by his enemies in 1321, and the great tower was then said to be on the point of collapse. A new town had been founded beside the castle in 1298, but it was destroyed, and the castle taken, by Owain Glyndwr in the early 1400's. It is clear that the castle was not completely destroyed, for it was regarded as a worthy gift from a grateful King Henry VII to his major supporter, Sir Rhys ap Thomas, after the Battle of Bosworth.

Dinefwr Castle, seat of The Lord Rhys

IN CARE OF private owner

OPEN viewing from the surrounding area only

LOCATION 1m W of Llandeilo

MAP REFERENCE 3 SN6122

COUNTY Dyfed

DOLBADARN CASTLE

Early 13th-century native Welsh castle, built by Llywelyn the Great to command the overland route to the upper Conwy. Most prominent is the well defended circular keep. Fine location and views.

Dolbadarn's solitary tower sits proudly on its rock, presiding now over the lake of Llyn Padarn and the mountain pass of Llanberis. The ruggedly-beautiful lower mountain slopes have changed much in these last two centuries, through the influence of slate quarrying and, lately, an ambitious hydro-electric scheme. Yet Dolbadarn Castle still stands, serene and timeless, silently watching over a reshaped landscape.

Although the place is never mentioned in records before the Edwardian conquest, we can be reasonably certain that its builder was Llywelyn the Great. Commanding the ancient route inland from Caernarfon to the upper Conwy valley, Dolbadarn's walls enclose a rocky boomerang-shaped knoll some 80ft above the waters of Llyn Padarn. Ir-

Dolbadarn Castle, Llanberis, faces quarry excavations on the opposite shore

regular curtain walls of unmortared slate slabs and foundations of rectangular buildings comprise what is probably the oldest work, dating from just after 1200. Here, close to the northern end, lay a hall – quite uncharacteristic of a native Welsh castle such as this – dividing the enclosure and still providing evidence of two open hearths.

Very different, both in build and character, is the great round tower, which stands near the castle's southern end. Far superior to the rudimentary and insubstantial defences nearby, this is a fully developed, strongly-fortified round keep, which proudly matches those similar structures built by Llywelyn's rivals in the southern Marches, like William Marshall's Pembroke or Hubert de Burgh's Skenfrith. The prince seems almost to have copied these southern keeps, for his tower at Dolbadarn is a most English-looking structure.

As now, the tower was entered through a door on its first floor. But the steps one climbs today are entirely modern and not at all like their early timber predecessors which could be pulled up when danger threatened. The entry door was stoutly barred and additionally defended by a portcullis, a feature seldom found in other round keeps. Only a trap door led downwards into the ground level basement, but a tiny circular stair, set in the thickness of the wall, climbs narrowly up to the floor above the entry and further up again to the battlements. Once a timber hoard might have hung from the walltops. Today the stair ends abruptly, penned in by an uncomfortable wire cage which limits an otherwise commanding view through the valley.

IN CARE OF Welsh Office

OPEN at all times

ADMISSION free

LOCATION ½m SE of Llanberis

MAP REFERENCE 10 SH5859

COUNTY Gwynedd

DOLFORWYN CASTLE

The castle of Llywelyn the Last, in ruins since the 14th century, is hidden in woodland above the Severn valley, near Abermule.

In June 1273, Edward I wrote a letter to 'Llywelyn, son of Griffin, Prince of Wales'. It forbade him to build a castle at Abermule near Montgomery and ordered that he cease building or repairing it 'so that the king may not be compelled to apply his hand otherwise'. Llywelyn's reply, a masterpiece of ironic politeness, is worth quoting, particularly since it summarises the different positions of the two men over three years before war broke out:

'We have received a letter written in the king's name ... forbidding us to build a castle on our own land at Abermule ... we are sure it was not written with your knowledge and would not have been sent if you had been in the kingdom (Edward had been on Crusade) ... for you know well that the rights of our principality are totally separate from the rights of your kingdom (and) we and our ancestors had power within our boundaries to build castles ... without pro-hibition by any one'. Llywelyn held his Easter court of 1274 at Dolforwyn, Edward or no Edward, but in 1277 it was taken by Roger Mortimer after a fortnight's siege, when the water supply failed. A survey of 1322 lists the buildings of the castle, including the round and square towers, both of which can be seen today, but by 1381 it was 'worth nothing'. Current excavation is beginning to reveal the castle of the last native Welsh Prince of Wales.

IN CARE OF Welsh Office

OPEN at all times

ADMISSION free

LOCATION 1m W of Abermule. Access via track off minor road

MAP REFERENCE 9 SO1594

COUNTY Powys

Above the fertile Severn valley are the fragmentary remains of Dolforwyn Castle

DOLWYDDELAN CASTLE

Native Welsh castle of c1200 and after, built by Llywelyn the Great, its square keep rising prominently above the mountain pass. Much restored in the 19th century. Fine views from battlements.

Like so many castles built by the native Welsh princes in the 13th century, Dolwyddelan now stands lonely and desolate, still guarding its landlocked mountain pass. Its one, solitary square tower rises starkly out of the hillside, above the modern road from Blaenau Ffestiniog to Betws-y-Coed,

The lonely ruins of Dolwyddelan Castle lie in the shadow of 2860ft Moel Siabod

strangely intact even to its crenellated battlements.

The castle is accessible along a rough track past a hillside farm, a short walk from a little roadside car park. Elevated upon its grassy knoll on the north west margin of the plain of Dolwyddelan, the castle once commanded the old medieval trackway from Meirionnydd to the Vale of Conwy.

We have no written record of the building of Dolwyddelan. Llywelyn the Great is said to have been born inside the castle, in 1173, but this is difficult to substantiate. An earlier medieval site, recently discovered lower down the valley, seems a far more likely location.

The castle is of three main building periods. Earliest, and now the most impressive, is the rectangular tower keep, a compact 31ft by 44ft, standing precipitously above a steep, rocky slope. Probably built around 1200 by Llywelyn the Great, it was originally of two storeys only. Approached, as now, by an external staircase, a small drawbridge and barred door resisted attack. A trapdoor led down to the basement, while a narrow stair, in the wall thickness, today leads past an upper floor (inserted in the 1400s but now vanished) to the roof. All the upper levels and battlements were restored in the 19th century, giving the tower a 'too good to be true' appearance, for they do not accurately reproduce the medieval arrangements.

Originally, this keep would have been surrounded by a courtyard enclosed by timber stockades. A little later in the 13th century, wood was replaced by stone, with a characteristically irregular curtain wall entered through a simple arched doorway.

During the Edwardian wars, Dolwyddelan occupied a position of vital strategic importance. On 18 January 1283, it fell to the English and was promptly refortified by Edward I. The second rectangular tower, on the west side of the courtyard, probably dates from this time. Apart from the keep, all is ruinous today, but the restored Victorian walltops still fulfil their 19th-century purpose, for the views from the top bring their own reward. The castle looks out to the rugged grandeur of Moel Siabod.

IN CARE OF Welsh Office

OPEN at all times

ADMISSION free

LOCATION 1m from Dolwyddelan off A470

MAP REFERENCE 11 SH7252

COUNTY Gwynedd

DRYSLWYN CASTLE

A lost town of the Middle Ages, with fragments of a castle, being excavated from just below the surface on the summit of a steep, isolated hill. The ruins comprise traces of a chapel and hall.

There is only one approachable side to the hill of Dryslwyn and its castle ruins, which command a narrow point of the Tywi valley. The view from the steep track which leads to the top of the hill is a fine one, for Dryslwyn is surrounded by rich farmlands rising to wooded uplands. But the castle remains are scanty, although more is being uncovered by excavation every year. This site has a long history, though we first hear of it in 1245, when John of Monmouth attacked the Welsh castle here.

After the death of Llywelyn ap Gruffudd ('the Last') the Lord of Dryslwyn, Maredudd ap Rhys, rose against Edward I. Maredudd had been one of the few Welsh lords to oppose Llywelyn, but had not been given Dryslwyn as his promised reward. Whilst Edward was still in Gascony, the Earl of Cornwall brought up an army of 11,000 men to besiege Maredudd. This famous siege lasted more than two weeks. Miners filled up the ditches, but an undermined wall fell on 150 men and the castle was finally taken by battering down the chapel wall. The incoming royal constable spent over £300 on repairs, including felling the trees round the castle and building a new mill. The castle was betrayed to Owain Glyndwr in 1403, and thereafter leased out; its last constable was appointed in 1439.

Today, humps and bumps – the remains of buildings just under the turf – cover the whole hilltop. There was a wall around the edge, and the clearest traces of the town which once stood here are the well-preserved house sites backing against this wall on the north side.

One upstanding tower fragment marks the outer ward of the castle and at the southern corner of the hilltop (overlooking the bridge) are the main surviving ruins: two buildings protruding from the line of the curtain wall. The upstanding wall with two rows of windows probably belonged to the hall. The other wall (with three narrow pointed windows) may have been the chapel, and the breach between them might be the result of the siege of 700 years ago.

DYSERTH CASTLE

Very fragmentary remains of King Henry III's castle built on the rock at Dyserth in 1241. Destroyed in 1263 by the Welsh.

A rocky hill forms the site of Dyserth's vanished castle (right)

Though Dyserth Castle today has remains that can most generously be described as scanty, this site was once of great importance during that troubled period of the early 13th century. The River Conwy was the innermost rampart that guarded the historical independence of mountainous Gwynedd, but the lands further east, as far as the River Dee, frequently changed hands with the variable fortunes of war.

In 1241, after the death of Llywelyn the Great, they fell to the English. King Henry III set about bringing them under permanent control by building a castle, on the high rock, just to the north of the present-day village of Dyserth. The inner ward is, in some respects, like that of his earlier fortress of Montgomery, having a twin-towered gatehouse, with two further towers astride the curtain wall and lodgings sited within the enclosure. The towers here are curiously angular and the whole site is surrounded by earthworks.

Today, it is only these earthworks that survive, for the few remaining masonry parts of Dyserth Castle disappeared, with quarrying operations, in 1914. They consist of a bank and internal ditch, partly enclosing the inner ward and outer bailey. But the site has been much confused by later garden features, so that it is now difficult to interpret the plan.

In 1256, the exactions of English officials and the king's own precarious position at court prompted Llywelyn ap Gruffudd ('the Last') to lay siege to Dyserth, but he was unsuccessful. In 1263, he tried again, this time taking the castle and succeeding in utterly destroying it.

IN CARE OF private owner

OPEN viewing from the surrounding area only (National Trust Graig Fawr property)

LOCATION ½m NE of Dyserth

MAP REFERENCE 11 SJ0679

COUNTY Clwyd

Dryslwyn's once-splendid castle stands on a hill on the north side of the River Tywi. It played an important part in 13th-century struggles between the Welsh and the English invaders, led by King Edward I

IN CARE OF Welsh Office

OPEN at all times (unless closed for excavation or consolidation)

ADMISSION free

LOCATION on B 4297, 5m W of Llandeilo

MAP REFERENCE 3 SN5520

COUNTY Dyfed

EWLOE CASTLE

This native Welsh castle is hidden in a wooded hollow just off the busy A55 near Hawarden. The D-shaped Welsh Tower was built by Llywelyn the Great c1210. The remainder of the castle, with its two baileys and round tower, was the work of Llywelyn the Last c1257.

Ewloe is a most uncharacteristic situation for any castle and not what we have come to expect, for today it can hardly be seen at all in its wooded hollow. If it were not for the green and white sign on the busy roadside along the A55 its presence might pass quite unnoticed. As it is, few drivers pull into its lay-by car park, but those who make the effort are rewarded, for this is an interesting native Welsh fortress.

The castle dell is reached by a short walk across an open field, through a wicket gate and down a tree-covered descent. At once, pink sandstone walls rise out of their deep-ditched hollow as if to ward off entry. But access is easier now, for a shallow flight of steps leads gently downward, skirting the curtain walls, towards a timber-staired entry.

THE EARLY CASTLE

The name Ewloe is English rather than Welsh. Lying close to Hawarden, in that much fought-over part of borderland Wales to the east of Offa's Dyke, at one time it changed hands constantly with the fortunes of war. Not until 1146 did it fall to the Welsh, when the men of Gwynedd captured nearby Mold. Shortly afterwards, Owain Gwynedd established a motte and bailey here, though not a trace remains today. From Owain, it passed to his son Dafydd, but he in turn was dispossessed by Llywelyn ab Iorwerth ('the Great'), who held the place

13th-century Ewloe Castle was a vital garrison during Welsh–English clashes and struggles between the Welsh princes

until his death in 1240.

Although we have not a shred of written evidence that Llywelyn built a castle at Ewloe, this is not unusual, for Welsh records of the time are notoriously sparse. We do know, however, from an English survey of 1311, that his grandson, Llywelyn ap Gruffud (the Last), established a castle in a corner of the woods at Ewloe. From looking at the masonry of Ewloe Castle, it is also quite clear that here stand two quite separate periods of building – one, its most note-worthy feature a great apsidal 'D' tower; the other, a two ward enclosure with a second, round tower.

Apsidal towers are common enough in native Welsh castles of Llywelyn the Great's time. Moreover, the junction of the masonry shows this tower to be of an earlier period than the remainder of the castle. We can therefore assume, with some degree of certainty, that this tower, the Welsh Tower, was built by Llywelyn the Great and that the rest of the enclosure must therefore be the work of his equally-famous grandson.

THE WELSH TOWER

This tower was probably built around the year 1210 and must have stood more or less alone, performing much the same function as a keep. It was entered, as was the fashion of keeps, at its first floor level. Although the stone steps that lead up to it now follow similar lines to their predecessors, they are without the additional protective screen wall to guard against enemy fire. Just inside the doorway, to the right, a small stair in the wall thickness led up to the battlements.

Here would have hung, once, a timber fighting platform, its presence now attested solely by the grooves, one foot wide and two feet deep, that run into the wall on this southern side. Visible too, on the flat west wall, is the outline of the tower's single gabled roof and the triangular hole for a drainage gutter. Only these south and west walls still remain to full height and it is difficult now to say what the internal arrangements might have been. No doubt, there was a living room and possibly one or two sleeping rooms. Accommodation must have been very limited, and there is not a trace of either kitchen or chapel.

ADDITIONAL BUILDINGS

Once the lower ward and round west tower were built, around 1257, far more space would have been available. Quite possibly there was extra accommodation for the lord within timber buildings, beside the Welsh Tower, in the upper ward. Or he may have been content to share with his garrison the hall, kitchen, buttery and pantry inside the lower ward. The visitor today must imagine all these structures in his mind's eye for, sadly, none remain. The West Tower is also in ruin, but still shows traces of the plaster once covering its walls.

In 1277, the English gained permanent control of this part of Wales, building their great fortress at Flint. Ewloe ceased then to serve a purpose. Held by the crown for many years, it was at last abandoned.

IN CARE OF Welsh Office

OPEN at all times

ADMISSION free autumn, winter, early spring, some charge late spring and summer

LOCATION 1m NW of Hawarden

MAP REFERENCE 12 SJ2867

COUNTY Clwyd

CASTLES OF THE WELSH PRINCES

Although about 14 earthwork castles are known to have been built in the early 12th century by Welsh princely rulers, they are totally indistinguishable in the landscape from their Norman counterparts. Built largely because of internal family squabbles that were so common, they can be identified only by the careful linking of records to ground features.

The later stone castles of the two Llywelyns ('the Great' and 'the Last') in the north are more easily recognized. They are to be found in naturally strong, isolated positions, away from the older centres of government. Perched high on the sides of landlocked valleys, they were built to guard the natural routeways around the borders of Gwynedd and through the mountains of Snowdonia.

CHARACTERISTIC FEATURES

Several common architectural features distinguish these native Welsh castles from contemporary English sites, making them almost instantly identifiable. All tend to have curtain walls that are low and comparatively insubstantial. They enclose areas of irregular shape and are often confined merely to a keep and a single ward. Normally, the gatehouses are not strong (Criccieth is the spectacular exception to this rule); indeed there is often no gatehouse at all to protect the entrance. Towers are rarely over two storeys high and do not usually include circular stairwells, although Dolbadarn is an exception on both counts.

Perhaps the most characteristic feature, however, are the apsidal ('D' shaped) and rectangular towers. These sometimes stand keep-like and alone, as at Ewloe, but are more often joined haphazardly to the curtain wall, as at Caergwrle, Dinas Brân, Castell-y-Bere, Criccieth, Dolbadarn and elsewhere. Where towers of any sort do join the curtain wall, though, rarely are they sited in such a way as to cover its outer face with a field of fire, as on an English castle.

EXPLAINING THE DIFFERENCE

As there are practically no records of the building of any of these Welsh princely foundations, we can only advance suggestions to account for the difference in their basic design. In the first place, the typical fighting man of North Wales, we are told, was a spearman and not an archer, as in the south. If this were so then the whole basis of castle defence – normally

Llywelyn the Great's coffin in Gwydyr Chapel, Llanrwst

so dependent upon the bow and arrow – would have been quite different. It would certainly account for what, to English eyes at least, must have seemed the totally ineffective siting of the wall towers.

Then, too, there would undoubtedly have been a marked difference in the monetary resources of a Welsh prince, compared to those at the command of a wealthy English lord. Partly because of this, but also because there was little tradition of stone building within Wales at this date, the quality and numbers of available, skilled craftsmen would have been that much less. Perhaps this explains why Castell-y-Bere is the only native site where any quantity of high-quality carving has come to light.

We must also consider the possibility that, in the planning of these castles, there may have been an almost unspoken reluctance to embark upon an ambitious programme of fortification for fear of provoking a hostile reaction from the other side (this happened in the end at Dolforwyn). Above all of these considerations, however, there was the over-riding difference in the two cultures. In Wales, the bonds between a lord and his followers were essentially those of kinship; in England authority was very largely maintained by fear and force of arms.

The ruin of Castell-y-Bere, Welsh native fortress, is dramatically set in the shadow of Cader Idris

FLINT CASTLE

Flint was the first castle of King Edward I's initial military campaign in Wales of 1277. Surrounded by water, it was built to an unusual square plan, with one large, isolated round tower. All traces of internal buildings have now vanished. In 1399, King Richard II was captured here by Henry Bolingbroke – a scene immortalised by Shakespeare centuries later.

Flint's Great Tower commands an eastern view of the sea

Flint Castle today finds itself, through no fault of its own, a victim of circumstance. Closeted away behind the main part of the modern industrial town, few people even realize that it is there; fewer still take the time to make a small detour and visit it. Left thus to itself, it is very much a prisoner of its own location. The castle was rather more literally a prisoner until a few years ago, for here, right in front of the castle ruins, stood an imposing, all-concealing block of the main county gaol, smothering the entire outer bailey.

Unfortunately too, the castle is located along a through-route in the extreme north east of Wales. Holidaymakers in their thousands stream through here in the summer months, pressing eagerly onwards along the last lap of their journey towards destinations further up the coast. So today, this once-great castle stands lonely and forgotten, hemmed in by development, by-passed by tourists and given altogether far too little recognition.

EDWARD'S FIRST CASTLE

Flint was the first base of Edward I's northern army as it pushed its way along the coast from Chester early in July of 1277. With great speed, measures were put in hand to assemble the large labour force who would build this, the first new royal castle in Wales. By the end of the month, there were 1,850 workmen here; on 9 August they were joined by another 300 diggers who had made a seven-day march from the Lincolnshire Fens, with three mounted sergeants to keep them from deserting en route. At the end of August, nearly 2,300 diggers alone were working at the place known, ever since, as Flint. The name had not existed before and we have no real hint of its exact origin. One guess is that it was an allegorical reference to the flint, or striking point, for Edward's whole campaign of conquest, but we shall never know for certain.

What, in the meantime, were all these diggers doing? The Welsh Chronicle of the Princes says that the king 'fortified a court in Flint with huge ditches around it' and we can perhaps infer from this what had been happening. The first task would have been the digging of a protective bank and ditch

around the site of the future castle and town for, by now, it must have been serving as a huge base camp for the army and labour force. Ditches were very important in the early stages of fortification, especially in hostile country. The sense of urgency is reflected here in a system of bonus payments for outstanding work and of deductions from the pay of those who shirked or went absent without leave.

A FORTIFIED TOWN

Flint, too, was the first of many fortified towns deliberately founded by King Edward in Wales. Having previously used planted towns, in his French lands of Gascony, as a means of settling the country and introducing new customs, the king now proposed to adopt very much the same procedure in his new Welsh realm. Flint's defences were of earth and timber, but today they can barely be traced, having been submerged long ago beneath the later buildings. The one lasting feature of the old Edwardian town is its rigid grid of streets, whose original layout still persists to the present day.

As for the castle, work proceeded rather more slowly after the initial scurry of ditching operations (the theatre of war had moved further west by this time, so completion was possibly not felt to be quite so pressing). The Great Tower seems to have taken the longest time – we have a record of payment for 44 bundles of straw thatch to protect its unfinished walltops during the winter of 1281–82. Although besieged briefly during the second Edwardian campaign, little damage was caused and, by 1284, it was practically finished, at a final cost of £6,068, 7s 5¾d (over £3½ million in today's terms).

SHAKESPEARIAN CONNECTIONS

As the first Welsh castle to be built by Edward, it is perhaps not so surprising that Flint should also have a rather unusual plan. The inner ward, described in Shakespeare's *Richard II* as 'the base court where kings grow base', is a strongly-built square, with a tower at each corner. At the south, the

corner tower is more like an old-fashioned keep – very much larger than the other three and isolated from the rest of the enclosure. This Great Tower, like the whole castle, was surrounded by a wet moat, fed by the River Dee, and was connected by drawbridge to the inner ward. The courtyard itself must have contained various domestic buildings ranged around its walls, but not a trace of them remains today. Grander private quarters would have lain in the Great Tower, which had its own well, storage in the basement, and a suite of lodgings and private chapel above for the constable and his family or, perhaps, for the justiciar of Chester when holding court in Flint.

The castle played little part in later history, but it has been immortalized by William Shakespeare, as the setting for the final capture of Richard II by his great rival Henry Bolingbroke. The king was here for his last three days in August 1399 and, on 22 August, he 'having heard mass went upon

Flint Castle possesses architectural devices which Edward I did not use again in his building programme

The south west tower of Flint, which last saw military action in 1647

the walls of the castle which are large and wide on the inside' and beheld 'the Duke of Lancaster as he came along the seashore with all his host'. From Flint, King Richard was taken to London, where the deed of abdication was signed.

IN CARE OF Welsh Office

OPEN at all times

ADMISSION free

LOCATION near town centre

MAP REFERENCE 12 SJ2573

COUNTY Clwyd

GROSMONT CASTLE

Grosmont, unlike Hubert de Burgh's other castle at nearby Skenfrith, is set on a hill, above the church and village. It is a fine example of a small border castle. Here was found a unique relic of the Crusades.

Grosmont takes it name from the French gros mont ('big hill'), an apt if prosaic description of the impressive ditched earthwork on which the castle stands. Originally a Norman earthwork castle with timber defences, it was probably founded by William FitzOsbern, Lord of Breteuil in Calvados and palatine Earl of Hereford, to whom William the Conqueror had given the task of subduing the South Wales borders. In 1138 the Welsh, far from being subdued, were giving King Stephen so much trouble that he had to make an exchange of lands with a baron, Payn FitzJohn. Through this exchange he created a defensible block of territory on the Welsh border around the Three Castles of Grosmont, Skenfrith and White Castle, which controlled the routes between England and Wales on this strategi-cally-important sector of the March.

HUBERT'S GAINS AND LOSSES

In 1201 King John granted the Three Castles to Hubert de Burgh (for Hubert's somewhat eventful career see Skenfrith Castle) who held them until 1204. In the merry-go-round of medieval politics they became his again from 1219 until 1232, when he fell from power and was again stripped of his castles and lands. Though he later recovered them for a few years, he was never again sufficiently secure in the king's favour to risk the 'provocation' of strengthening his castles. (The Three Castles remained in one ownership until the 19th century.)

What we see today at Grosmont represents in stone three phases of the castle's history. Grosmont I was built by Hubert between 1201 and 1204. Grosmont 2 represents a major rebuilding, also by Hubert de Burgh, in 1219–32. Grosmont 3 is a remodelling of the castle as a nobleman's residence by the Earls of Lancaster in the 14th century.

THE FIRST STONE STRUCTURE

When Hubert acquired the castle, it still had the timber defences and buildings of the Norman ringwork. Its first stone building was the rectangular hall block which the visitor finds on his right after crossing the castle bridge and passing through the entrance. The hall was on the first floor, reached by an external wooden stair (the doorways cut into the hall at ground-floor level are the result of later alterations). The back of the hall fireplace and its flanking windows can still be seen, and at one end would have been Hubert's private rooms.

After Hubert had recovered Grosmont in 1219, he set about rebuilding it in the new

Grosmont's moat is a relic from an earlier wooden castle

mode of fortification of the 13th century. The simple blank curtain walls and box-like keeps of Norman days were replaced by what is now considered typical of the medieval castle, with half round towers projecting out at intervals from the curtain wall, thus covering the ground in front of the castle with cross-fire from its arrow-slits. At Grosmont, the earlier hall was retained, but the Norman palisade around the bailey was replaced by a trapeze-shaped ward with round towers at three of the corners and an entrance gateway tucked into the fourth corner, beside the earlier hall.

TOURING THE TOWERS

Travelling clockwise from the entrance, the first tower was re-modelled by the Earls of Lancaster, the impressive tall arch facing the courtyard belonging to their time (Grosmont 3). The second tower is unaltered, but the third was demolished to make way for the suite of private apartments for the Earls of Lancaster, distinguished by a tall 14th-century chimney. Only the round basement of the earlier tower can now be seen. All three of Hubert's towers had deep circular basements for storage (his considerable experience of castle sieges had perhaps impressed upon him the importance of adequate space for storage of food and munitions) and the rooms above are equipped with sets of arrow-slits.

The rooms on the upper part of the first tower, with their fine fireplaces, are 14th century. Another relic of this period was an Arabic faience jar from Rakka in Syria found here during excavations. This relic of the trading cities of Crusader Palestine is now in the National Museum of Wales, Cardiff.

Edmund Crouchback, Earl of Lancaster, was the father of Henry Grosmont, born here in about 1281. Henry was one of the leaders of the English army in France in the early part of the Hundred Years War and his share of ransoms and pillage may have helped pay for his rebuilding of Grosmont. With the merging of the Duchy of Lancaster with the Crown, Grosmont lost its importance, and by the 16th century it was in ruins.

The castle's influence, however, is still with us in one unexpected way. The village church of St Nicholas is unusually large and magnificent for such a small community. Both village and church are a direct result of the presence of the castle, the village having borough status until 1857, with its own mayor, ale-taster and corporation. Jack O'Kent, a 15th-century wizard and hero of a remarkable cycle of local tales, is buried at the church. The devil promised to take him whether buried in church or out of it. His grave can be seen beneath the wall of the church, neither in nor out.

IN CARE OF Welsh Office

OPEN at all times

ADMISSION free

LOCATION on B4347, 10m NW of Monmouth

MAP REFERENCE 5 SO4024

COUNTY Gwent

Beautiful stained glass windows are a feature of Gwrych's hall

GWRYCH CASTLE

Another interesting example of a 19th-century house built in a then fashionable castellated style is this castle at Abergele. It is more romantically than authentically medieval.

In the 19th century, it became fashionable to build houses in the style of the castle. This architectural trend had its roots in the Romantic Movement and a growing interest in the Middle Ages and all things antiquarian. Many wealthy barons of industry and landowners conscious of their status and the styles of the time indulged their fancies by building so-called castles which contained accommodation as luxurious as that in any grand conventional house.

Gwrych, started in 1815 by Bamford Hesketh of a wealthy Lancastrian family, is such a castle. Hesketh employed a Brighton architect, C A Busby, who built a castellated Georgian house with Gothic windows. Unfortunately, the finished structure was not to Hesketh's tastes, so with the aid of Thomas Rickman, a Liverpool architect and respected historian, he added to it. Through this later rebuilding, Gwrych became more than ever a fanciful fantasy castle, its character altered by the addition of a vast arrangement of yards, screen walls and false towers. These features, all inspired by nearby Conwy Castle, ultimately created the splendidly picturesque and striking façade now visible from the coast road at Abergele.

Rickman used standard windows with cast-iron Gothic tracery. These were also used in the lodges and farms which, with the wall surrounding the park, were designed to match the house.

IN CARE OF private owner

OPEN usually at regular times, in spring, summer and early autumn. Please check in advance

ADMISSION some charge

LOCATION just off B5443 1m W of Abergele

MAP REFERENCE 11 SH9277

COUNTY Clwyd

HARLECH

Built in 1283, as part of King Edward I's iron ring of castles to contain the Welsh in Snowdonia, Harlech is perhaps the most impressive of them all today. It stands 200ft above the old sea level, astride a high outcrop of rock, its massive inner walls and towers still almost at full height. Noteworthy features are its dominant gatehouse and defended stairway to the sea. Harlech was captured in 1404 by Owain Glyndwr and held by the Welsh for five years before being lost. It stands in a wonderful location, with memorable views from its battlements.

Of all the overworked adjectives used by writers to describe the grander castles of North Wales 'spectacular' and 'dramatic' would no doubt top the list. Yet at Harlech they seem all too readily relevant. From the foot-worn boss of rock at the southern edge of the little town the view of castle, sea and mountain is breathtaking. The greystone bulk of the castle sits astride a rocky promontory, towering nearly 200ft above the green flatlands of Morfa and the sea, its backcloth the wide, distant panoply of Snowdonia.

Small wonder that this place has received the attentions of countless visitors, past and present. Small wonder too that, of all castles in Wales, Harlech is perhaps the most familiar to those who live elsewhere. Even after seven centuries, it still displays with clarity the genius of that architect, Master James of St George, who created it. The twin requirements of defence and accommodation have been perfectly adapted to suit a restricted, rocky crag and the whole structure possesses great elegance of line, an unmistakable sense of power and a position of strength.

THE IRON RING

Harlech was built during the second and final campaign of King Edward I in North Wales. It was the southern link in the iron ring of castles surrounding the coastal fringes of Snowdonia; a ring intended to prevent the region from becoming, ever again, a focal point of insurrection and a last bastion of resistance. Towards the end of Edward's campaign, the native stronghold of Castell-y-Bere finally fell in April 1283. This enabled the English army, under its commander, Sir Otto de Grandison, to march up through the mountains of Meirionnydd and establish a base at Harlech.

Work began on a new castle here almost immediately. Strangely, for a royal foundation such as this, the records of its first three years are surprisingly few, but one or two snippets of information here and there help to fill in the gaps. By the middle of June, we learn that 20 stonemasons and quarriers, together with a packhorse to carry their tools, had been dispatched from their base at Conwy to travel over the hills and report for duty at Harlech. The following month, they were followed by another 15 masons and a squad of carpenters, so things were evidently progressing.

Part of Harlech's stout defences, a portcullis groove

Harlech Castle's groundplan shows its massive gatehouse and towers

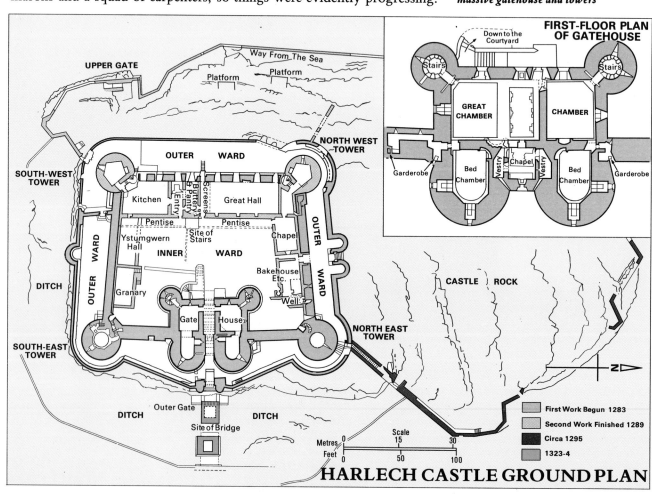

HARLECH CASTLE GROUND PLAN

*Alan Sorrell's impression of
Harlech as it might have been*

WORK IN PROGRESS

Not until the summer of 1286, when work here was at its height, do we
manage to glean an overall picture of the building in progress. The labour
force built up steadily that year, from only 60 in the slack winter months of
January and February, to almost 950 by midsummer. Of these, we have a
full breakdown by occupation – 227 masons, 115 quarriers, 30 smiths, 22
carpenters, 546 labourers and minor workmen. Materials for building, too,
were being shipped in almost daily – limestone from Anglesey and
Caernarfon, better quality freestone (for carving) from the quarries at
Egryn, seven miles to the south, and iron and steel from Chester.

The bills and accounts for Harlech, as for most of the major Edwardian
fortifications, are still preserved in the Public Record Office. They record
in minute detail the amounts of money paid out, who received it, and what
he had done in return for his payment. The records for 1289 are
particularly comprehensive, the men being paid on a piecework basis. A
certain Master William of Drogheda, in Ireland, was paid £111 7s 6d for his
work on the 'north tower towards the sea' (ie the North West Tower)
49½ ft high @ 45s per foot. Two men, Robert of Frankby and Reginald of
Turvey, built 18½ ft of the southern stair turret in the gatehouse and were
paid £12 6s 8d, at the rate of 13s 4d per foot. Again, William of Thornton
was paid the sum of eight shillings for making a fireplace in one of the
upper rooms on the south side of the gatehouse.

THE CASTLE COMPLETED

By the end of 1289, after seven seasons of work, the castle of Harlech was
virtually finished. It was the smallest of Edward's new works in North
Wales and its final cost was over £8,000. Today, we should have to
multiply this and all the other figures, by 600 or more, to arrive at an
equivalent, so that Harlech's price would now be £5 million.

Harlech is very much a concentric castle. Its outer walls may seem low
and insubstantial when compared with Beaumaris, but Harlech enjoys the
ready-made natural advantage of a high rocky site and also, on the more
level ground to the south and east, a deep rock-cut ditch. In most places,
however, this outer wall is ruinous. Only on the north, with its postern
gate, does it survive to anything like full height, so the effect today is not
really comparable to what it would have been in the 13th century.

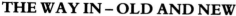

Harlech's gatehouse (left) gave a daunting display of power to would-be attackers

The castle's inner ward (above) shows foundations of domestic buildings

The vaulted ceiling of Harlech's gatehouse (below)

THE WAY IN – OLD AND NEW

Another false impression is given now by the approach. Today's visitor enters through a ticket office, carefully hidden at the outer edge of the ditch. From the inner side of the ditch, a veritable tower of solid-looking oak stairs then leads to the outer gate – an arrangement which, in original medieval terms, is all quite wrong. For a more authentic first impression, initially look at the castle from the children's playground. Even after all these years, that fortified east front still throws down its haughty challenge, the sense of might and power quite overwhelming. This, after all, was the only possible direction of attack. Once, a great bridge would have thrust across the ditch (its piers still visible) and straight up to the outer castle gate – at its ends, a drawbridge and beyond, inside the great inner gatehouse, three stout, barred doors and three more portcullises. After the dark of the gate passage came the inner courtyard. Instead of today's mown greensward and open aspect, it would once have presented a very different picture, its three now-blank and vacant walls surrounded by buildings which formed the castle's public areas – on the right, a Great Hall with a kitchen to its left, with a second hall, chapel and service areas to either side, all safe and protected by the massive curtain walls around.

PRIVATE QUARTERS

The main private accommodation at Harlech was above the guardchambers of its gatehouse. Within this imposing structure, standing defiantly astride the eastern curtain, lay two self-contained suites of grand residential quarters (just look at their fireplaces and the remains of those traceried windows). On the upper floor was probably a guest suite for visiting dignitaries – the king, perhaps, or the chamberlain.

The lower floor, with its controls for all three porcullises and direct access to the courtyard, must have been the lodgings of the constable, or castle governer, and his family. In 1290, and for the following three years,

Harlech's constable was none other than its own architect, Master James of St George. During this period, he received a salary of 100 marks a year (£66), which would have been enough to keep him in conditions of considerable comfort.

SEA AND SHIPS

The castle's other remarkable feature is the defended 'Way from the Sea', a gated and heavily-fortified stairway plunging almost 200ft down the castle rock on its west side. Today, one can drive down to the base of the cliff, then cross over the railway and enter the castle up these steps. But at one time, there could have been neither railway nor road, for the sandy flatlands at the foot of the castle would have been covered by sea. Like all King Edward's new castles in the north, Harlech was built so that it could be supplied and victualled by ship; this stairway provided the necessary link. Its purpose is no longer very evident today, because the sea has receded half a mile or more, leaving the castle isolated now upon its rock. The painting by Alan Sorrell of Harlech in its prime shows it as it might have looked.

In 1294, the 'Way from the Sea' fully justified its existence, when it enabled Harlech to be supplied by ship from Ireland and thus stand firm against the blockade of Madog and his rebels. Perhaps the most famous event in the castle's history was its taking, in the spring of 1404, by Owain Glyndwr. For nearly five years, it became the residence of his court and family. It was the meeting place for parliaments of his supporters and here, so it is said, he crowned himself Prince of Wales.

'MEN OF HARLECH'

Harlech saw action again during the Wars of the Roses, when it was held for the Lancastrian side by its Welsh constable. It was surrendered, at last, after a prolonged siege, forever immortalised in the song 'Men of Harlech'. The final curtain fell with the Civil War. Harlech was the last castle to fall to Parliament, ending forever its role as a place of defence.

So we find the place today, a Crown property still, its gates, its towers and curtain walls standing perpetual guard over the reclaimed Morfa dunelands, looking vainly out to sea for the ship that will never come.

IN CARE OF Welsh Office

OPEN all reasonable times (standard hours)

ADMISSION some charge

LOCATION near centre of town

MAP REFERENCE 8 SH5831

COUNTY Gwynedd

ALAN SORRELL RWS

Devotees of ruined castles up and down the country will have become familiar, by now, with the reconstruction paintings which are often on display there, showing their likely appearance when first built. Often painted in sombre colours, with dramatic shafts of light breaking through the clouds, they are almost all the work of one remarkable artist – the late Alan Sorrell, member of the Royal Watercolour Society.

Born in London in 1904, the son of a master-jeweller, Sorrell spent his formative years and almost all of his subsequent life in remotest rural Essex. After training at the Royal School of Art, he won a scholarship to Rome and it was there that he met with the archaeological stimulus that was to dominate so much of his later work.

In the later 1930s, he formed a personal link with the National Museum of Wales, undertaking several reconstructive interpretations of the Roman and prehistoric sites which were then being excavated. This link continued and he soon formed a further, regular contact with the *Illustrated London News*. But it was not until 1956, when Sorrell carried out some reconstruction drawings of Hadrian's Wall for the then Ministry of Works, that his career as a reconstruction artist par excellence became firmly established.

Working in close collaboration with the Ministry's inspectors of ancient monuments, he produced what are generally reckoned to be the most carefully researched and artistically pure imaginative depictions of ancient monuments ever undertaken. Until his death in 1974, he produced 70 such paintings for the Ministry throughout the country. Fourteen were of historic sites in Wales, some of which are his castle views reproduced in this book.

HAVERFORDWEST CASTLE

Fragments of a two-ward castle beside the county museum on a hill overlooking the town in the county of Dyfed.

Haverfordwest's name was originally simply Haverford, the 'West' being added in order to distinguish it from the similar-sounding Hereford. For centuries after the reign of Henry VIII it was a separate county all by itself, an anomaly which only ended within living memory.

The castle occupies a strong ridge, with a natural scarp on all sides except one, where the site is cut off by a defensive ditch. The outer ward is now occupied by a museum, once the old prison. There are the remains of one square tower nearby, and also the former prison governor's house. The museum itself contains excellent material on the life and history of Pembrokeshire.

Recent clearance of the Victorian prison buildings beyond the museum now allows a good view of the medieval castle with two round towers, a chapel and a hall. Interestingly, the large windows of this latter building are placed too high for scaling-ladders set up against the curtain wall to reach them. Local gritstone is used for most of the buildings, but a lighter-coloured sandstone was brought in for decorative use – around the window-frames, for example.

Next to the chapel is a small dungeon and a postern passage through the wall of the round tower leading to a small terrace which could be used for counter-attack by the forces within the garrison. On the other side of the chapel is a sharp angle of the curtain wall, marking a corner of the original keep, probably belonging to the first castle mentioned by the medieval chronicler, Giraldus Cambrensis.

Haverfordwest Castle was held against Owain Glyndwr, despite his French reinforcements who were landed nearby in Milford Haven. By the 16th century the castle was derelict, but like others was hastily refurbished at the beginning of the Civil War. It is said to have fallen to Parliament without a single shot being fired when the garrison fled, having mistaken a herd of cattle on the skyline in the twilight for a besieging army. Recaptured the next year, Haverfordwest was then properly stormed, and Cromwell's letter ordering the destruction of the castle is still preserved locally.

A striking landmark, Haverfordwest Castle stands on an 80ft hill above the River Cleddau in the town centre

IN CARE OF local authority

OPEN at all reasonable times

ADMISSION free

LOCATION in town centre

MAP REFERENCE 2 SM9515

COUNTY Dyfed

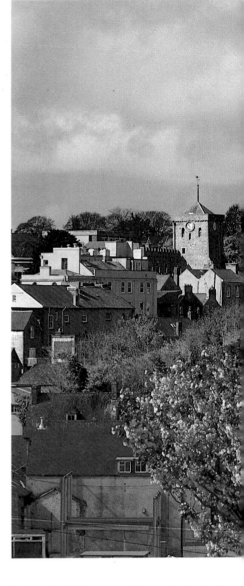

HAWARDEN OLD CASTLE

Lordship castle of c1280 on an ancient fortified site. Its attack in 1282 sparked off the second and final Edwardian campaign. A circular keep, surmounting an earthwork motte is enclosed by an inner ward.

Hawarden Old Castle – built on the first high ground in Wales after the English border at Chester

Today, the visitor to Hawarden Old Castle passes through the pleasant parkland setting of a later-period castle house. Suddenly, a mound of impressive earthworks comes into view, from the top of which the old castle once dominated its surroundings 200ft above the valley floor.

The site has long been used for fortification, being the first high ground for those heading west after crossing the Cheshire Plain. Evidently, its strategic value was first recognised by prehistoric man, for the castle's outer earthworks are in fact those of an Iron Age hillfort, whose banks and ditches were re-adapted by the medieval castle builders. The most prominent feature is a round tower, elevated upon its mound. The mound, on close examination, proves to be an earlier Norman earthwork motte. The circumstances of its building are unknown to us, but its presence is hardly surprising, for this part of Wales, to the east of Offa's Dyke, was continually changing hands between Welsh and English and some kind of fortification would have been needed.

The present masonry castle is also largely undocumented, though it almost certainly dates from around 1280. In 1267, after the destruction of the earlier foundation, the lordship was restored to Robert de Mohaut (or Montalt) upon condition that no castle should be built on the site for 30 years. We do know, however, that a castle had been re-established here by 1282 for, on Palm Sunday that year, Llywelyn ap Gruffudd's brother Dafydd swooped down, in the dead of night, upon Hawarden killing the garrison and taking prisoner its governor, Roger de Clifford. It was this action that forced Llywelyn's hand, precipitating the final uprising that was to lead to his and his brother's deaths and to King Edward I's crushing campaign of 1282–83.

The circular keep would fit well with a date of c1280. A 40ft-high two-storey structure, it has an octagonal inner chamber on its main first floor, with a small chapel leading off from it and an almost continuous mural passage. In style, it matches well with other Edwardian castles such as Flint and Caernarfon, possibly because the king's architect, Master James of St George may have had a hand in its design. The remainder of the castle consists of an inner ward enclosed by a curtain wall. There are remains of an original gateway on the north side, but the most striking features are two fine Early English style windows, marking the site of what was once a Great Hall.

IN CARE OF private owner

OPEN regular times, spring, summer, early autumn. Check in advance

ADMISSION some charge

LOCATION in the park

MAP REFERENCE 12 SJ3265

COUNTY Clwyd

HAY CASTLE

Hay Castle, on the boundary of Wales, has a 13th-century gatehouse, a tower built by one of the luckless Dukes of Buckingham and a Tudor mansion, and is located in an attractive borderland town.

The present castle of Hay-on-Wye replaced an earlier timber castle whose motte can be seen near the parish church. The date of the move is not known, but it had

Part of Hay's castle wall can be traced in local back gardens

probably taken place by about 1200, for an attack on Hay Castle in 1215 is usually thought to refer to the present site. A circular area on a hill top was enclosed by a substantial earth bank, now almost entirely removed. Later, this bank was faced with a masonry wall. A length of this survives together with a gateway with portcullis groove. These defences seem to have been the work of Humphrey de Bohun soon after he recovered Breconshire from Llywelyn ap Gruffudd ('the Last') in 1272, though the remains are not closely dateable, and could be a little later.

In the 15th century Hay passed, with the lordship of Brycheiniog, into the hands of the Dukes of Buckingham. But the family were, to say the least, dogged by misfortune. Humphrey, the first Duke, was killed in battle in 1460, Henry, the second Duke, was beheaded by Richard III as was Edward, the third Duke by Henry VIII. Their memorial at Hay is the square, heavily-buttressed tower built down the scarp next to the medieval gateway.

After Edward's execution, Hay passed to the Crown and its castle fell into disuse. The large, late-Tudor mansion was lived in by a succession of gentry families and in the 19th century was let to' the vicar of Hay. It now belongs to Richard Booth, the bookshop owner, who has gathered at Hay one of the world's largest collections of second-hand books.

IN CARE OF private owner

OPEN viewing from the surrounding area only

LOCATION in town centre

MAP REFERENCE 7 SO2342

COUNTY Powys

HOLT CASTLE

Lordship castle built by the Earl of Surrey after the second Edwardian campaign of 1282–83. Now little more than foundations upon a rocky knoll remain of this historic site near Wrexham.

The scant remains of Holt Castle rest upon a picturesque boss of red-toned sandstone rock

Holt was a lordship castle of the second Edwardian campaign against Wales of 1282. In that year the king granted the lands of Bromfield and Iâl to John de Warenne, Earl of Surrey, but nothing is known of the building of his new castle here. Very little survives of the place today. The most prominent feature is the artificially-shaped boss of sandstone rock on top of and against which the castle was built, for it stands now some 20ft above the surrounding meadow. At one end the top of the rock is fenced against all but the most intrepid visitors, but a walk around the base of the rock will reveal some traces of walling and corner towers.

That great traveller and cartographer John Norden made careful record of the castle in 1620 at which time it was 'nowe in great decay', though clearly still intact. From Norden's drawing we know it was a single ward castle, planned as a regular pentagon, with buildings ranged against each curtain wall and a tower at each angle. Four towers were round, with watch turrets and battered plinths while, at opposing ends, there were square towers, one of which acted as a gatehouse barbican. Attached to the castle were various outbuildings such as 'garners for corne barnes, stables for cattell, killne, brewhouse and one pidgeon house' but, at the time, they were all decayed and are now quite untraceable.

IN CARE OF local authority

OPEN at all times

ADMISSION free

LOCATION near town centre

MAP REFERENCE 12 SJ4153

COUNTY Clwyd

LIFE IN A MEDIEVAL CASTLE

The bare walls of a castle standing above a rough turf or manicured greensward give little idea of that castle when lived in. Apart from missing battlements and walltops, the time traveller would see many wooden features – stairs and half-timbered buildings lining the inner walls and, above, galleries and gables.

Inside the rooms, stonework would be plastered and usually painted over the fine white finish. Patterns of squares outlined in red were most common, imitating fine dressed limestone. There were other decorative features too – Chepstow Castle, for example, had painted shields and bands of yellow and red.

Even during their heyday, we have to remember that castles were rarely fully occupied. When the lord was not in residence, the occupants would consist only of the garrison and a few officials. Usk Castle in 1185 had 25 cavalry, 10 archers and four sentries – 40 in all with the commander. The lord would arrive with a wagontrain, for his furniture; tapestries and even crockery would be carried around from castle to castle. If he was with his army, his soldiers would encamp in the outer enclosure.

The size and complexity of medieval households can be seen in the arrangements necessary to feed them. The doors of the castle would be shut and all would be seated according to their rank and degree. At Raglan in its last days, seven tables were spread, from the Marquess and his family, who were served by gentleman's sons, through the knights and honourables waited on by footmen, to the yeomen grooms with their beer and the separate tables elsewhere in the castle for the clergymen and the lady's maids.

Most castles had their own bakehouses and breweries, and household accounts list truly impressive quantities of wine, game, meat, birds and fish. Self-sufficiency within the castle walls was, of course, a necessity. Clearly, comfort and good food were important considerations even in medieval times.

KIDWELLY CASTLE

Founded within a short time of the Norman Conquest, with powerful earthworks to protect both town and castle. A remarkably complete and perfect stone castle, added to by a local baronial family in the reign of King Edward I. Members of the House of Lancaster enlarged it with an outer ring of walls and towers and a Great Gatehouse which had to be rebuilt after being damaged during Owain Glyndwr's rising. A final re-modelling was carried out in Tudor days. A well-preserved site.

Roger, Bishop of Salisbury, founded the castle and priory of Kidwelly shortly after 1106. Kidwelly lay on the main highway through South Wales, at the limit of tidal water on the Gwendraeth river. The other major castles in this part of Carmarthen Bay – Laugharne and Llanstephan – are similarly sited on their respective river estuaries. All three guarded a coastal route by-passing Carmarthen which could be used at all states of the tide. Thanks to their coastal locations, each castle could be easily supplied with food and ammunition by sea if cut off by hostile forces from the land.

Kidwelly's 14th-century chapel projects on to the scarp above the river

THE MEDIEVAL TOWN

Today the town of Kidwelly lies on both banks of the river, mainly on the lower left bank. The last medieval house was knocked down about 50 years ago, but the 14th-century priory church still stands, with its splendid stone spire. Most tourists make straight for the castle on the other bank. But it is worth taking a short stroll between castle and priory, past the town gate.

Norman Kidwelly was defended by a bank and ditch, enclosing a long triangular area around the castle on its river-cliff. Most of the town embankment was destroyed apart from one gate, and now only the deep ditch remains around the perimeter of the medieval town to remind us of its fortifications as they were in Norman times.

A WALK AROUND KIDWELLY

The gutted interior of the town gate can be seen at the far end of the road leading away from the castle. Closer to, the square towers on each side of the entrance archway can be examined, with their several arrow-slits. From here, a footpath turning sharply to the left leads down to the castle mill and on to the bridge over the river.

The mill house incorporates a little of its medieval predecessor. A path, accessible through the gate just to the left of the house, runs across the watermeadow beside the leat – the channel providing a water supply to turn the millwheel – to the medieval weir just below the castle.

The river bridge is medieval. Although it has been widened for modern traffic, the two pointed arches of the original bridge can be seen from the paved path. From both here and the churchyard there are excellent views of the shale ridge, falling sharply to the Gwendraeth inlet, off the Tywi estuary, on which castle and walled town stand.

NORMAN EARTHWORKS

Outside the castle walls, the deep dry ditch curving around in a semicircle is a remnant of Bishop Roger's first castle, with the steep cliff forming the diameter. Most of the palisaded bank inside the ditch was removed when the outer ring of stone walls and towers were added 200 years later.

The small hill outside the gatehouse might have been a Norman motte – a mound carrying a timber tower – but this is uncertain and the knoll may merely have formed part of a bridgehead. A ditch would have been unnecessary on the steep slope leading down to the river. The only evidence we have of early stone buildings on the site is a small piece of Norman carving built into the later hall.

THE CHAWORTHS BUILD A STONE CASTLE

Llywelyn ab Iorwerth ('the Great') finally threw the Norman castle to the ground in 1231, but the English owner, Patrick de Chaworth, restored Kidwelly's defences sufficiently for it to withstand a further Welsh attack in 1258. Patrick and his sons lived here until about 1280, and the square inner ward, with its four round towers, is attributed to this time.

The new castle was built inside the old

Medieval life is depicted by these authentic period pieces, taken from a book known as the Luttrell Psalter, written 1330–1340 for . . .

defences. Its entrances are simple archways in opposite walls, closed by doors and protected by a portcullis apiece, worked from the battlements above. The round towers at the corners differ in their details – in particular, the two near the cliff edge are not set four-square like the others but are slewed round, not only to prevent their collapse down the slope if the shale slipped, but also to cap the ends of the hall along the cliff. One of these two towers was fitted up as a residence, with fireplaces in all of the main rooms.

LANCASTRIAN REBUILDING

Edmund of Lancaster, the king's brother, was given charge of the heiress of the Chaworths – and of Kidwelly. When she was married in 1298 to Edmund's second son, her new relatives extended the castle,

regarding it as a great prize. The rebuilding began with the hall, which was put on the first floor over a range of store-rooms. Excavation of a rubbish pit near the hall 50 years ago produced four complete pots which must have been broken simultaneously, one being a decorated wine-jug made in Gascony about 1300. During the rebuilding, the residential tower was downgraded, and a small kitchen built alongside.

At the lower end of the new hall, a chapel tower was built down the slope, its angles canted off into huge spurs reflecting those of the contemporary priory church across the river. The high-set row of windows, framed in white stone contrasting with the darker local materials used elsewhere in the castle, were fitted up for shutters, but not glass. A small square annexe alongside the chapel formed a strongroom; notice the cross-

Alan Sorrell's impression of Kidwelly Castle shows the fortress as it might have appeared towards the middle of the 15th century

gables of the stone roof. Below the chapel and strongroom was a private flat for the chaplain, with fireplace and latrine, all reached by steps from the hall.

OUTER WARD

The Norman palisade and much of the bank was swept away by the Lancastrian builders to give a good foundation for a stone curtain wall flanked by six half-round towers and a Great Gatehouse. Two of the towers were planted close together to flank another but smaller entrance on the far side of the castle.

The other four half-round towers were originally open-backed, so that they would

. . . the Luttrell family. The term Psalter . . .

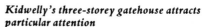

Kidwelly's three-storey gatehouse attracts particular attention

kitchen built inside the inner ward, a bake-house and a lodging or barrack-block.

THE GREAT GATEHOUSE

Unusually, at Kidwelly the Great Gatehouse forms part of the outer rather than the inner defences. A lack of solid ground within the earthworks provides the explanation – the inner ward had to be very small so that its towers could be built on firm foundations, leaving insufficient room for a gatehouse.

The present gatehouse is a very odd building, not at all symmetrical and very unlike those at Caerphilly or Harlech. Originally the only staircase was one awkwardly sited in the left-hand front room, leading up to the hall on the first floor facing into the outer ward. The castle well seems to have been in the other front room. The entrance passage was closed by doors and a portcullis at each end of the passage, and the gatehouse was connected to the former residential tower of the inner ward by a thick wall with doors defended by portcullisses at each end. The gatehouse could therefore be held independently from the wards.

OWAIN GLYNDWR ATTACKS KIDWELLY

The gatehouse had only been begun a few years before Henry of Lancaster succeeded to the English throne in 1399, and was not complete when Glyndwr's forces captured the town and attacked the castle. Although the gatehouse was burned, it was repaired over the next 20 years. The rebuilt parts can be clearly distinguished by the use of thin stone slabs (for example, the three murder hole arches over the entrance, the vaults inside the rooms and the new staircase turret on the inside wall).

The accounts for the rebuilding (which cost £500) include a number of interesting sidelights on castle life during the assaults of Owain Glyndwr's men. Garrison sent messengers in a little boat to Bristol for help, laid in supplies between attacks and cut loopholes through the walls. The garrison itself was tiny: two men at arms and six archers, plus civilians from the town, later strengthened by more archers and a gunner.

IN CARE OF Welsh Office

OPEN all reasonable times (standard hours)

ADMISSION some charge

LOCATION near town centre

MAP REFERENCE 3 SN4107

COUNTY Dyfed

Boiling liquids and missiles were thrown at attackers from murder holes. Kidwelly Castle had three murder hole arches

provide no cover for attackers who captured them against fire from the defenders still holding the inner castle. The round towers of the inner castle were heightened in order to overtop the new outer walls. Evidence of this strengthening is still visible, for the old battlements can be seen walled up solidly below the new tops, in such good condition that the bases of the sentry-boxes, on top of the stair-turrets, are still in place.

Two of the half-round towers on the outer curtain collapsed in the Middle Ages, probably owing to their poor foundations on the old bank. Several large buildings were put up in the outer ward by Sir Rhys ap Tewdwr about 1500: a hall, with a nearby

... tells us it was a psalm book, though today it is admired for its lively series of marginal illustrations

LAUGHARNE CASTLE

A large, mysterious castle, in a remote corner of Dyfed. Excavations are revealing its complex story, entwined with that of Carew Castle.

Laugharne is best known for its associations with the Welsh poet Dylan Thomas, and only recently has the castle been opened up for consolidation and conservation. The site, at the junction of the Corran and Taf rivers, must have been that of Robert Courtmain's castle of Aber Corran, mentioned in 1113. Rhys ap Gruffudd, the Lord Rhys of Deheubarth (South West Wales) came to terms with King Henry II here in 1172. But upon the king's death Rhys seized the castle, as did the two great Llywelyns in turn during the 13th century.

The stone castle we see today was built a little later, by the de Brian family around the year 1300. Of that date are the two large round towers and part of the inner gatehouse, built in a red-coloured stone. By contrast, most of the later work uses stone of a greenish hue. In the 15th century the castle passed into the hands of the Earls of Northumberland, who secured a royal licence to wall and ditch the castle and the town of Laugharne in 1464.

TOWERS AND CANNONBALLS

The outer ward is diamond-shaped, with a dry ditch in front of the gate, running back to the riverside in either direction. The gatehouse, with its two angular towers, probably dates from the time of ownership by the Northumberlands; notice the stone steps leading up to the battlements of the curtain wall. The spurred bases of the gatetowers not only deflected battering rams and other missiles, but also acted as buttresses and gave added protection against undermining. The gate was partly rebuilt about 1580, and cannonballs from a Civil War siege have been found embedded in the battlements.

TUDOR ALTERATIONS

Within the castle there is a hall range inserted between the old medieval round towers, with a great semicircular stair tower built onto its outside. The simpler inner gate seems to have been extended forward (and upward) at the same time. It is not known who did this, nor when it was done, but there are several close resemblances to the work undertaken for Sir Rhys ap Thomas at Carew Castle. Since Sir Rhys also held Laugharne for a time, we can assume that he was probably the builder.

THE LATER TUDOR HOUSE

The southern angle of the castle overlooks the Taf estuary. This part of Laugharne castle has been excavated down to the Tudor levels, although some of the walling belongs to the medieval (de Brian) buildings. Sir John Perrott, said to have been a bastard son of Henry VIII, leased the castle between 1587 and 1591, and seems to have converted it into a Tudor mansion, with a formal garden in the outer ward.

Noteworthy features in the castle include the kitchen's large fireplace and the pent-roof over the latrine projecting out from the curtain, to discharge into the river at high tide. The trenches inside the ward mark the line of the foundations of the inner walls of Sir John Perrott's hall, which seems to have been of half-timbered construction, apart from the standing wall (with fireplaces and windows) which is the old curtain wall of the castle itself. The medieval well is still buried under the floor of this later hall – the Tudor well is just outside it. A little further on is a passageway leading to a postern gate, giving access to the shore below the castle. This served as a possible escape-route if siege conditions became intolerable, or even for a pleasant sail or row after a meal in the Great Hall.

The courtyard between the two Tudor halls would have been paved with patterns of cobblestones, and the base of an ornamental water-fountain (and its supply pipe) has been found. Laugharne was captured by the Royalists in 1644, but was surrendered on easy terms once the besieging Roundheads began undermining in earnest. The Tudor mansion was apparently knocked down soon afterwards, since little rubbish of later date was found in the excavations. In later times, the painter Turner, absorbed by the castle's ivy-clad beauty, captured it memorably on canvas.

IN CARE OF Welsh Office
May be closed for repairs. Can be viewed from the surrounding area

LOCATION on A4066 14m SW of Carmarthen

MAP REFERENCE 3 SN3011

COUNTY Dyfed

Deep in Dylan Thomas country is the pretty castle of Laugharne, seen from the air (right) and against the Taf (below)

LLANDOVERY CASTLE

An early Norman motte and bailey castle, given stone walls in the 13th century and still in use 200 years later.

This must be one of the most easily-accessible castles in Wales for the motorist. It immediately adjoins the market car park just off the main trunk road, the A40, in the middle of an attractive county town. The taller earth mound (the motte) now carries stone walls around its top, amongst which there is a large, D-shaped tower with turrets on each side of the entrance. Alongside the motte is the larger, but lower, bailey, complete with ditch. Both overlook the crossing-point of the River Bran, a tributary of the main Tywi.

The 'castle of Cantref Bychan' was attacked in 1116: this may refer to the underlying earthworks of the castle at this crossroads, a site of early importance. Llandovery was the Roman Alabum, with roads leading to both Abergavenny and Carmarthen as well as to the gold mines at Pumsaint nearby (off the modern A482). The masonry dates from the late 13th century, when the castle was attacked frequently. It was still strong enough to merit the attention of Owain Glyndwr's forces during his rising in the early years of the 15th century, some time before the enigmatic leader disappeared.

The town of Llandovery grew up around the Norman castle (right) and became an important centre for the assembly of cattle that were being driven to England

IN CARE OF local authority

OPEN at all times

ADMISSION free

LOCATION in town car park

MAP REFERENCE 6 SN7633

COUNTY Dyfed

LLANSTEPHAN CASTLE

On a headland occupied since prehistoric times, the Norman castle was modernized from time to time right up to the end of the Middle Ages. Interesting evolution of fortifications. Fine views of the Tywi estuary.

Where the estuary of the Tywi widens into Carmarthen Bay, a ridge runs down from the west, ending in a steep bluff. This is a site of great antiquity, for long before any castle was built here the bluff formed an Iron Age promontory fort, charcoal samples from which have been dated to the 6th century BC.

Just when the prehistoric fort was re-occupied is not known. We hear of it first in 1146 when it was captured by the princelings of Deheubarth, 'throwing down the English scaling-ladders into the ditch'. But the English eventually won, and the castle was held by five de Camvilles in turn, right down to the middle of the 14th century. The first de Camville borrowed money to fortify Llanstephan in 1192, and part of the wall around the inner ward could be as old as this.

THE FIRST CASTLE AND INNER GATE

The Normans clearly took advantage of the existing site, clearing out the ditches of the Iron Age fort and making part of the fort into an inner ward on the summit of the ridge. To understand the castle's development and the way in which it functioned, it is best to go straight inside and walk up to the top of the hill.

The conspicuous square tower acted as the gatehouse to the inner ward. It stands on top of the earlier curtain wall, with its passage defended by doors and a portcullis in vertical slots, now gone. The room over the passage could only be reached from the battlements of the curtain wall, and the room above that by a staircase in the thickness of the wall.

The curtain wall was heightened a little later; this shows up as a well-defined horizontal line on the outside, and in blocked-up battlements on the inside. Elsewhere the wall was thickened with vaults, to provide a wider walk behind the new battlements. Excavations here have revealed several 13th-century buildings, including a round tower.

IMPROVEMENTS TO THE OUTER WARD

In 1257 an English army marching to Carmarthen was destroyed by the Welsh. That army contained nearly all the garrisons of the castles nearby, and the Welsh, pressing home their advantage, captured Llanstephan for a time. This must have prompted the de Camvilles to improve their defences soon afterward by walling in the lower ward and flanking it with large D-shaped towers, each fitted up for permanent residence, with fireplaces and latrines.

The D-tower above the beach is both larger and stronger than the other, with two turrets respectively carrying the spiral staircase and the latrine block. It was probably intended for occupation by the lord of the castle, giving him relative comfort and privacy. The right-angled turn in the curtain wall nearby was another set of toilets, serving the hall between the angle and the D-tower.

The hall has vanished completely, and its site is occupied by a great barn whose roof is carried right over the top of the curtain wall.

The barn probably dates from the ownership of Jasper Tewdwr at the end of the 15th century. For the next 400 years, the castle was occupied by farm buildings.

GREAT GATEHOUSE

Llanstephan's most imposing feature is undoubtedly its twin-towered gatehouse to the outer ward. This became the castle's main living quarters and was converted by the Tudors into a house by walling up both ends of the passage and building a simple new entrance alongside, defended only by a murder hole above the gate.

Originally the gatehouse was of the common 'Edwardian' pattern, with a passage protected by at least two portcullises and doors, murder holes in the vault above and arrow-slits in the side walls. Rooms extending right across the upper floors were reached by spiral stairs in corner turrets and lit by large windows looking safely into the outer ward. Geoffrey de Camville's mason copied many of the ideas of the inner east gate of Caerphilly Castle, down to the letterbox-like 'water-chute' over the front arch, through which boiling liquids were poured onto attackers, but here the design was not a practical success.

IN CARE OF Welsh Office

OPEN at all times

ADMISSION free

LOCATION on headland 8m SW of Carmarthen

MAP REFERENCE 3 SN3510

COUNTY Dyfed

Perched high on a wooded hill above the mouth of the River Tywi, Llanstephan Castle (below) commands fine views of countryside and coastline

Undulating farmland makes pleasing contrast to the rugged ruin of Llanstephan Castle (above), an important fortification in the 13th century

LOUGHOR CASTLE

Small residential castle of the de Breos family, built on the site of a Roman fort in the county of West Glamorgan.

The direct road from Swansea to Llanelli (A484) crosses the Loughor river between two headlands which were once part of the same glacial moraine. This made a tidal inlet, fordable at low tide, with a sheltered harbour above the present road and rail bridges.

The road passes through the site of a Roman fort, the centre of which is marked by St Michael's Church. The medieval castle was built on the crest of the spur, over the buried remains of a corner turret of the Roman fort. An oval enclosure was made by cutting a ditch six feet deep and piling the spoil inside, though the castle was burnt by the Welsh in 1151. Recent excavations have revealed burnt Norman chessmen together with traces of later wood and stone buildings against the earth bank.

In about 1220, the castle was given to John de Breos, Llywelyn ab Iorwerth's son-in-law. The new owner probably added the curtain wall whose foundations now lie just under the turf. This curtain would have been entered on one side of the present ruined tower, which is probably slightly later than John de Breos's time. Originally, there would have been more than one tower on this site: note the separate entrances to each floor from the courtyard, and the evidence of comfortable residence – windows, fireplaces and toilets – in both standing and fallen masonry.

Loughor Castle has yielded many interesting Roman finds, as well as this early 13th-century tripod pitcher

IN CARE OF Welsh Office

OPEN at all times

ADMISSION free

LOCATION on western edge of town near bridge

MAP REFERENCE 3 SS5697

COUNTY West Glamorgan

MANORBIER CASTLE

Birthplace of Giraldus Cambrensis, the 12th-century writer, and ancestral home of the de Barris. The castle is very well preserved, complete to its battlements, and shows how a 13th-century knightly household was organized in times of peace as well as in war. Beautifully located in Pembrokeshire Coast National Park.

'Maenor Pyrr is the pleasantest spot in Wales', wrote man of letters Giraldus Cambrensis at the end of the 12th century. 'It is excellently well defended by turrets and bulwarks, and is situated on the summit of a hill . . . a fine pond of fish and an orchard and wood remarkable for the projecting rocks and tall hazels, a mill lake and never-failing stream . . .'

Giraldus's grandfather had come from Barry (South Glamorgan) as a follower of Gerald of Windsor in the first Norman expedition into South West Wales. But for all its beauty, Manorbier was only a poor manor, and the de Barri's family lands were to be mainly in Ireland.

Situated as it is away from it all on the extreme south coast of Dyfed, Manorbier was never attacked by the Welsh after the de Barris arrived. Although taken by force in 1327 during a family quarrel, it had degenerated into a farm by the 16th century, in common with many other castles in West Wales. In 1654 during the conflicts of the Civil War, it was surrendered to Parliament.

FIGURE-OF-EIGHT PLAN

Manorbier is built of limestone quarried not far away. The excellent state of preservation of so much of the castle is due to this building material, for limestone is extremely durable both as a building-stone and for mortar. The castle plan resembles a figure-of-eight, with two walled wards in line, situated on a low spur in a valley running down to the sea. In this direction are a dovecot and a ruined mill beside a marsh, the successors to Giraldus's lake and mill.

The path to the inner ward crosses the outer, of which a length of curtain wall with

a 13th-century round tower can be seen on the right. The 17th-century great barn covers a big V-shaped defence, stone-faced with a ditch and terrace, of a common Civil War type, loosely called a ravelin. (There is a similar one at Carew Castle.)

THE HOUSE OF THE DE BARRIS

There is another 17th-century barn within the inner ward, into which a modern house and outbuildings have been inserted. Beyond, on the farthest side of the inner ward, is the manor-house of the de Barris. The original Norman hall can be reached by the right-hand staircase; it stands on top of dark, unlit, storage rooms. The windows and fireplaces of the hall were improved in the 13th century, but the end wall with its fireplaces and round 'Flemish' chimney-stack, next to the Norman doorway, could well have been there when Giraldus Cambrensis was born in the castle in 1146.

The left-hand staircase leads to the main floor of the vaulted chapel, which is almost as large as the hall. Originally the chapel was in a separate building from the hall, but the two were shortly linked together by a new chamber-block carried over the passageway leading to the postern gate.

On the far (right-hand) side of this block

of buildings is the great kitchen, with its enormous hearths and ovens, and also the castle well. For a kitchen it has very fine windows, with side-seats and traces of shutters. Was it originally intended to be a new hall, but never completed?

CURTAIN WALL AND ENTRANCE

The original Norman manorhouse was enclosed later within a polygonal curtain wall, which still surrounds most of the inner ward. However, the seaward end was demolished when it proved inconvenient. On the other side, the castle shop is basically a 13th-century guardroom on one side of the entrance. The other side is formed by a Norman tower, high but thin-walled, which has partly collapsed.

The first gate was a simple doorway in the curtain wall protected by a portcullis, but later in the 13th century the passage was lengthened and a second portcullis added at the inner end. The ditch outside was crossed by a turning-bridge which landed on the stone pier: the holes for the pivots of the bridge are still there, but the position of the chains is incorrect.

On each side of the gateway is a round tower at an angle of the curtain wall; another angle has a turret perched astride the top of the wall. The round tower reached by the stairs behind the shop is the better of the two – it has two floors of fine arrow-slits, and the old parapet has been roofed over to form a

GIRALDUS CAMBRENSIS 1146–1223

We owe a lot to Giraldus. Giraldus Cambrensis – Gerald of Wales – was, throughout his eventful life, many things: a scholar, a monk, a pilgrim, an archdeacon, a traveller, and, most important of all, a writer. Born about 1146 at Manorbier Castle, near Tenby, his famous chronicles paint a unique picture of life in medieval Wales just after the coming of the Normans. His two works, *Itinerary through Wales* and *Description of Wales*, bring into sharp focus a distinctive country and its people, still resilient under the overlordship of the Normans.

Giraldus's work has a lasting authority because it avoids polemic. He observes the strengths and weaknesses in both Welshman and Norman, a rare impartiality which must have come from his background. Born of mixed Norman-Welsh descent, Giraldus admitted, 'I am sprung from the princes of Wales and from the barons of the Marches, and when I see injustice in either race I hate it'.

In his early career, Giraldus entered the church and was sent to the University of Paris, where he distinguished himself. But his talents could never be confined with an ecclesiastical straightjacket, and it was as a writer that he gained lasting recognition. In 1188 he accompanied Archbishop Baldwin on a tour of Wales, in effect a recruitment campaign for the Third Crusade. His journal of the tour, published in 1191 as his *Itinerary* is, thankfully, much less prosaic than its title suggests. This is no straightforward diary of events, for in the book Giraldus plays the part of the roving reporter, casting a perceptive eye over life in 12th-century Wales.

His second work, *Description*, was published in 1194. Taken together, his two books give an insight into Wales and the Welsh character which even today – as any honest Welshman will admit – is uncannily accurate. On the negative side, Giraldus tells us of the endless internal feuding and vindictiveness that so debilitated and disunited the Welsh, of their chronic impulse 'to avenge not only recent but ancient affronts'.

Welshmen might ruefully recognize that trait; but at the same time be proud of their hospitality, love of music, poetry and talk, their gifts of eloquence and liberality that Giraldus praised in his writings.

Less contentiously, he records a Welsh lifestyle largely unaffected by the Normans; of a pastoral people eating more meat than bread, sleeping communally on beds of rushes in the same scant clothes they wore by day, having no taste for trade, paying 'no attention to commerce, shippings and manufactures'.

Giraldus, the objective reporter, does let the mask slip occasionally. His tremendous affection for his birthplace, Manorbier, 'the pleasantest spot in Wales', is evident throughout his work. And so, too, is his ultimate affection for the Welsh who, whatever their faults, he found passionate and warm in comparison to the cold, calculating Normans.

fighting-gallery between tower and gate like that at Cilgerran. Indeed all the parts of the curtain wall have been raised at least once – that on the other side of the entrance no less than three times, the old battlements being visible on the outer side of the wall.

IN CARE OF private owner

OPEN at regular times in summer. Please check in advance

ADMISSION some charge

LOCATION 5m SW of Tenby

MAP REFERENCE 2 SS0598

COUNTY Dyfed

Manorbier Castle still retains traces of the domestic and religious aspects of life that sustained a privileged medieval environment

MONMOUTH CASTLE

One of a chain of 12th-century forts built by William FitzOsbern, this castle was later the birthplace of King Henry V, victor of Agincourt. The site is still in military occupation.

Monmouth Castle was part of a highly-effective Norman defence system

Once a centre for cap-making, Monmouth's close-fitting caps were mentioned in Shakespeare's **Henry V**

Monmouth is one of the main gateways to Wales. The cliffs of the Wye valley to the south are a strong natural barrier, at the two ends of which – at Monmouth and Chepstow – major Roman roads entered Wales across the river. Very soon after the Norman Conquest, William FitzOsbern, one of William the Conqueror's most trusted barons, built castles at the two crossings from which he overran most of Gwent. Monmouth Castle is still in military occupation, as the headquarters of the Royal Monmouthshire Royal Engineers, the senior non-regular regiment of the British army.

The buildings of the castle stood around what is now the parade ground. The oldest is the 12th-century hall-keep like that at Chepstow, with a row of Norman slit windows at ground floor. The hall was on the floor above and in about 1270 was replaced by a separate hall built onto the keep in an L-plan. A round keep like that at Skenfrith fell down in 1647, as we know from the diary of a local schoolmaster, Reverand More Pye. In its place the first Duke of Beaufort, after the Restoration of Charles II, built Great Castle House in 1673 to replace Raglan as his family's residence in the county. In 1875, the house became the official headquarters of the Royal Monmouthshire Engineer Militia.

King Henry V, 'Harry of Monmouth', was born in the castle on 16 September,

1387. Shakespeare refers to Monmouth several times in his play, mentioning appreciatively the Wye salmon and recounting, through his Welsh soldier Fluellen, how the Welsh 'did goot service' on the Agincourt campaign patriotically 'wearing leeks in their Monmouth caps'.

IN CARE OF Welsh Office

OPEN viewing from the parade ground

LOCATION on western edge of town

MAP REFERENCE 5 SO5113

COUNTY Gwent

MONTGOMERY CASTLE

Montgomery's ruins look down from a high rock ridge above the small town onto the Severn valley. Castle and town were created by King Henry III in 1223, replacing an earth and timber castle a mile away. Fine views.

A few years after the Battle of Hastings, Roger of Montgomery, from St Foi de Montgommeri in Calvados, built a motte and bailey castle of earth and timber, commanding an important ford on the River Severn, as a military base for his campaigns in West Wales. By the early 13th century, with Llywelyn the Great near the height of his power, it became obvious that such a key point of the border could no longer be defended only by an obsolescent wooden castle. In the autumn of 1223 the advisers of the boy King Henry III gave orders that a new castle was to be built on a high narrow ridge, a mile from Roger's old castle, which in time became known as Hen Domen ('the Old Mound').

FROM WOOD TO STONE

Work on New Montgomery began immediately. Forest of Dean miners were set to work to divide the ridge into two wards with ditches cut across its width and to dig the castle well, whilst carpenters quickly ran up a timber castle which could be replaced in stone over the coming years.

At the northern end of the ridge is the inner ward. This was the only part defended in stone in the first phase of the castle's history. A large twin-towered gatehouse occupies the full width of the ridge, with a massive rock-cut ditch in front of it and the ward itself behind. Projecting out from one side of this ward is the Well Tower, with the well cut through the rock to a depth of about 220 feet.

The timber defences of the middle ward were replaced in stone in 1251–53, when the present curtain wall was built. But with the conquest of independent Wales by Edward I, Montgomery lost its role as a front-line military castle. In the 14th century, it belonged to the Mortimers, Earls of March, and it may be significant that the additions which they made were inspired by domestic and manorial, rather than defensive, considerations.

HOME COMFORTS

In the inner ward, their kitchen can be seen; the stones in the floor of its great circular domed oven set on the edge to resist the effects of fire. Next to it is the castle brewery. In the middle ward is a building containing an oven for drying grain, a reminder that a castle was not only a military work but was usually the centre of a sizeable and busy agricultural estate. During

Battle reconstructions often take place at Montgomery – scene of many real battles

Montgomery's ditch and gatehouse

the long reign of Henry VIII, Bishop Rowland Lee, President of the Council of the Marches, restored Montgomery, which he described as 'the second key of Wales'. Throughout the castle, lightly built two-storey lodgings were assembled for the numerous servants and minor officials of his household.

Later in the century, the castle passed to the Herberts. Lady Magdalene Herbert was a friend of John Donne the poet, and the mother of another poet, George Herbert. Donne stayed with them at Montgomery and wrote a poem about a primrose growing on the castle hill. Lady Magdalene's magnificent tomb is in the Montgomery Church, her effigy alongside that of her husband. This was erected in her lifetime (like Donne's tomb in St Paul's), but she later re-married and, in contradiction to best-laid plans, was buried in Chelsea.

CIVIL WAR STRIFE
Her son, Lord Herbert of Chirbury, became tired of the quarrels of Charles I's London and retired to Montgomery, building himself a fine brick house in the middle ward. He lived here peaceably until the night of 4 September 1644, when a Parliamentary

commando force placed a bomb under the outer gatehouse and forced him to surrender the castle. A Royalist force under Lord Byron besieged the castle in an attempt to recover it and when the Parliamentary relief column arrived, a major battle followed. The Battle of Montgomery was a crushing defeat for the Royalists.

Lord Herbert of Chirbury died in 1649. His son had been a Royalist colonel and Parliament thought it safer to have Montgomery Castle demolished. Since no one could be found locally to do the work, Lord Herbert demolished his own castle, the costs being deducted from his fines for 'malignancy', a euphemistic reference to loyalty to King Charles.

A small museum in the town exhibits some of the finds from recent excavations.

IN CARE OF Welsh Office

OPEN at all times

ADMISSION free

LOCATION reached by Castle Hill

MAP REFERENCE 9 SO5113

COUNTY Powys

MORLAIS CASTLE

Morlais, a castle of Gilbert de Clare isolated on high, windy moorland above Merthyr Tydfil, was probably never finished. Superb views of Brecon Beacons can be gained from the site.

In 1290, two of Edward I's greatest subjects, Humphrey de Bohun, Earl of Hereford and Lord of Brycheiniog and Gilbert de Clare, Earl of Gloucester and Lord of Glamorgan, were contestants in a celebrated legal action in the king's court. The cause of this was a castle which Gilbert had begun in disputed border territory between the two lordships, and a minor private war between the two involving cattle raids and looting. The castle referred to must have been Morlais.

To day, unfinished rock-cut ditches sur-

round a moorland plateau on the borders of Mid Glamorgan and Powys. Not a great deal of masonry remains above ground, but from the turf-covered mounds which mark the lines of walls and towers, it is possible to trace the outline of a great pointed-oval ward with some six substantial towers. Morlais's most interesting and unexpected feature is beneath ground level – an intact vaulted basement of what may have been a great tower or keep, with its central pillar and ribbed vault.

In the centre of the ward, a vertical shaft

Morlais has a spectacular vaulted basement – possibly once part of a keep

is cut through the rock. It is not a relic of recent mining, but a medieval attempt at a well. In the 19th century, it was 70ft deep, but the Victorian archaeologist and engineer G T Clark estimated that a shaft of 400ft would have been necessary to reach water.

IN CARE OF private owner

OPEN at all times

ADMISSION free

LOCATION on N edge of Merthyr Tydfil Access by path from minor road

MAP REFERENCE 4 SO0409

COUNTY Mid Glamorgan

NEATH CASTLE

At Neath, Edward II sought refuge from his queen and her lover, but was captured nearby and later murdered.

Around 1130, the Norman knight, Richard de Granville built Neath's first castle close to the Roman fort of Nidum and the abbey which he later founded. His castle has disappeared and the present one, around which the town of Neath has grown up, is across the river from fort and abbey.

The second castle began as a D-shaped mound protected by wooden palisades on its flat northern side by the river. In the early 13th century it was given a stone curtain wall and a round tower on each end of its northern side. The entrance was a simple arch inside one of the towers (as at Chepstow), approached by a flight of steps. The siting of the towers is odd, since they would have left most of the perimeter unprotected, though there may have been others on the south, to give protection to the remainder of

The 13th-century main gateway, its two towers, and parts of the curtain wall are all that remain of Neath Castle

the curtain wall.

Neath Castle was sacked by Llywelyn the Great in 1231 and by the dissident barons opposed to Despenser in 1321. It seems to have been ruined before it was rebuilt in the 14th century, when the tower flanking the entrance was supplemented by a second to form an Edwardian style gatehouse and the castle was generally renovated. Neath played its part in high tragedy in 1326 when Edward II sought refuge, shortly before being captured near here and taken to Berkeley Castle, where he was horribly done to death.

IN THE CARE OF local authority

OPEN viewing from the surrounding area only

LOCATION near town centre

MAP REFERENCE 4 SS7597

COUNTY West Glamorgan

New Castle once controlled a ford on the River Ogmore

area with its flat rear face backed up against a steep slope. This curtain probably follows the line of the bank of an original earthwork castle, to which the stone defences were later added. The way in which the curtain is built – in short straight lengths with 'hinges' of squared dressed stone where it changes direction – is typical of the 12th century; also typical are the two small square towers of similar size which protect the castle's southern and western faces.

These are like miniature keeps and had their entry doors at first-floor level, reached by an external stair, probably of timber. This feature can best be seen in the tower by the Norman gateway, where the present ground floor door is a later insertion. The other tower is more ruined, but what is left is basically similar.

Next to the South Tower is the decorated Norman gateway of about 1175–80. Outside churches, Norman architectural work of this quality has rarely survived later rebuilding and destruction. New Castle's well-preserved gateway is valuable evidence of the quality which 12th-century secular buildings might achieve in these parts. Twin columns are recessed into the angles of its outer arch and a bold roll-moulding is carried around the top of the arch from their decorated capitals. Inside this first arch is a door-like inner arch with flattened head, its stone carved with Romanesque ornament.

Within the ward are the foundations of a lightly-built structure, probably a Norman hall with timber-framed walls. Overlying it at one end are the remains of a 16th-century building.

IN CARE OF Welsh Office

OPEN at all reasonable times (standard hours). Key from keeper

ADMISSION free

LOCATION near town centre on A4063

MAP REFERENCE 4 SS7597

COUNTY Mid Glamorgan

NEW CASTLE

William, Earl of Gloucester's gateway shows the high standards of architectural decoration of some Norman castles in Wales. It makes this little-known castle in Bridgend well worth a visit.

The New Castle on the banks of the Ogmore already existed by 1104, when Robert FitzHamon granted the adjacent church to the monks of Tewkesbury. The Old Castle, which the name suggests must have existed nearby was probably Coity. New Castle belonged to the Lords of Glamorgan, and the stone defences may be

the work of William, Earl of Gloucester, who died in 1183. With its neighbours at Coity and Ogmore, it guarded the river crossings which controlled access into Glamorgan from the west at a time when much of this western territory was in Welsh hands.

The curtain wall encloses a D-shaped

MEDIEVAL WARFARE

Medieval warfare was usually a summer occupation, for in winter roads became impassable with mud, food was hard to find and armies starved or froze. In spring, when the campaigning season opened, a lord would lead his army into hostile territory, burning villages and crops, carrying off cattle and seeking to reduce the land and its ruler to submission. The campaign's two 'set piece' events were the battle and the siege.

BATTLE PLANS

In battle, the basic pattern of warfare between cavalry and foot soldier, once it had evolved, did not radically change. The cavalry sought to ride down the ranks of infantry with the cold steel of lance and sword. The infantry tried to break the formation of the advancing cavalry with concentrated archery fire and then to receive the survivors with an impenetrable hedge of pikes. Tactics were not basically different centuries later at Waterloo, except that musket and bayonet had replaced longbow and pike.

Among the cavalry, knights performing military service in exchange for land were gradually replaced by paid professionals, organized into troops and with a small group of bannerets (subalterns) and troopers to each knight. Light cavalry were used for scouting, intelligence work and for raids.

Welsh longbows were soon famous. Giraldus Cambrensis described the people of Gwent in the south east as 'more used to war, more famous for valour and more expert archers than other Welsh'. When they attacked Abergavenny Castle in 1175, arrows aimed at soldiers fleeing across the bridge to the motte penetrated an oak door four fingers thick. One of William de Braose's knights was transfixed by an arrow which passed through his armoured thigh and his heavy military saddle, and mortally wounded his horse. Another, similarly transfixed, turned his horse around and was promptly pinned through the other thigh also.

Crossbows were used for defending castles. They were powerful weapons and easier to handle in the confined space of an arrow-loop than ordinary bows, but their mechanisms were sensitive to damp, which made them unsuitable for use on campaign. Since they enabled a peasant infantryman to kill his armoured social superior, one 12th-century church council tried to ban them as 'weapons hateful of God'.

SIEGE WARFARE

The purpose of a castle, in peace or in war, was to control a particular area of territory. Since it would be unsafe for a hostile army to advance further leaving an unsubdued castle in its rear, it was often necessary to besiege and capture a castle. Methods of attack and defence depended upon the type of castle and its situation. Fire arrows and 'Greek fire' – an incendiary weapon brought back from the Crusades – were useful against timber defences or against the wooden parts of stone castles. But against stone castles it was often necessary to used heavy stone-throwing catapults and battering rams to break down the walls, scaling ladders and siege towers to storm them, or miners to undermine them.

When it was thought that a castle was ready to surrender, a summons to the defending commander might be sent in. If he felt secure, the commander could simply reject this; otherwise he might open tentative discussions with the besiegers. This stage could involve elaborate bluff and counter-bluff and one eminent historian has compared negotiations of this kind to a game of poker, though willingness to talk was often a sign that the garrison's resolve was weakening.

This sword, thought to date from the 14th century, was found at Heyop in the old county of Radnorshire, now known as Powys

NEWCASTLE EMLYN CASTLE

The only stone castle built by the Welsh in Dyfed. One of the last to hold out for King Charles I during the Civil Wars.

The 'New Castle in Emlyn' was so called to distinguish it from Cilgerran Castle, a few miles away, not the earlier motte and bailey castle just across the river. The rocky promontory, surrounded on three sides by the River Teifi, was fortified about 1240 by Maredudd ap Rhys Grug. In 1287, another Welshman, Rhys ap Maredudd, escaping from the siege of Dryslwyn Castle, again evaded the English forces here and turned the tables by capturing the leader of the English garrison. An enormous effort was put into a second siege, and eventually the castle was taken. Five years later the royal garrison deserted, but local officials held the castle until Rhys was finally defeated and killed.

Newcastle was rebuilt soon afterward, and a new town was founded outside its walls. Only parts of the castle gatehouse still remain standing, though its plan shows that the castle must have resembled those in better condition at Carreg Cennen and Laugharne. In the inner ward, tapering to the point of the ridge, some foundations of the hall and chapel can be traced. We know that in 1340 the hall had a shingled roof and wooden gutters; 200 years later the roofs were slate, and the gutters lined with lead.

The town was half destroyed by Owain Glyndwr in 1403, and the castle was seized by the Crown in 1531 (see Carew Castle). During the Civil Wars the local Royalists retreated to the castle and inflicted a severe defeat on their opponents. But after the general surrender in these parts, the castle was blown up to make it untenable should fighting have broken out again.

IN CARE OF local authority

OPEN at all times

ADMISSION free

LOCATION on A484, 10m SE of Cardigan

MAP REFERENCE 3 SN3140

COUNTY Dyfed

Now a serene ruin, Newcastle Emlyn Castle was intended as a country seat rather than a military post

Arrow-slits, like the one above at Carreg Cennen Castle, were up to 6ft high but only inches wide. A chamber accommodated two crossbowmen, who would load and shoot in turn

DEFENDING THE CASTLE

The castles of Wales give us many fine examples of the way in which military architecture evolved under the influence of medieval warfare. A second line of defence was necessary to fall back on should the first be taken by the enemy. This second, preferably stronger line would have additional strongpoints which, in the last resort, could be held separately, or used to tie down sections of the attackers.

The evolution of castle architecture illustrates this strat-egy. With a motte and bailey, the defenders could retreat to the motte. A circular stone keep on the motte gave a better strongpoint, with a lethal all-round field of fire, and a strongly-defended inner ward, as at Montgomery, an even better one. At Skenfrith, the circular central keep overtops the surrounding curtain so that the attackers scaling the walls would be point-blank targets for its archers.

This, the concentric principle, is fully developed in the great Edwardian castles of North Wales. A low outer curtain wall encloses a higher inner curtain, which covers the outer line from its arrow-loops. Vulnerable corners and gateways are protected by circular towers and massive gatehouses, which can themselves be shut off as separate strongpoints. Their water defences make mining impossible and access to the river or sea make them difficult to starve out. The art of medieval military architecture reaches its zenith.

NEWPORT CASTLE

Newport Castle is enigmatic. Moved at some date from the hilltop beside the present cathedral down to the bank of the Usk, what remains is the residence of a later medieval nobleman, seemingly unfinished.

Until 1314 Newport was part of the Lordship of Glamorgan. When Gilbert de Clare died on the battlefield of Bannockburn, Newport became a separate lordship and passed to his sister Margaret and her husband Hugh d'Audele. Its castle was then a motte and bailey at the top of Stow Hill, where its mound was visible until buried in spoil from a Victorian railway tunnel. Margaret's sister was married to the royal favourite Hugh le Despenser, who ejected d'Audele from Newport, which he only recovered on Despenser's fall and execution in 1326. The move downhill to the existing site may have been due to d'Audele, who wanted a new castle for his new lordship.

After d'Audele's death, Newport passed by marriage to the Earls of Stafford. Much of the existing castle may be the work of Hugh, Earl of Stafford. The three towers on the riverward side may be basically his, but maps made before the railway and a canal destroyed much of the castle area in the 19th century show that, in contrast, the other three sides were protected by a blank wall with no towers. This is surprising, for a landward block would usually match an existing river frontage, with at least a land gate to match the watergate. But Hugh died unexpectedly in 1386 and may have left the castle unfinished. In 1405, at the height of the Glyndwr crisis, large numbers of masons were working here on what was clearly an emergency building programme, perhaps putting Hugh's unfinished castle into a defensible state with a simple curtain wall.

Hugh's grandson, Humphrey Stafford, came of age in 1424 and a few years later began transforming Newport into a residence worthy of his rank. In 1444 he became Duke of Buckingham. By great good fortune, we have several of the annual accounts listing the expenses of rebuilding which tell us much about the castle, the sources of building stone and the masons who built it. The castle was now in its final form. At the north (railway) end was the hall with its tall window and fireplace. The central tower had a presence chamber where the lord sat on ceremonial occasions under a vaulted roof with carved ornaments. Below was the watergate, above the chapel. From the presence chamber a wall passage led to the south tower, by the bridge, with its richly-appointed ducal apartments.

Newport's most substantial remains are a gateway and flanking tower

IN CARE OF Welsh Office

OPEN viewing from the surrounding area only

LOCATION near town centre

MAP REFERENCE 5 ST3188

COUNTY Gwent

OGMORE CASTLE

Ogmore Castle guards a ford across the Ewenny river now marked by a series of stepping stones. This explains its low-lying site and disregard for strong defensive siting. The Norman keep of the de Londres family and the later buildings form a striking group in this fine setting.

Ogmore Castle stands beside a ford on the Ewenny river. With the neighbouring castles of Coity and New Castle – Bridgend, it controlled the fords into Glamorgan from the Welsh-held territory to the west. It was the centre of the extensive lordship of the de Londres family (de Londres – of London). William de Londres had arrived here by 1116 and the earthworks of the castle may date back to his time. The defences and buildings of this early castle would have been of timber. We may picture a solidly built palisade and fighting platform around the perimeter, a gate tower of wooden posts, a wooden hall and a clutter of smaller buildings in the interior.

THE STONE KEEP

Ogmore, like most of the important Norman castles of the area, later acquired a stone keep. This was probably the work of William's son, Maurice de Londres, whose fine tombstone can be seen in Ewenny Priory, which his father had founded. This

Ogmore overlooks a ford on the River Ewenny, famous for its stepping stones

keep still stands three storeys high beside the entrance to the inner ward. The ground floor was originally an unlit basement with no external access, the present entrance having been cut through the walling at a later date (originally, the ground floor would have been reached by ladder from the floor above). On the first floor was the hall, accessible from the ward of the castle by an external staircase. Two round-arched Norman windows remain in one wall and there is a fine fireplace, with a projecting hood supported by circular columns. A stair leads to the upper floor, added slightly later as a private suite for the lord and his family.

AN ANCIENT FIND

The building with a cellar on the opposite side of the ward may also be 12th century. When the steps leading down into it were conserved, one step was found to be part of a pre-Norman cross, much older than the castle, recording the gift of some land in the area to a local church by a man named Artmail: 'Be it known to all that Artmail has given this field to God and to St Glywys and to Nertat and to Ffili the Bishop'. Nothing is known of these people, but the inscription is important as evidence relating to the Welsh church in a very obscure period of its history. A cast is on display here, the original being in the National Museum of Wales, Cardiff.

In the early 13th century, the wooden hall and defences which would have survived alongside the stone keep were replaced in stone. The new hall stood at the north end of the ward. A series of small slit-like windows light the ground floor room, which was probably a basement serving for storage and the like. The hall itself would have been on the upper floor, reached by a stair from the

Original earth banks and ditches dating from the 12th century remain at Ogmore Castle to this day

ward of the castle. There would probably have been a solar, or private room, for the lord of the castle at one end and service apartments and a detached wooden kitchen at the other.

From the hall, a stone curtain wall encircled the ward. Where it joined the earlier keep, a turret was built projecting out over the ditch and housing two sets of latrines, serving the hall and the upper chamber within the keep. There is another latrine in a small projecting turret behind the building with the cellar.

On the opposite side of the keep is the main gateway, its arched passage set back into the ward. Originally, a bridge would have crossed the ditch, its inner side protected by a drawbridge whose pit can be seen in front of the gate. A small postern gate tucked in beside the hall on the opposite side of the ward was later blocked and turned into a fireplace. At about the same time as the building of the curtain and hall a small range of buildings was added on the south for accommodation or storage.

LATER TIMES

The lands of the de Londres eventually passed to Payn de Chaworth of Kidwelly whose niece, Matilda, married Edmund, Earl of Lancaster, the castle remaining in the hands of the Duchy of Lancaster to the present day. By the later Middle Ages, with independent Wales conquered, the military importance of Ogmore, like that of other Welsh castles, declined and it became merely the centre of administration and justice for its lordship. The outer ward of the castle held, as usual, the manorial buildings. Two are still visible – a large lime kiln and a later building which would have housed the manorial court. Outside the walls are Ogmore's picturesque stepping stones across the river.

IN CARE OF Welsh Office

OPEN at all times

ADMISSION free

LOCATION 2½m SW of Bridgend on B4524

MAP REFERENCE 4 SS8877

COUNTY Mid Glamorgan

OXWICH CASTLE

This gigantic six-storey 16th-century tower has been likened to a 'latter-day Raglan' for its lavish appointments. It is perhaps built on the site of an earlier castle here on the Gower Peninsula.

We know from documents that there was a castle at Oxwich by the end of the 14th century, but whether it stood on the site of the present one is very uncertain. The present site contains clues to its origins – the ruined dovecot, with its pigeonholes lining the interior, and the fragments of early wall at the base of the tower could equally have belonged to an unfortified manor-house or monastic grange as to a castle.

A public footpath runs past the site, mainly occupied by a farmhouse and its outbuildings. The show-front has a gateway over which is carved the coat of arms of Sir Rice Mansel, who completed the present building as a Tudor mansion in 1541. Above and behind the gateway is the Great Hall, at first-floor level. The enormous 'battlements' above are, in fact, the lower halves of great rectangular windows to a Tudor 'long gallery' on an upper floor, like that at Carew Castle and elsewhere. Beyond the hall is an enormous tower six-storeys high, with numerous windows, forming a lavish suite.

Soon after its building, the castle was the scene of a tragedy. On Boxing Day 1557, a French ship went aground in the bay, and its cargo was seized by Mansel's tenants. They refused to hand over their booty to Sir George Herbert, Vice-Admiral of the Crown, and an affray took place when Herbert attempted to enter Oxwich Castle to make a list of the disputed property. A thrown stone hit Anne Mansel on the head whilst she was trying to pacify the menfolk, and she died soon afterwards.

IN CARE OF Welsh Office

OPEN viewing from footpath only

LOCATION off A4118, 11m SW of Swansea

MAP REFERENCE 3 SS5086

COUNTY West Glamorgan

OYSTERMOUTH CASTLE

Situated in a commanding spot not far from Mumbles Head in West Glamorgan, Oystermouth has many beautiful windows. The whole castle still stands to its original height.

Although Oystermouth overlooks the sea, its name has nothing to do with shellfish. The Normans turned the Welsh 'Ystumllynwynerth' into 'Osterlaf', and then the English vernacular into the recognizable words 'Oyster Mouth'. Swansea Bay lies below, with its splendid anchorage, and the castle has wide views of the Gower coast.

Oystermouth is said to have been given to John de Breos by Llywelyn ab Iorwerth ('the Great') as a bribe for his support, at which time it probably consisted of only the central keep. Most of the present castle was begun a little later in about 1280, the building stone coming from the site itself.

INSIDE-OUT ENTRANCE

The entrance to the single triangular ward is of the 1280s. The concave faces on each side of the present passage are the insides of round towers which once flanked the gate, but were entirely demolished after the Civil War. Still visible are the rows of square holes which took the ends of the joists carrying the upper floors.

The passage was protected by two sets of doors as well as a portcullis (although the present portcullis is modern, it hangs in the original grooves). A flight of steps on the left leads up to the 'White Lady's Room' over the passage. With small side-chambers off it, and a southerly view to Mumbles Head, this room must have been one of the most desirable medieval residences in Gower.

The long building next to the 'White Lady's' steps was the kitchen, with remains of large fireplaces and ovens. On the other side of the entrance is a set of lodgings with smaller fireplaces and access to a toilet block. As at the palace at Llawhaden, these lodgings may have been for important guests, although equally they could have housed a small garrison if pressed. Since there is another kitchen beyond, the long building might originally have been a barrack or lodgings at some period during the castle's long life.

THE KEEP AND CHAPEL

Across the courtyard from the entrance stands the keep, formed from a central block between two other ranges. Its date and original layout have not yet been worked

Oystermouth's sturdy fortress stands on the site of earlier wooden castles

The Mansel family made their home at Oxwich Castle (right) in the first half of the 16th century. Their family crest (above) adorns the gateway

out, and are confused by the numerous Early English (13th century) windows, the vaulted porch and the fine fireplaces inside. The top floor was re-modelled in the 14th century, when the castle became the favourite residence of the de Mowbrays. A hint of an earlier origin lies in the very thick walls, one of which contains two stairs spiralling upward and also through its thickness.

To the right of the keep block is an even taller building, with large and splendid Decorated (14th century) windows and its own stair-turret. The basement and first floor were purely domestic, each with a fireplace and latrine passage backing onto those from the lodgings described earlier. The windows of the chapel were restored in 1845 from the one perfect example left and from fragments found lying about nearby. Previously the windows had been blocked up at some time of trouble, and loopholes for muskets cut through the blocking. Inside the chapel, the aumbry (cupboard for communion wafers) and piscina (drain for rinsing the chalice) can

be seen, and in some lights, wall paintings can be glimpsed in the deep recesses on either side.

THE LODGINGS

To the left of the keep block is an L-shaped range, each wing having one large and two smaller rooms. The central pillars in one range were reputedly used to chain-up prisoners, but this was not just a gaol. The large fireplaces in the other wing, and its drain for a sink above the so-called cells, suggest that it was another kitchen. The general good finish to the details of the masonry indicate that this was probably the private hall and chamber of the Mowbrays in the 14th century, for the keep by then would have been old-fashioned and inadequate for their needs.

About 1350 the castle was converted into a residence for the steward of the Seignory of Gower, with a courtroom in the old keep and cells and in the old lodgings. Unlike other castles in South West Wales, Oystermouth appears to have played no part in the Civil Wars of the 17th century.

IN CARE OF local authority

OPEN at regular times in summer. Please check in advance. In other seasons by arrangement with groundsman

ADMISSION some charge

LOCATION on A4067 at The Mumbles, 4m SW of Swansea

MAP REFERENCE 3 SS6188

COUNTY West Glamorgan

PEMBROKE

First founded during the original Norman scramble for South West Wales, Pembroke Castle was completely rebuilt in stone by William Marshall, the greatest English knight of the Middle Ages. His magnificent castle, never captured by the Welsh, remains unaltered to this day. Birthplace of Harri Tudur, the Welshman who became the first Tudor monarch, it had otherwise an unexciting history until the Civil Wars, when it withstood a seven-week siege led by Oliver Cromwell himself, finally surrendering through lack of water.

Pen-fro, the 'land's end' in Welsh, is a suitable name for this area and, in a different way, for Pembroke town. For although the westernmost part of Wales is, to be geographically correct, away at St David's Head, Pembroke itself stands at the west of a peninsula on the Milford Haven. The tip of the peninsula is fringed by rocky cliffs above two parallel tidal creeks. Modern barrages, however, mean that they are tidal no longer.

On the death of the Welsh ruler in South West Wales in 1093, Earl Roger of Montgomery moved rapidly across the backbone of Wales and built a castle at Pembroke of stakes and turf, giving it to his son, who had made the journey by sea. This early castle must have been more than adequate, for alone of the Norman castles in Dyfed, Pembroke withstood the Welsh attacks in the following years. In 1105 Gerald of Windsor, Giraldus Cambrensis's grandfather, became the constable of the castle 'where he deposited all his riches, his wife and family and fortified it with a ditch and wall and a gate with a lock on it'. During one siege, Gerald indulged in a gory medieval ruse when he cut up his last four hogs and threw the pieces out. By this elaborate bluff he hoped to convince the Welsh that he was well supplied with food.

WILLIAM MARSHALL'S CASTLE

Gilbert de Clare was made Earl of Pembroke by King Stephen. His son Richard ('Strongbow') took a leading part in the conquest of Ireland, so Pembroke from the first became the regular port of embarkation for those crossing the Irish Sea. King Henry II spent Easter 1172 here while on his way to assert his overlordship over Strongbow in Ireland. Strongbow's daughter married William Marshall in 1189. William had risen from

Pembroke's gatehouse had a complex barbican and three portcullises. This mighty defence was the work of William Marshall

humble origins to become the greatest nobleman and statesman of his day, the epitome of chivalry (see page 57). During the next 30 years he was to build practically all of the Pembroke Castle that we see today.

When the Marshall family died out in 1245, the castle passed to King Henry III's half-brother, William de Valence. During the next 50 years he improved the domestic buildings of the castle, but wisely left the enormously strong defences alone. During the invasion scare of 1377 the garrison was enlarged to three knights, 67 sergeants and 70 archers, but the castle thereafter was neglected to such an extent that, during the Glyndwr rising, the Constable had to ransom both himself and the castle!

HENRY VII AND OLIVER CROMWELL

Jasper Tewdwr was created Earl of Pembroke by his half-brother King Henry VI. In 1456, Jasper gave hospitality to his sister, the newly-widowed Lady Margaret Beaufort, who gave birth here in 1457 to Harri Tudur, first of the Tudors (see page 27). Where this event took place is disputed. Most of the so-called Henry VII Tower is modern (as is the name) and a room over the gateway seems poor hospitality for one's sister!

Pembroke was the only town in South Wales to declare its support for Parliament at the beginning of the Civil Wars. Under its mayor, John Poyer, it remained a secure refuge despite Royalist threats. However, in 1648 Poyer, disappointed in his demands for reward for services rendered, threw in his lot with a band of Roundheads unwilling to be demobilized. Trounced by a regular Parliamentary army near St Fagans, Cardiff, they fell back on Pembroke, and Cromwell himself came up to besiege the town.

The siege dragged on for seven weeks, an attempt to scale the walls failed, but eventually the water supply was cut off and a train of siege cannons arrived to start a proper bombardment. The garrison surrendered on terms allowing the soldiers to go free, but the officers were to leave the country and the ringleaders were to be tried.

THE 'PEMBROKE FLOUNDER'

In plan Pembroke Castle is egg-shaped, with its apex cut off to form an inner ward containing the great round keep. The whole town and castle was compared by its Victorian owner to 'The skeleton of an ill-conditioned flounder, the Castle precinct being the head, the donjon (tower) the eye, the great south curtain its gills, the only street representing the vertebral bone and the various gardens its rays'.

THE GREAT GATEHOUSE

Approaching the castle from the town, do not be deceived by the apparently excellent state of preservation. Cromwell blew out the barbican walls in front of the gatehouse and the fronts of all the towers to prevent their future use after the surrender, and they were only restored early this century. One charge – that in the tower to the right of the gate – literally backfired and blew out the back instead of the front!

The gatehouse, with rooms on either side as well as above the passage, is one of the finest – as well as the earliest – of its kind. In the passage is a long series of successive defences: grooves for three portcullises, three murder holes in the vaulting and four arrow-slits in the side walls. One tower alongside has a prison cell in its basement, and there are two upper floors reached by stairs spiralling opposite ways. The rooms there have fireplaces and other domestic features, and lead on to wall passages forming fighting-galleries. In particular, those on the left (as seen from inside the castle) lead to and through a well-appointed round tower.

GATES AND GRAFFITI

The outer ward is completely bare of standing buildings, and the curtain wall on the left has been doubled in thickness, probably to resist cannon fire during the Civil Wars. To the right the bastion housing the modern toilets originally protected a narrow doorway reached by a steep path from the quayside below. The Monkton Tower on the opposite side of the outer ward is interesting, not only for the two postern passages at the different levels which it guards, but also because the plasterwork in the room on the other side still has medieval graffiti.

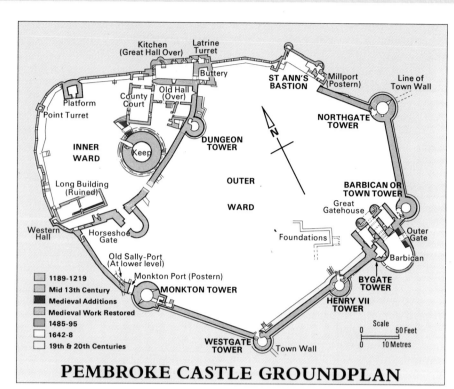

PEMBROKE CASTLE GROUNDPLAN

Labels within the plan: Kitchen (Great Hall Over), Latrine Turret, Buttery, ST ANN'S BASTION, Millport (Postern), Line of Town Wall, County Court, Old Hall (Over), Platform, Point Turret, NORTHGATE TOWER, INNER WARD, DUNGEON TOWER, Keep, OUTER WARD, BARBICAN OR TOWN TOWER, Long Building (Ruined), Great Gatehouse, Western Hall, Horseshoe Gate, Foundations, Outer Gate, Barbican, Old Sally-Port (At lower level), Monkton Port (Postern), MONKTON TOWER, BYGATE TOWER, HENRY VII TOWER, WESTGATE TOWER, Town Wall

Legend:
- 1189-1219
- Mid 13th Century
- Medieval Additions
- Medieval Work Restored
- 1485-95
- 1642-8
- 19th & 20th Centuries

Scale: 0 — 50 Feet / 0 — 10 Metres

Pembroke's groundplan shows its massive cylindrical tower

Pembroke's great dome as seen from the keep

The view from the top of Pembroke's Great Keep is magnificent

THE HORSESHOE GATE

Between the Monkton Tower and the great round keep are the foundations of much of the inner curtain wall, pierced by a great U-shaped tower with its main entrance in one side and a very narrow postern in the other. This Horseshoe Gate and the Monkton Tower were sited so as to support each other in controlling all approach to the inner ward. This ward has only a low parapet wall around the cliff edge: no more was necessary. The long building to the left of the Horseshoe Gate seems to have been a minor hall, downgraded to stables. Across the inner ward, the large square platform supported a huge medieval catapult aimed at any attacking ships.

THE ROUND KEEP

The solid squat proportions of the round keep disguise both its height – 75ft – and its very slight lean. It had four floors under its domed top, reached by a single spiral staircase. Each floor was divided into two rooms with one arrow-slit or more, but only two of these rooms had a fireplace and window. Unfortunately, defensive considerations meant that the windows had to face northward, so they received no sunlight. An upper doorway gave an emergency exit on to the top of the curtain wall. There is a fine view from the top of the stone dome, where the details of the battlements are worth examining. But the large square holes below the battlements, designed to enable defenders to drop things on to attackers from a point of safety, can be best seen from the ground.

The other round tower (of lesser size) nearby is a grim fighting-deck over a prison, defending the other side of the keep and the hall buildings.

DOMESTIC BUILDINGS

In the corner behind the keep is a complex of buildings, one of which (the building nearest the stair leading up to the keep) housed the county court from at least the 14th century. Between it and the round tower just described was William Marshall's hall, later converted into the solar chamber of de Valence's hall which occupied the space beyond, with its service rooms at the right-hand end. The kitchen lay below the hall proper.

THE WOGAN

Pembroke is probably the only castle in Britain built over a natural cavern. A spiral stair leads down from the hall into a large cave known as the Wogan. The front of this cave can be seen from the quayside, blocked off by a wall with two rows of arrow-slits and a window (like those in the keep) nearly above a watergate. It must have been a boathouse, suitable for a ship on slender lines like a Viking galley.

IN CARE OF a local trust
OPEN all reasonable times
ADMISSION some charge
LOCATION on NW edge of town
MAP REFERENCE 2 SM9801
COUNTY Dyfed

TOWNS AND THEIR DEFENCES

On the top of the mountain north of Pwllheli are the foundations of 150 huts within a defensive wall, occupied by the native population both before and during the Roman period. The Romans themselves built only two fortified towns in Wales, at Caerleon and Carmarthen, both of which had been abandoned before the Normans constructed castles outside them. Rhuddlan, however, has been occupied as a town for over one thousand years, first as an Anglo-Saxon fortified burgh, next as a dependency of the Norman motte and bailey castle, and then as a bastide attached to the Edwardian stone castle.

NORMAN TOWNS

Giraldus Cambrensis states that town life was alien to the Welsh spirit, and that towns had no place in Welsh society. But in the Middle Ages the Welsh certainly engaged in trade, and moved into urban settlements when they could. The neighbourhood of a castle was an obvious place for a town to grow up. Traders were attracted by the wealthy customers living nearby (or at least passing through regularly), and the protection afforded against attack. Workmen discharged after building the castle might decide to settle nearby, together with other pioneers. Abergavenny, Brecon, Chepstow, Monmouth and Pembroke Castles all had towns at their gates soon after their foundation. The Bishops of Salisbury founded many a new town in England (including New Salisbury itself) and built an early one at Kidwelly. All had earthwork defences.

ORGANIZATION

The lord of the manor, particularly where he owned a castle, found it profitable to allow a community to develop nearby, both to provide for his needs and for those of each other. Settlers would be attracted by land grants, low rents and other privileges. An organized trading monopoly offered security in economic terms, and the rights of controlling one's own property within the town. Each freeholder had one or more long narrow plots of land in the town, with a house abutting on to the street acting as home, workshop and trading premises combined.

THE BASTIDES

Both King John and Henry III planted new towns in Wales. Montgomery is the best remaining example, even though it had only earth and timber defences at first. Henry's son, Edward, had seen and built new towns on a rectangular grid plan within stone walls during his campaign in Gascony, France, and brought the bastide idea back to Britain. Each of Edward I's new Welsh castles (with the exception of Harlech) was thus accompanied by a new bastide, the first being built in timber, but the later ones in stone. The fine betowered walls at Caernarfon and Conwy survive complete to this day, living examples of this French-influenced system of town defences. There were baronial new towns as well, at Denbigh and Ruthin. Tenby's town walls, probably built in the late 13th century and later refortified, will stand quite intact along certain sections. Historically, they protected the town far more effectively than its ruinous castle.

The economic importance of the town made it a prime target all over Wales during Owain Glyndwr's rising in the early 1400s. In these later medieval times, town records show a fairly heavy turnover of property ownership and the emergence of dominant groups, family oligarchies and the persistence of archaic legal institutions. Local taxes had to be raised to keep the walls in repair (sometimes the lord contributed out of self-interest). Sometimes a new market developed on a better site nearby, and the old fortified area was abandoned altogether, as at Denbigh, Flint and Kidwelly.

The defences of the town of Caernarfon, with its betowered walls and castle, are best seen from the air

PENHOW CASTLE

Penhow, birthplace of the Seymour family, stands perched on its rock near Newport. With its medieval keep, 15th-century hall and lavish late Stuart house, it is now a showplace for the enjoyment of visitors and is a good example of the smaller type of fortified manor house.

The Seymours are one of the great historic families of Britain. The Seymours of Penhow, the senior branch of this important family, took their name from Sir William St Maur, the landowner who probably began the castle in the early 13th century.

Penhow stands on a rock overlooking the Roman road from the nearby Roman town of Caerwent. It consists of three successive houses, gathered around a central courtyard, each built by three successive families. The medieval keep and its curtain wall were the work of the Seymours. Their male line became extinct about 1400 and Penhow passed to the Bowles family, who

Penhow Castle, where the Normans protected their knightly seats

The 15th-century hall at Penhow Castle has a welcoming atmosphere

built the 15th-century hall block, one of its first-floor windows bearing the arms of Seymour (a pair of wings) and of Bowles (a Griffon).

Sir Thomas Bowles died in the mid-16th century and, after passing through various hands, Penhow was eventually bought by Thomas Lewis of nearby St Pierre in 1674. He added the third house in a fashionable style of the period, with fine woodwork, plaster ceilings and paintings. His other house, at St Pierre, with its magnificent park, is now a golf club. His son, George Lewis, died in 1703 and Penhow thereafter gradually declined to a farmhouse.

THE NORMAN KEEP

This square keep is of three storeys. It is now entered from the courtyard through a doorway of about 1280–1300. This may be a later insertion into an earlier tower, for there

are some indications that the tower could be 12th century in origin. There is no direct access from the ground floor to those above, which must have been reached by an external stair from the courtyard. The ground floor is now the kitchen of the present house, but the upper floors have been furnished in medieval style.

The 15th-century hall block is a splendid example of a late medieval domestic house. It shows strong connections with South West England, for the Bowleses or their builders may well have come from those parts. Of greater interest, though, is the way in which the usual planning of a medieval house, centering on a large hall, with services (pantry, buttery for drink, and kitchen) at one end and a chamber of private rooms at the other has changed with a changing society.

CHANGING TIMES

A small door in a corner of the courtyard now gives access to the ground floor of the 15th-century hall, with its large fireplace and rectangular terraced window. This is not the original arrangement, for in its time the entrance would have been by way of a passageway between the kitchens (rebuilt in the 18th century) and the hall. Although the basic medieval pattern is adhered to – services, hall, chambers – the emphasis is radically different. The hall, no longer the focus of the whole building, has shrunk to something of its modern role as an antechamber to the main living room, which is on the floor above.

The twin chambers or private rooms usual in domestic houses of this time have also shrunk to a pair of small cupboard-like rooms, one of them cut away by the inserted entry door. The hall itself probably served as the manorial court building, and for the payment of rents, with the pair of small rooms storing rent books, cash and the like.

THE GREAT CHAMBER

The upper hall or Great Chamber is on the first floor, reached by a spiral stair with a lamp niche at its dark mid turn. The screen at its lower end has been restored (the surviving upper beam of the original giving the necessary evidence) and fragments of the original late 15th century flat panelled wooden ceiling have been incorporated in it. A wall passage leads through to the upper room of the tower.

Across the courtyard, the 17th-century house originally had mullioned windows, but these have long vanished. The principal rooms have decorated plaster ceilings, boldly moulded door and fireplace surrounds (the former enriched with inset panels with landscape painting), and panels of woodcarving in the style of Grinling Gibbons.

Comparatively recent work has excavated and restored the rock-cut ditch on the approach to the castle and added the handsome pair of stone gateposts.

IN CARE OF private owner

OPEN at normal times in spring, summer and early autumn. Please check in advance. Other times by appointment

ADMISSION some charge

LOCATION 2½m N of Junction 23 on M4

MAP REFERENCE 5 ST4291

COUNTY Gwent

PENNARD CASTLE

Drifting sand has made two successive castles here uninhabitable in turn. Consequently the site has very little history, though it lies amid fine scenery to the east of Oxwich Bay on the Gower Peninsula.

Pennard is a simple enclosure castle, with round towers flanking the entrance and the surviving angle of the curtain wall. Time and weather have left their mark here, and most of the south side has gone completely, where the ground falls away steeply to a stream. The castle is best viewed from the north, where the curtain wall is almost intact. Opposite the entrance a large square room has been added to the outside of the curtain wall. The masonry has a curious appearance; local red sandstone was used for the lower parts of the walls, with a grey or yellow limestone higher up, probably because it was easier to quarry and work into shape. The gatehouse stands to its original height, and the traces of floors and the remains of arrow-slits are clearly visible.

This was the castle of the de Breos family, built about 1270 and abandoned by 1400. An earlier hall has been excavated inside, with rounded corners and a bench along two adjoining sides. Sometimes the shifting sand moves to reveal this hall. It must have looked quite smart, with purple walls picked out with white stone dressings to the doorways and window-frames. From an even earlier period traces of a timber palisade were found running along the side of the cliff.

IN CARE OF Pennard Golf Club

OPEN all reasonable times

ADMISSION free

LOCATION ½m S of Parkmill on A4118. Access by coastal footpath

MAP REFERENCE 3 SS5488

COUNTY West Glamorgan

Pennard's attractive remains, reached via a footpath, are best seen from the north

PENRHYN CASTLE

A gigantic, mock-Norman sham castle of 1820–37, built by the architect Thomas Hopper for Lord Penrhyn. Covering over five acres near Bangor in the County of Gwynedd, it has a high, four-storey keep, impressive and richly ornamented state rooms and extensive servants' quarters. Considered the best example in Britain of the Norman revival, its architecture is elegantly, if heavily proportioned.

As a castle, Penrhyn is an elaborate and gigantic sham. No archer ever loosed his arrow from its battlements, no army ever camped in siege around its walls. Built not out of military need, but upon the lucrative, commercial proceeds of sugar and slate, Penrhyn was erected in the decade before Queen Victoria ascended the throne of Britain.

This splendid, mock-Norman castle stands, imperious and somehow statuesque, at the eastern outskirts of Bangor town, almost hidden from the sight of traffic along the busy A5 road. There is just a brief glimpse, here and there, of tower or battle-mented turret to entice the car-borne visitor through its grand entrance gate and up the long, winding carriage drive. Around a bend, one is caught quite unprepared for the vision which suddenly rises up amongst the streets; astride a grassy mound sits an enormous Norman keep, four-storeys high and complete from massive battered plinth to battlemented turrets. On again, the elevated entrance terrace swings into view, heavily machicolated all around and half obscuring the great, turreted residential block that looms, massively, behind. Beyond the terrace, the entrance drive travels past lengthy service wings and stables to the car park near

Penrhyn's battlements cut into the sky from an impressive setting in wooded parkland overlooking the Menai Strait

the far end. Here, in its carefully manicured parklands, with splendid views out across Anglesey and down the coast, stands Thomas Hopper's best-known essay in the Norman revival – more than five acres of grand, castellated limestone architecture.

EARLY PENRHYN

The early history of Penrhyn does, in fact, begin in the Middle Ages, when its lands became linked with those of the great family of Tudor and a manor house was built on the site, but not a trace of this early structure remains today. By the middle of the 18th century, the estates had passed, through marriage, to Richard Pennant. He owned large sugar plantations and other properties in Jamaica and was later to develop the slate trade in North Wales. As a Member of Parliament for Liverpool, Pennant's Caribbean interests made him actively oppose the abolition of the slave trade. Finally, in 1783,

The spacious and comparatively unadorned dining room houses part of Penrhyn's collection of paintings

interlace, or ornamental arrow-loops.

Lord Penrhyn was certainly well-endowed with ample funds for such an ambitious project. His Jamaican interests were exceedingly lucrative and the Penrhyn slate quarries, here at home, were just beginning to make him huge profits. The neo-Norman creation which resulted served to obliterate completely the earlier house and achieve an unrivalled degree of virtuosity and self-confidence. Not only is it Hopper's most notable accomplishment, it is the acknowledged high point of the Norman revival in British architecture.

INSIDE THE CASTLE

Interior matches exterior in its lavish decoration. The most striking feature of Penrhyn's rooms is the extraordinary woodwork. Everywhere there are enormously thick, high oak doors, all heavily decorated. The embellishment is continued in the timber panelling and in the furniture, much of which was specially designed for Penrhyn by Hopper. Thus you will see, in these lavish interiors, many of the familiar exterior architectural motifs carried through to the castle's inner contents. The decorated plasterwork and carved stone, too, are quite breathtaking – especially so in the Great Hall and in the grand staircase, where it is hard to find a single undecorated surface and which took a further ten years to complete after the main house was finished. Whether or not you find it to your taste, you most certainly cannot ignore it.

A BED OF SLATE

Around the house are decorated brass grilles let into the floor. These are vents for an extensive and quite early system of under-floor heating, which warmed much of the house. The beds upstairs include the King's Bed of elaborately worked brass, made specially for the visit of Edward VII, when Prince of Wales in 1894, at a cost of £600; a massively heavy, decorated slate bed, weighing over a ton, in which Queen Victoria is said to have refused to sleep; also a richly-carved state bed, designed by Hopper, in which the queen did sleep when she visited Penrhyn in 1859. Other items of interest within the castle include a doll museum and natural history collection.

Penrhyn has much in common with Cardiff Castle in the south. A latter-day mock Norman castle, Penrhyn was, like Cardiff, designed for its wealthy owner essentially as a showpiece, an uncompromising statement of supreme self-confidence. The lifestyle which it was built to support largely vanished with the First World War. Ironically, although the castle is much closer to us in time, it is almost as far removed from present-day realities as the more authentic, but less perfect remains of its medieval counterparts.

IN CARE OF National Trust

OPEN at regular times spring, summer and autumn. Please check in advance

ADMISSION some charge

LOCATION 1½m E of Bangor

MAP REFERENCE 10 SH6072

COUNTY Gwynedd

A collection of dolls, dolls' houses and other hand-made toys can be seen in the children's room or doll museum within Penrhyn Castle's lavish interior

he was created Baron Penrhyn, of Penrhyn, County Louth, in Ireland.

Shortly before, he had set about rebuilding the medieval house which, fairly typically, seems to have ranged around a courtyard. Choosing the Gothic revival style, then just coming into high fashion, he appointed as architect Samuel Wyatt and, during the 1780s, acquired an undistinguished structure in yellow brick, with crenellated roof and Gothic windows.

HOPPER RE-CREATES A NORMAN CASTLE

Samuel Wyatt's castle lasted barely a generation. It was evidently not to the liking of its new owner, George Hay Dawkins Pennant, for he commissioned Thomas Hopper to rebuild it in 1820. Hopper had earlier worked for the Prince Regent at Carlton House and, by this time, had built up a very

considerable practice. Although he possessed that happy ability to work in any style that suited the whims of his client, he was particularly fond of castellated structures, so the 1820s must have proved both highly fulfilling and profitable for him.

Hopper's first essay in Norman architecture had been at Gosford Castle, County Armagh, in 1819. This is now hailed as the prototype of the Norman revival in Britain and both its plan and treatment clearly foreshadow Penrhyn. Though he was certainly not the only architect to appreciate the possibilities of the Norman style for domestic architecture, Hopper's singular achievement lay in his careful study of form and judicious use of detail, bringing that touch of authenticity and continuity so lacking in previous attempts. Happily blending together several elements, to emphasize a skyline or add weight to an overall design, he would use elaborate crenellation and heavy machicolation. These he linked to carefully-organized groupings of widely differing height and weight, decorated with chevrons and billets, blind arcading and

PENRICE CASTLE

Large but weak enclosure, with an unusual gatehouse and medieval barn forming the stronghold of a family which took their name from the place. Located on the beautiful Gower Peninsula.

Henry de Beaumont, Earl of Warwick, is said to have built a castle at Penrice in 1099 during the Norman conquest of Gower. This site, sometimes known as Old Penrice Castle, is today represented by 'Mounty Bank', the scarped earthwork beside the road across the green from St Andrew's Church in the village of Penrice, near Oxwich Bay. Before the sand dunes formed, the bay would have been a sheltered harbour between Oxwich and Nicholaston.

Modern Penrice Castle, the grand, occupied house, is located in nearby parkland on a sheltered south-facing slope of a side valley running into the bay. Historically, the most significant site here is a third castle, a medieval stone fortress built some time after Old Penrice. This stone castle stands above the modern house in the park which is normally closed to the public because of the ruinous state of the castle.

Penrice's stone castle has a very strong site, at the angle of two valleys with an almost precipitous slope. Its area is enormous – about ten times that of 'Mounty Bank' – but its defences are poor, with roughly-built masonry from local stone outcrops, and the accommodation is modest.

The earliest feature is a small round keep tower, to which a polygonal curtain wall was later added to form a single ward, with a long building, probably a barn, opposite the keep. Later on, another storey was added to the keep and several square towers (with rounded corners) added to the curtain wall. It may have been built by Roger de Penrice, who died in 1283 or by his son William. William was excused knighthood (an expensive business) for seven years after his father's death, perhaps so that he could afford to strengthen or rebuild the family castle.

Three of the square towers were added to make a gatehouse like a cheap version of that at Denbigh Castle – one inside the old curtain wall to form a gate-hall behind the original doorway, and the other two, one on each side in front of the same doorway to protect it. The Penrice family held the castle until 1410, though not without difficulty. One member of the family was accused of stealing property belonging to King Henry II, and another of murdering a woman in Laugharne. Although the castle was ordered to be repaired against a potential French threat in 1367, it seems to have been reduced to a mere farm (a Tudor pigeonhouse has been traced near the barn). Penrice took no part in the Civil War, though it was partly blown up to make it indefensible.

The main gatehouse at Penrice, built from local stone outcrops

Modern Penrice is a grand, occupied house, privately owned and set in spacious and attractive grounds

IN CARE OF private owner

OPEN Old Penrice (Mounty Bank) can be viewed from the surrounding area.

LOCATION in private park not generally open to public, 1½m NW of Oxwich

MAP REFERENCE 3 SS4988

COUNTY West Glamorgan

PICTON CASTLE

Never vacant throughout a long history, the castle, near Haverfordwest, has been occupied by one family for more than 500 years.

A large mound in Picton represents the first Picton Castle, a Norman fortification of earth and timber. The present medieval castle was probably built by Sir John Wogan, who was descended from a Welsh prince and prominent Fleming settler in Pembroke. Wogan was Justiciar of Ireland under King Edward I, and is said to have called the first Irish Parliament together in 1295. From the Wogans, Picton passed by marriage first to the Dwnns and then, when the heir was killed at the Battle of Banbury in 1469, his daughter married into the Philipps family who hold Picton to this day.

Picton Castle, with its fake Norman additions, now houses an art gallery

The interior of the castle is not open to the public. But the exterior, visible from the gardens, shows the usual 'Edwardian' plan of large round corner towers, although here they are set so close together that there is no room for a courtyard but only space to squeeze in a first floor Great Hall above a vaulted store. The same plan can be seen in several Irish castles attributed to Wogan's patron, William de Valence.

In 1643 the castle was captured from the Royalists by a trick, as opposed to the accepted methods of warfare. This proved to be something of a blessing in disguise, the lapse in military etiquette given as the reason for Picton not being 'slighted' like other castles by Parliament.

The Philipps family were closely associated with educational and evangelical work in Wales. A new four-storey block was built at the back of the castle about 1800, and the fake 'Norman' porch and windows added to the entrance about 1850. The so-called 'Norman' stables higher up the hill, are, however, a delightful touch. The castle now houses an art gallery with a fine collection of Graham Sutherland paintings.

IN CARE OF private owner

OPEN viewing from gardens only. Graham Sutherland Art Gallery and gardens open at regular times. Please check in advance

ADMISSION some charge

LOCATION on minor road 3½m SE of Haverfordwest

MAP REFERENCE 2 SN0113

COUNTY Dyfed

POWIS CASTLE

On first impressions the name 'castle' as applied to this stately country house at Welshpool seems merely a courtesy title. Yet the shell of Powis Castle, alias Castell Coch, is a strongly-fortified border castle, with a medieval Great Gatehouse and keep. Its formal gardens are a delight.

Powis is one of several Welsh castles known as Castell Coch ('Red Castle'). The red limestone of which it is built, and on which it stands, provides the reason. It was a castle of the Welsh Princes of Powys and a square keep and medieval stone hall, much altered, form the earliest part of the present buildings.

Owain, last of the Princes of Powys, took the Norman surname of de la Pole. It was probably he who built the large double-towered gatehouse which forms the entry to the inner ward, after his change of status from Welsh prince to English baron in 1283. His heiress, Hawys 'Gadarn' – Hawys the Hardy – married a Shropshire gentleman John de Charlton in 1309.

Hawys's uncle, Griffith de la Pole, disputed de Charlton's right to the lands and in 1312 besieged Powis Castle. But Owain's strongly-built castle defied the Welsh attack and eventually an English relief force under Roger Mortimer arrived, the de Charltons remaining Lords of Powis until up to the 15th century.

ORIGINS OF GRANDEUR
The last Marcher Lord of Powis, Edward Grey, died in 1551 and within a few decades

the castle had passed to Sir Edward Herbert, who bought it in 1587. His grandson was an active Royalist and went into exile with the future Charles II. After the Restoration he began to transform the medieval castle and Elizabethan house into a residence fit for a grand nobleman, but the 'Glorious Revolution' overthrew James II and for a second time a Herbert of Powis Castle followed his Stuart king into exile.

William III, 'Dutch William', installed his nephew William van Zuylesteyn at Powis and created him Earl of Rochford. He gave the house its celebrated gardens and wall paintings, but in 1722 the Herberts returned and the Powis earldom was restored to them. The castle is still the residence of Lord Powis, though it was necessary to make a third creation of the title in 1804, after the marriage of the Powis heiress to Lord Clive, son of the conqueror of India, whose son assumed the surname of Herbert.

MEDIEVAL REMNANTS
The twin-towered gatehouse of Owain de la Pole, its passageway strongly defended with two portcullis slots and by arrow-slits, forms the entrance to the inner court around which the buildings are grouped. In the

The elegance of Powis Castle has been preserved by continued occupation

outer court a stretch of the medieval curtain wall remains, with a round turret midway along its length.

The medieval hall, now (appropriately) the dining room, is on the left through the inner gatehouse. Opposite, Elizabethan classical columns form an arcade under the long gallery. The architect Sir Robert Smirke, who did much work here in 1815–28, closed in the originally open arcade, this later building concealing the fact that the outer wall of the court on this side is the medieval curtain wall. The east gate, towards the town, is 15th century. Its upper floor was added by Smirke, who also restored its statues of the Saxon Kings, Offa and Edgar.

SUMPTUOUS APPOINTMENTS

The solidly grand Great Staircase, of Restoration date, leads to the main apartments on the upper floor, with paintings added after

The formal gardens and period architecture of Powis Castle make it a delight both outside and in

1688 by Lord Rochford. The long gallery, an essential feature of an Elizabethan great house, has an exuberant plaster ceiling and panelled walls painted to trick the eye by their resemblance to raised panels. There are two dates on the plaster-work – 1592 in the frieze and 1593 on the fireplace.

Next to the long gallery is the state bedchamber of about 1668, a truly extraordinary room built inside the early medieval keep. The state bed, like those of the French kings, stands in a stage-like recess behind railings, with much carving and gilt complete with the crowned monogram of Charles II. It was presumably built in expectation of a royal visit, but Charles never in fact came here. A 17th-century Covent Garden actress would probably have felt more at home in this bed, quite literally a

theatrical piece of furniture.

The celebrated gardens lie below the castle on a series of long terraces. They were the work of Lord Rochford in the late 17th century in Italian style with fine use of brick, sculptured stone and lead statuary. These ornate, spacious and well-tended gardens are a spectacle in themselves.

IN CARE OF National Trust

OPEN at regular times spring, summer and early autumn. Please check in advance

ADMISSION some charge

LOCATION 1m S of Welshpool

MAP REFERENCE 9 SJ2106

COUNTY Powys

RAGLAN CASTLE

The imposing rose-red towers of Raglan tell the story of the rise of the Herberts of Raglan, from an ambitious royal servant of obscure origins who built himself a tower-keep under King Henry VI to the time when the same family abandoned the war-wrecked shell after the Restoration of Charles II. Outstanding is its Great Tower. Although more decorative than Wales's earlier medieval castles, Raglan endured the longest siege of the Civil War from June to August in 1646.

Fifteenth-century warfare could be a profitable business, if one was lucky, and a number of castles of that period were built with the help of the ransom of rich prisoners or a share of the booty from campaigns in France. Sir William ap Thomas was a characteristic figure of his time. From a modest local family, he had risen to wealth and importance as steward of royal lordships in South Wales and as a professional soldier in the French Wars. He also had more than a touch of the professional gangster and with his large retinue of armed and liveried servants controlled many of the local sources of influence and profit.

He inherited Raglan by marriage, and in about 1435 began to build a Great Tower recalling contemporary castles in Brittany and northern France which he may well have seen in the wars. A modest domestic manor house stood on the site, probably the successor of a Norman motte and bailey. The outline of this early castle can still be traced at Raglan, with its Great Tower built on top of the remains of the motte.

THE GREAT TOWER

This was known to contemporaries as 'Sir William ap Thomas's Tower' and to later generations as 'The Yellow Tower of Gwent'. Its strength was almost sufficient to defy Cromwell's demolition engineers, but after 'tedious battering the top thereof with pickaxes', they eventually undermined two of its six sides and brought them down, leaving the tower in the state in which it is today.

The visitor approaches it by a bridge across the castle's wide moat. The inner span of the bridge (now in timber) would have been a drawbridge, the elaborate slots for which, above the entrance arch, can be more easily paralleled in France than in England. The drawbridges were later replaced by a stone forebuilding (now demolished) when the present entrance arch was inserted. Traces of these changes can be seen in the masonry above the arch.

Evolution in weaponry can be traced in the round port-holes below the cross-shaped arrow-slits in each face of the tower near ground level. These are for hand guns or light cannon, mounted on wooden frames and perhaps intended against siege engines or siege guns rather than against enemy personnel.

Inside the tower is one large room on each floor – in ascending order, a kitchen, dining hall, private sitting room and bedroom, with, before Cromwell's pickaxes,

Alan Sorrell's romantic reconstruction shows Raglan Castle in its prime (top)

The handsome towers of Raglan were built in the later Middle Ages

another bedroom and an elaborate tower top matching those on the Great Gatehouse. The tower filled several roles – as a residence, stronghold, bank vault for gold or for equally valuable deeds. But above all it was a perpetual reminder to all of the power, influence and wealth of the Herberts.

WILLIAM HERBERT REBUILDS

Ap Thomas died in 1445. His son, William Herbert, Earl of Pembroke, was a leading Yorkist during the Wars of the Roses and his Welshmen played a significant part in bringing Edward of York to the throne as Edward IV. In 1469 he was defeated and captured at the Battle of Edgecote. Warwick 'The Kingmaker' wanted no rival in that role and Pembroke was beheaded on his orders. A man of great wealth and political power, William Herbert was one of those overwhelming subjects who came to represent for the Tudors the unacceptable face of feudalism.

Most of what we see at Raglan is William's work. His father had added the South Gate and an earlier version of the present hall to the buildings around the Fountain Court. The son now added a second great court, the Pitched Stone Court, with the Great Gatehouse which still forms such an imposing entry to the castle. William also rebuilt the Fountain Court as a series of formal state apartments for himself and his household.

The Fountain Court takes its name from 'a pleasant marble fountain in the midst thereof, called the White Horse, continually running with clear water', but this must now be left to the imagination. Around it were the principal apartments, with a roomy range of cellars below, which even at the end of the siege contained 'great store of corn and malt, wine of all sorts, and beer'. At the angles of the Court are the Grand Staircase and the South Gate leading to a terrace on which King Charles I played bowls.

THE GREAT HALL

Between the two courts is the Great Hall. In its present form, it is Elizabethan. The porches from the two courtyards lead to the lower end of the hall. At the upper end, beside the great oriel (bow) window and under the carved stone shield bearing his arms as Knight of the Garter, was the high table where William Somerset, Third Earl of Worcester, dined in state. The windows were filled with stained glass bearing the arms of the Herberts and of related families, while above were the shadowy spaces of the hammer-beam roof of Irish oak, traces of which can be seen on the end wall.

At first-floor level along one side of the hall was a long gallery for indoor exercise and recreation, an indispensable addition to the amenities of an Elizabethan great house. Its sculptured stone fireplace remains, as does its splendid view over the Gwent hills, but all else is gone.

Around the Pitched Stone Court were the service buildings. The kitchen is in the corner tower, and its great ovens and fireplaces remain. One oven has a circular gun hole in its back – in an emergency the fire would be put out and a hand gun or small cannon brought into action, at least in theory! From the other corner tower, by the gatehouse, the steward ran his estate office, with a strongroom for valuables and a prison for poachers and trespassers.

The magnificent Great Gatehouse was again the work of William Herbert. It repays careful examination. Of particular interest are the circular gun ports in the lower part and the masons' marks (the 'signatures' of the individual masons who dressed the stones). Their purpose was to enable faulty workmanship to be traced.

Raglan's grandeur is a product of social rather than military ambition

RAGLAN DURING THE CIVIL WAR

When Civil War broke out, Raglan was garrisoned for the king. Edward, Fourth Earl of Worcester (and later First Marquess), was reputedly the king's richest subject and poured out his wealth in the Royal cause. Prince Charles was here at the beginning of the war, when many Welsh gentlemen gave their silver plate to be melted down to pay the Royalist troops. His father was here twice, in less happy times after the destruction of his army at Naseby. It was perhaps the last time that the unhappy king enjoyed some moments of tranquillity as he played bowls on the terrace outside the Fountain Court, overlooking the village. The local champion was called in to give him a game, scandalizing the protocol-conscious courtiers by pointing out his house to the king.

By June 1646, Raglan itself was under siege. Heavy artillery pounded the castle from the higher ground to the east (a brick water tank on the slope beyond the farm marks the site of the battery). Remains of the earth defences dug by both sides can be seen in places, as can the gap made by the Parliamentary guns in the wall next to the gatehouse.

On 19 August, Raglan surrendered. Its soldiers were allowed to march out 'with horses and arms, colours flying, drums beating, trumpet sounding and . . . with . . . powder, match and bullet'. Inside the castle, the 70-year old Marquess stood with his household and watched through the great window of the hall as Fairfax and his officers entered the castle 'as if a floodgate had been left open'.

FALL AND DECAY

The fall of Raglan marked the virtual end of the Civil War. The Marquess was removed to London by Parliament and was dead by the end of the year. Gun-battered Raglan was stripped of its timber, lead and anything

else saleable and was left totally derelict.

After the Restoration of Charles II, the Marquess's grandson was created Duke of Beaufort by the king. He began to build a new family mansion at Badminton in Wiltshire and Raglan was stripped of any fittings which remained useable. Panelling and other fittings at Badminton may well be from Raglan, but the castle itself was never again occupied and fell into decay. By the 19th century it had become an ivy-clad attraction for tourists and seekers after the picturesque. It is still the property of His Grace the Duke of Beaufort.

Raglan's impressive hexagonal Great Tower of Gwent, surrounded by a moat, endured a long siege

IN CARE OF Welsh Office

OPEN all reasonable times (standard hours)

ADMISSION some charge

LOCATION Just off A40, 7m SW of Monmouth

MAP REFERENCE 5 SO4108

COUNTY Gwent

PRESERVING A CASTLE FOR POSTERITY

Although Wales is known today as the 'Land of Castles', practically all of them were deliberately damaged beyond repair, or else lapsed into disuse, after one single, cataclysmic conflict – The Civil War of 1642–1648.

Only a very few, like Chirk, Powys and Penhow, managed to weather the political storm that followed and survived with only superficial damage. The rest were blown up, or knocked down, stripped of their fixtures and fittings and left to the elements, all too often becoming a convenient source of stone for later builders.

Of the 82 castles described in this book, 40 of them, all ruined to a greater or lesser degree, are looked after by the Ancient Monuments Branch of the Welsh Office. Three furnished and complete examples are run by the National Trust and the remainder are privately owned, or in the care of local authorities.

Once a building has lost its roof and is open to the weather, the rot soon sets in – joints in the stonework become loose, ivy roots push them apart, large parts of the masonry become unsafe and, if left unattended, eventually collapse. It is in the care of such ruined sites that the Ancient Monuments Branch specialises. After careful excavation of what remains below the soil, the only lasting way of dealing with the upstanding masonry is to strip off the creeper, dismantle all loose stonework, grout, replace and repoint. The result may not be then the romantic, overgrown ruin that it was before, but it will, at least, still be there for the generations who come after us.

The fragmentary remains of Dolforwyn Castle, in the care of the Welsh Office, are under excavation

RHUDDLAN CASTLE

To carry Rhuddlan's supplies from the sea the River Clwyd had to be diverted

Rhuddlan was the second major castle of King Edward I's initial campaign in Wales. Begun in November 1277, the River Clwyd had first to be made navigable by digging a canal passage to the sea. This is a good example of a concentric castle, with a protected river dock for ships and a massive, diamond-shaped inner ward.

Rhuddlan is rather more fortunately placed than its southern neighbour, Denbigh, for it is situated just off the road from Prestatyn to Abergele, which many people take to by-pass Rhyl. Even so, the visitor has to drive down into the little town before catching a glimpse of the high towers of the castle's inner ward. By far the easiest and certainly the most impressive way to approach it is from the A55, along the fast dual carriageway road from St Asaph. From here, Edward I's great castle rises majestically above the river bank, dominating the plain to its west. From here, too, you can see, to its right, the large earth mound of Robert of Rhuddlan's earlier Norman castle, built in 1073 during the early years of baronial penetration into Wales. Known today as Twthill, it can be reached by walking down the waymarked path, close to its grander successor. The outline of its bailey may still be traced in the adjoining fields.

AN ANCIENT SITE

Situated at the lowest fording point of the River Clwyd, Rhuddlan has long been a place of settlement. This site has been, in turn, a Saxon English colony, a Welsh princely seat of Gruffudd ap Llywelyn in 1063 and, ten years later, a Norman emplacement and springboard for military expansion further west.

In 1277, Edward I led his army along the coast from Chester, in a war that was intended to bring to heel Llywelyn ap Gruffudd, the last native Prince of Wales. Rhuddlan was the second major base to be established after Flint. It was chosen in preference to rebuilding Henry III's old hill castle of Dyserth, just a few miles to the east, because Dyserth had already been cut off and destroyed by the Welsh once and might well suffer the same fate again. The much older Norman centre of Rhuddlan, on the other hand, was on low-lying ground and, having access to tidal waters, its strategic advantages were very much stronger.

ACCESS BY SEA

The king's master plan was founded upon the concept of seaborne access to his new castles. Without such access, the mountainous nature of the territory which they were built to control, and the difficulties of landward approach, would pose a constant risk of isolation. Thus, apart from the inland site of Builth, the other castles of his early campaign (at Flint and Aberystwyth) could be supplied by ship. His later fortresses, too, at Conwy, Caernarfon, Harlech and Beaumaris, were all provided with seaward communication, a facility that was to prove a decisive factor at times in their later history.

In order to put the plan into effect at Rhuddlan, a great deal of digging had to be done, for the River Clwyd then meandered over a shallow course towards the sea. A new deep-water canal was cut over a two- to three-mile distance, taking three years of continuous work at the cost of nearly £800.

It has been estimated that, with 3d a day as the normal rate for a digger, this represents the continuous employment of 66 men for six days a week over the entire period, although seasonal fluctuations would have increased this number considerably. At any rate, this great feat of civil engineering has stood the test of time, for the river course today follows, by and large, Edward I's diversion of over 700 years ago.

MASTER JAMES'S FIRST WELSH CASTLE

Work on the castle itself began in November 1277. Significantly, it is here that the king's military architect, Master James of St George, is first recorded as being in charge of building operations. Rhuddlan Castle is concentric in plan, although not uniformly so. On the west, the outer ward extends down to the river, where the access to its small dock is well-protected by arrow-slits. Outside this wall, a large, flat-bottomed, dry moat still encircles the castle as it always did, with the modern entry bridge across it following the line of the medieval original. Within this outer ward once stood ancillary buildings, such as granaries and stables, a forge and other workshops.

The inner ward, by contrast, is quite symmetrical and diamond-shaped, having two massive, twin-towered gatehouses. Their battlements may have disappeared long since, but their former strength can still be imagined in the entrance beneath those gloomy portals through to the inner courtyard. Today all is bare stone and mown grass, but 13th-century visitors would have seen a rather different picture. The walls were lined, then, by timber-framed buildings – the King's Hall and its painted chamber, a Queen's Hall and chamber, the kitchens and the chapel. Now, almost all that remains are the beamholes and roof creasings cut in the curtain wall.

Neither is there any indication of something else that appears in the records, for Queen Eleanor evidently added her own feminine touch in this severely military establishment, as she was later to do with her gardens at Conwy and Caernarfon. Near the castle well, with its boarded roof, she located a little fishpond, lined with four cartloads of clay from the marshes and set around with seats. The remainder of the courtyard was laid with 6,000 turves and fenced with the staves of discarded casks.

Rhuddlan town, built alongside the castle by Edward I, seems to have been a story of lost causes. A projected new cathedral, to replace nearby St Asaph, was never built; its proposed status as the shire town was conferred, instead, on Flint; and an almshouse, endowed by Queen Eleanor, was soon put to other uses for want of inmates. Perhaps it was all the inevitable result of new and greater fortifications now rising beyond the Conwy.

STATUTE OF RHUDDLAN

The castle's place in history is assured, however, by the issuing there, in March 1284, of the Great Statute of Wales (otherwise known as the Statute of Rhuddlan) – a settlement for the country which lasted until Wales was merged with England in 1536, at the Act of Union. According to tradition the king, on hearing news of the birth of his new son, Edward, at Caernarfon in April 1284 named him before the assembled Welsh leaders at Rhuddlan as their prince who was 'born in Wales and could speak never a word of English, whose life and conversation no man was able to staine.'

IN CARE OF Welsh Office

OPEN dawn to dusk

ADMISSION some charge

LOCATION 3m S of Rhyl on A525

MAP REFERENCE 11 SJ0377

COUNTY Clwyd

Alan Sorrell made Rhuddlan Castle the subject of one of his famous series of reconstruction paintings

ROCH CASTLE

This mysterious isolated tower of unknown age stands on a lone stone outcrop on an old border between England and Welsh-speaking areas.

A lordship of de Rupe ('Rock') is said to have existed since about 1200, but the earliest reference to the castle dates from the 15th century. Legend has it that Adam de Rupe built the castle on a pinnacle of rock for fear of adders. Unluckily one was brought in among a bundle of firewood, and bit Adam, causing his death.

The masonry tower, shaped like a letter D in plan, covers the top of an igneous rocky outcrop. Double banks and ditches below mark the limits of a castle bailey. A modern wing was added when the castle was reconstructed about 1900, and the whole structure has recently been turned into holiday flats.

Since the castle stands on the boundary between the English and Welsh-speaking parts of the old county of Pembrokeshire, it could be argued that the tower's plan shows that it was put up by a Welsh lord in the 13th century. But the details of some of the windows support the documentary evidence for a 15th-century date. This is particularly so in the case of the slightly-projecting top of the wall, which is carried on a corbel-table (a row of alternately projecting stones). A similar corbel-table can be seen around the walltops of nearby Carew Castle.

Roch's remaining 13th-century tower can be leased for self-catering holidays

IN CARE OF private owner

OPEN can be leased for holidays only. Closed to the public, but may be viewed from the surrounding area

LOCATION 1½m SE of Newgale

MAP REFERENCE 2 SM8721

COUNTY Dyfed

RUTHIN CASTLE

Begun after Edward I's 1277 campaign, Ruthin became a lordship in 1282. Once a cause for the Glyndwr uprising, the castle is now a hotel.

Set in attractive gardens, Ruthin has been converted into a luxury hotel, where medieval banquets take place

In its latter day largely incorporated into a castellated house of the 1830s that is now a fine hotel, Ruthin is indeed a strange mixture of authentic and neo-Gothic styles.

The castle's origin is a little obscure, though we know it was begun as a royal castle of Edward I's after his first campaign in 1276–77. After the war, this area of Dyffryn Clwyd was granted to Llywelyn's brother, Dafydd, the castle works then presumably becoming his responsibility. The situation changed in 1282, when Dafydd's rebellion sparked off the second war. Dyffryn Clwyd was regained by Reginald de Grey, Justiciar of Chester, and work on the castle restarted almost at once. There is some scant evidence of the personal involvement of Edward's chief military architect, Master James of St George. However, the king soon granted the entire lordship to de Gray, at which time the castle became his.

The castle consists of two wards, separated by a ditch; the inner ward has five sides, whose curtains still partly remain, but the present entrance is modern.

Ruthin stands traditionally at the root of the Owain Glyndwr uprising. An old quarrel over land between de Grey and Glyndwr apparently resulted in its sacking and burning by the Welsh in 1400, an apparently parochial affair which escalated into a full-scale revolt.

Today, the blood and thunder atmosphere has gone and the castle echoes, instead, to the sound of nightly medieval banquets, traditional evenings of food, wine and musical entertainment.

IN CARE OF private owner

OPEN by appointment only to non-residents of hotel

ADMISSION some charge

LOCATION in middle of town

MAP REFERENCE 12 SJ1258

COUNTY Clwyd

On the site of a medieval fortress, Ruthin incorporates some of the old walls

Despite the ravages of time St Quintin's gatehouse is still virtually intact

ST QUINTIN'S CASTLE

The overgrown ruins at Llanblethian near Cowbridge belong to a short-lived castle of Gilbert de Clare, probably left unfinished when its young owner was killed in battle at Bannockburn in 1314.

When Earl Gilbert de Clare was killed at Bannockburn in 1314 he was 23 years old and the last of his line. In the official survey of his lands which followed his death, Llanblethian Castle – alias St Quintin's – was noted as newly begun. It was probably never finished.

Its overgrown ruins stand on a spur with steep natural slopes on all sides save the east, where a large three-storey gatehouse dominates the approach. Through the gateway one enters a rectangular bailey with the remains of towers at three of its angles.

In the centre of the ward, a spectacular grass-covered heap of debris seven-feet high has fragments of walling projecting from it, one with traces of a stair. This appears to be the remains of a square keep, a surprising thing to find in a castle of the Edwardian period. It might possibly belong to an earlier castle, which Gilbert de Clare planned to remove when he had finished his new castle, but until its ruins have been cleared and studied, we can only speculate.

Llanblethian was among the castles captured in 1321 by the Marcher barons during their attack on the strongholds of the unpopular royal favourite, Hugh le Despenser. Thereafter it disappears from history and must have fallen into decay.

IN CARE OF private owner

OPEN by appointment only

LOCATION 1m W of Cowbridge

MAP REFERENCE 4 SS9874

COUNTY South Glamorgan

SKENFRITH CASTLE

Skenfrith stands, with its church and village, beside the River Monnow in a setting of great beauty and tranquillity. Built in the early 13th century by Hubert de Burgh, copying the style of the castles of his adversary, Phillip Augustus, King of France. Notable for its fine round tower and well-preserved curtain walls.

Skenfrith is one of the 'Three Castles' – Y Tair Tref – of northern Gwent. This triangle of fortresses – Skenfrith, Grosmont and White Castle – controlled the routes from England into Wales in the gap of fairly open country between the cliffs of the Wye valley and the Welsh hills. There was a timber castle here from soon after the Norman Conquest and excavation has produced evidence of a 12th-century stone building (perhaps a hall like that at Grosmont). All that we see today, however, is the work of one man, Hubert de Burgh, Earl of Kent.

Hubert had a variegated career, his lands and castles being confiscated by the king more than once, despite a consistent record of loyal service to the Crown. He was from an unimportant family of Norfolk landowners and made his name as a civil servant and diplomat rather than as a soldier. In 1201 King John granted him the Three Castles as a reward for his service, but in 1204 he lost them when he became a prisoner of war in France after holding the castle of Chinon for John in a siege. Whilst poor Hubert was locked away, John granted the Three Castles to his notorious rival William de Braose of Abergavenny (who was soon to lose the fickle favour of John and to be hounded to his ruin by the king). Hubert was more fortunate, but did not fully recover his lands until 1219.

THE FRENCH INVADE

By the time Hubert recovered his castles, he had a wide experience of warfare and of French and English castles. In the national crisis which followed the death of John, when Hubert's old adversary Phillip Augustus, King of France invaded England as the ally of the rebellious barons, Hubert rose to the occasion. With his neighbour on the Welsh March, William Marshall of Chepstow, he was largely responsible for defeating the invasion, adding a sea victory and hard-fought siege of Dover to his battle honours. Between 1219 and 1232 he rebuilt the largely timber castles of Skenfrith and Grosmont in stone. They were also constructed in the new military style of the 13th century, with curtain walls protected by projecting semi-circular towers whose arrow-slits provided covering cross-fire to the area in front of the walls.

The plan of Skenfrith is bold and simple. It is dominated by the round keep which stands in the centre of the rectangular ward. The curtain wall around the ward has a round tower on each of its angles, well-equipped with arrow-slits to cover the adjacent walls. The tower half way along the side facing the village is a later addition. Inside the west curtain (the one towards the village) is the basement of a range of domestic buildings which would have included the hall with its associated chambers and service rooms.

The whole castle is built of the local warm-toned 'Old Red' sandstone. This durable stone served both for rubble walling and for dressed masonry, so there was no need to import fine dressed freestone from elsewhere during the construction of the castle. Although the area in front of the castle is now flat greensward, the walls would originally have been protected by a wide and deep moat filled from the adjacent river.

THE ROUND TOWER

This notable tower stands on a low mound. It was once thought to be an earlier motte, but excavation has shown that the mound was piled against the tower during its building and is contemporary with it. It was probably intended to protect the base of the tower against battering rams and similar siege engines in the event of the rest of the castle falling.

In medieval times, the tower would have looked somewhat different. Traces of its white plaster rendering can still be seen and on top would have been a projecting wooden gallery or hoard running right around it to give 360° covering fire. This would probably have had a low conical roof. The present entrance at ground-floor level is a much later addition – entry would originally have been at first-floor level via a wooden stair and the round-headed door above the modern entrance. Still visible on each side of the top of this door are the holes for the beams of a wooden porch.

CHARACTERISTIC FEATURES

The sloping base of the tower and the bold roll-moulding above it are characteristic of

These 13th-century chessmen were found at Skenfrith Castle

Skenfrith lies on the banks of the River Monnow on a main England–Wales route

the South Welsh round keeps and though very similar keeps were built by Phillip Augustus, they do not have this feature. Inside, the ground floor is a simple basement and the first floor would have acted as ante-chamber to that above, reached by a spiral stair in a semi-circular turret (another characteristic feature of the South Welsh round keep). This second-floor chamber has a large fireplace and was probably the private chamber of Hubert de Burgh.

The corner towers of the ward have deep basements for storage and their doors raised above ground level for security. The original entrance to the castle was not, as it would have been a few years later, a twin-towered gatehouse, but a simple doorway raised above ground level and reached by a timber porch.

IN CARE OF Welsh Office

OPEN at all times

ADMISSION free

LOCATION On B4521, 11m NE of Abergavenny

MAP REFERENCE 5 SO4520

COUNTY Gwent

SWANSEA CASTLE

In the centre of Swansea is a castle with a picaresque history as a Norman mint, a medieval Bishop's palace, and a debtor's prison whose conditions became a Victorian scandal.

'The olde Castle of Swinesaye was built ... by the Normans. And it stood by the Bishop of St David's castle that now is there.' Thus a 16th-century writer described the relationship of the two. The Norman castle stood north of the existing one in an area now built over. One 12th-century lord struck silver pennies here to pay his soldiers, but the motte was removed in 1804 and no trace of the early castle remains.

The existing castle is the work of Henry Gower, Bishop of St David's 1328–1347, and is similar to his palaces at St David's and Lamphey, particularly in the arcaded parapet. A symbol of Gower's rank and status as much as fortification, it stood in the corner of the outer ward of its predecessor. His Great Hall stood on the first floor of the southern range (on the right when viewed from the street) over a series of vaulted basements. The range has an impressive series of showy arrow-loops, decorative rather than functional. There are signs in the masonry here of changes of plan in the course of construction, the hall being added behind an existing curtain wall.

The northern block also has a number of medieval features, but was re-modelled in the 18th century as a debtor's prison, a feudal survival and private property of the Duke of Beaufort. A third block, now vanished, linked the other two along the line of the present street frontage. Inside the north block, the cells remain unaltered and give all too clear a picture of conditions in a prison whose state became a Victorian scandal. After long controversy and revelations in *The Times* it was closed by special Act of Parliament in 1858.

The castle later became the site of the offices of the *Swansea Evening Post*, where the young Dylan Thomas worked as reporter, but the newspaper buildings have now been removed.

IN CARE OF Welsh Office

OPEN viewing from the surrounding area only

LOCATION near centre of city

MAP REFERENCE 3 SS6693

COUNTY West Glamorgan

In the background some of Swansea's newer towers, in the foreground the 'olde Castle of Swinesaye', once the scene of a Victorian scandal

TENBY CASTLE

The castle's scanty remains are supplemented by the most complete town walls left in South Wales, with arrow-slits and a barbican.

'Dinbych' – the little fortress – was anglicized as Tenby (and elsewhere as Denbigh). The site of the castle is one of great natural strength – a steep-sided promontory with a narrow neck, but the castle remains are disappointing. A small square gate with a D-shaped barbican wall guards a watch-tower and another wall fragment built into the present museum. These ruins are all that remain of the castle probably built here in 1153 on the site of an earlier earthwork. During the Civil Wars 490 years later, the castle took part in an unusual battle, a cannon-duel with Parliamentary ships lying offshore.

By contrast to the castle, much of the town wall still stands, especially in South Parade. Elsewhere, particularly along the cliff edge, the walls have gone. Along the walls themselves, one gate and six towers survive of the three gates and twelve towers there were originally.

The walls are unique in Wales in having two tiers of arrow-slits. The upper tier of slits were fought from the wallwalk behind the battlements and the lower tier from the banked-up ground behind the wall. Nearly all the towers are half-round and stand at intervals varying between 50–100ft, so that they could give covering fire to their neighbours. The one square tower was residential (with a fireplace and latrine) and equipped with gun-loops (holes looking like an upside-down keyhole).

Tenby's most fascinating feature is its 'Five Arches'. This is not a wall-tower, but is a D-shaped barbican in front of the South Gate. Four of the arches are rough breaks in the wall, but that on the left has the vertical groove for a portcullis, and must be the original doorway. Thus Tenby had a flank entrance like those at Caldicot and Pembroke Castles. The two tiers of arrow-slits run round the front of the barbican at a higher level than those of the town wall proper, and were reached by open stairs. This arrangement allowed defenders to fire both outward and into the killing zone within the barbican itself, before the attackers could breach the inner gate.

Tenby was sacked in 1187 and again in 1260, latterly by Llewelyn ap Gruffudd ('the Last'). Architectural evidence suggests that the town wall was built in the late 13th century. A later refortification was agreed between the townsmen and Jasper Tewdwr in 1457, each party paying half of the cost towards the raising by ten feet in height and

Tenby Castle, on a green headland

extension of the town walls, together with the scouring and widening of the moat to 30ft. A date stone near the 'Five Arches' refers to rebuilding during the Spanish Armada scare. During the Civil Wars, the town was besieged by each side in turn.

IN CARE OF local authority

OPEN at all times (but no access to wall-tops)

ADMISSION free

LOCATION castle on headland, west of the town centre; town walls on farther side of parish church from the castle

MAP REFERENCE 2 SN1301

COUNTY Dyfed

TRETOWER CASTLE AND COURT

The tall round medieval keep of Tretower stands within an earlier ring of Norman masonry. Across the field is Tretower Court, a large and carefully restored late-medieval building ranged around a grassy courtyard which gives an insight into gracious living during this period.

The castle of the Vaughans of Tretower announces itself from a distance as a tall round tower rising from the flat floor of the Rhiangoll valley. The visitor, travelling towards this, arrives at what seems to be an unremarkable country hamlet, until, turning the corner, he finds himself in a medieval street. On one side is the bulk of a great barn, on the other the gable and upper floor of a range of medieval buildings, entered below through a moulded archway with (as the observant will note) two pistol loops above in case of hostile intent.

Through the gatehouse, one enters the courtyard of a large medieval house, remodelled in the years before the Civil Wars, though the newer square windows of this period make little impact on the older medieval whole. On one side, a wooden gallery runs along the upper floor, giving access to the upper rooms and to the battlements above the gate tower. Straight ahead is the doorway to the house, a similar plan to the colleges of Oxford and Cambridge with a stone gatehouse leading to a courtyard.

THE CASTLE

The older Tretower – the castle as opposed to the court – is to be found across an open meadow to the rear. Here the Norman Picard chose the site for his wooden castle, controlling routes down the valley, yet protected at close range by the surrounding stream and flat marshy ground. It was probably his son Roger Picard who, in about the middle of the 12th century, replaced its timber defences in stone. His stone shell keep (virtually a circular stone palisade) now forms an outer shell around the circular keep which was built within it in the 13th century.

The stone castle stands on top of a slight mound, the remains of the earlier Norman earthwork castle. It was entered through a small square gate tower with a pit in its floor for the end of the drawbridge.

The Norman domestic buildings within the castle were demolished to make room for the round keep, though their outer walls formed part of the shell keep and survived within it. The outlines of their widows,

A stately home of the late Middle Ages Tretower Court is set in the beautiful Usk Valley. Its plan is thought by some to resemble the colleges of Oxford and Cambridge in England

The stout oak timbers and ancient walls of Tretower Court Castle capture something of the flavour of gracious living as it must have been in late medieval times

blocked up with stone, can still be recognized standing out against the rubble masonry.

These Norman buildings comprised a kitchen (its fireplace still survives) next to a hall with a solar (suite of private rooms) at right angles, forming an L-shaped block. When they were demolished and their openings blocked, the shell keep wall above was raised, with cross-shaped arrow-slits in its upper part.

A FRENCH INFLUENCE

The round keep is an imposing example of a type characteristic of the southern March. This structure was probably copied from France by such men as William Marshall of Chepstow and Pembroke and Hubert de Burgh of Skenfrith, both with long experiences of French castles and warfare, and then adopted by such lesser lords as the Picards of Tretower and Walter de Clifford of Bronllys Castle.

The Tretower keep, of 1220–40, has a sloping reinforced base and roll-moulding above, features characteristic of these borderland keeps.

Entry was at first floor, through a timber porch, traces of which remain against the masonry of the tower. The present entrance is a gap in the masonry below this door. Inside, above an unlit basement, can be seen the hooded fireplaces of the lord's apartments on the upper floors. The castle bailey is now a farmyard, surrounded by its curtain wall and towers.

TRETOWER IN LATER TIMES

The oldest part of Tretower Court is the 14th-century north range, with its gallery. This was rebuilt in the early 15th century by Sir Roger Vaughan, who also added the hall range, with its magnificent roof timbers, at right angles to the earlier block. The curtain wall around the courtyard with its wallwalk and gatehouse was added later in the century. The Vaughans lived here until 1783, their best-known member being the 17th-century metaphysical poet Henry Vaughan.

The rooms contain many interesting details, particularly the woodwork, so important in medieval buildings, but which so rarely survives. The sliding wooden shutters of the gallery, the gallery itself and the panelled timber partition in the hall are particularly memorable. Some parts are, of course, scholarly reconstruction in modern timber of evidence found during restoration of the farm buildings which Tretower became after the Vaughan family had departed from it.

IN CARE OF Welsh Office

OPEN all reasonable times (standard hours)

ADMISSION some charge

LOCATION 3m NW of Crickhowell

MAP REFERENCE 5 SO1821

COUNTY Powys

THE DECLINE OF THE CASTLE

The castle, like the battleship, became obsolete as it reached its zenith. Later castles differ from the 13th-century Edwardian fortresses as an anti-missile cruiser from a World War II battleship. However, military needs were often not the only consideration – changes in the castle were also due to fashion and social pattern. A castle was not only a military structure. It also accommodated the large and complex household of the lord, an institution which, like all others, was subject to change. The lord seated in a hall with all his retainers soon gave way to a more social pattern, where he and his family sought privacy away from noise and smells.

At the same time his officials began to have their 'flats' within the castle, appropriate to their status. Roger Bigod III's hall complex at Chepstow was for the household of one of the greatest magnates of Edward I, but standing across the ward,

by comparison, is a tower where he had his private suite and chapel. By the 15th century, castles, such as Raglan, were sometimes dominated by a 'Great Tower' with lodgings for the household in courtyards below.

In Britain, the introduction of artillery into warfare had no great influence on castle design (far less, for example, than changes in society and fashion). This is in direct contrast to Europe, where curtain walls became low and massive to resist cannon, and towers became bastions built to house artillery. Despite the Wars of the Roses our castles saw little serious warfare at this time and Raglan, regardless of its gunports, would have seemed old-fashioned to an Italian or Turk. This castle eventually fell to Parliament's cannon and the hole made in its walls can still be seen. It is interesting to speculate the outcome had Cromwell faced up-to-date fortifications.

USK CASTLE

The 14th-century gatehouse of Usk Castle is still a family house. The Norman keep looks down on the flowerbeds and lawns of a fine garden which occupies the outer ward of the castle of William Marshall.

When the Normans were fighting to conquer Gwent, they built an earthwork castle in the Usk valley at a meeting place of natural routes of communication. It is no coincidence that the same place was chosen over a thousand years earlier by the Romans for the legionary fortress of Burrium during their conquest of the same area. The castle plan is the same as that of nearby White Castle, with a central oval plateau for the inner ward, a crescent-shaped earthwork protecting the approach from the higher ground to the north and a large outer ward to the south where soldiers and supply trains could camp behind earthworks.

THE FIRST STONEWORK
In the late 12th century, like most South Wales castles of significance, Usk acquired a square stone keep. This still stands, much altered, overlooking the gardens of the present house, which occupy the outer ward. It is three-storeys high and most of the doors and windows which now pierce its masonry are later insertion. Originally, as is usual with such keeps, the ground floor was a basement with no access from outside and entry was by an external stair to the first floor.

The outline of the original doors and windows, although filled in with later

masonry, can still be recognized. The door which faced the house and garden is on the east, whilst in the opposite (west) face, the original entry door can be seen at the left-hand side of the wall. On the floor above, the blocked round-headed Norman windows can be made out, their arches outlined in squared blocks of freestone. Two of the windows can also be seen on the outside, from the garden.

A NEW GENERATION OF CASTLES
In 1189 William Marshall the Elder married the de Clare heiress and acquired Usk and Chepstow. His curtain wall at Chepstow is one of the earliest in Britain with projecting round towers in the new defensive mode of the early 13th century. His rebuilding of Usk is an important example of this first generation of new castles where the ground in front of the walls is covered by cross-fire from the towers, replacing the passive defence of the square keep of earlier Norman times.

William Marshall was perhaps influenced by the castles that he had known in France, where he had spent much of a distinguished military career. Though strictly speaking octagonal, Usk's shape may be regarded as a rectangle with a tower on each of its angles, one being the earlier Norman keep. Of the three round towers, one has disappeared over the edge of the steep slope on which the castle stands, one was rebuilt by the ubiquitous Gilbert de Clare, and only one remains.

THE SURVIVING TOWER
What does remain is the Garrison Tower, a large round tower set in the centre of one of the longer sides, opposite the entrance. The latter is a simple archway through the curtain wall, like that in Marshall's work at Chepstow, for the twin-towered gatehouses typical of later castles were to come in the next generation.

The Garrison Tower is really a round keep integrated with the line of the curtain wall. Like other round keeps of the area (for example, Bronllys or Skenfrith), entry was by a first-floor door, the present entrance a later addition. Each floor has three arrow-slits covering the surrounding ground and the second floor has a curving passage in the wall, ending in a latrine.

Gilbert de Clare made additions to the

Fine gardens surround Usk's 12th-century keep, still a family home and reached via a lane along Raglan Road

castle, including the North Tower with its cross-shaped arrow-slits. After his death, Usk passed to his sister Elizabeth, but Hugh le Despenser, favourite of Edward II, had married her sister and he forced Elizabeth to grant Usk to him. She recovered it after his execution, when she proved that at the time of the 'voluntary' exchange, she and her baby had been in Despenser's prison. She lived to enjoy Usk for almost 40 years more and the hall and chapel in the inner ward are hers.

In the 14th century, the Earls of March added the gatehouse to the outer ward, which is still lived in. The castle was at-tacked by Owain Glyndwr's forces in 1405, a disastrous Welsh defeat after which 300 Welsh prisoners were massacred by the English. This was the last warfare that the castle saw. By 1536 it was in ruins.

IN CARE OF private owner

ADMISSION by appointment – apply Castle House, Usk

LOCATION reached by lane along Raglan Road

MAP REFERENCE 5 SO3701

COUNTY Gwent

WEOBLEY CASTLE

The tall box-like towers of Weobley Castle are remarkably complete. An important late medieval fortified house, combining domestic comfort with security, it is one of Gower's most important monuments.

The early history of the Lordship of Weobley is obscure. However, we do know that David de la Bere was Steward of Swansea in the 1290s, at a time when its lord was the notoriously improvident and hard-up William de Braose (not to be confused with the much earlier and notorious William de Braose of King John's time). Although direct evidence is lacking, it may have been David de la Bere who established his family at Weobley and began building the castle, aided perhaps by his master's willingness to sell land for hard cash.

The late 13th-century buildings are grouped around three sides of a square. On the north was the hall, its lower floor serving as the castle kitchen. Inside, a modern wooden gallery has been inserted at one end, so that the visitors can view the hall from its proper level. At the far end can be seen the hall fireplace, opposite to which is the window that lit the high table.

At the gallery end of the hall is a tall two-light window and a door leading through to a first-floor guest chamber and to a latrine block in a tall square projecting turret. At the other end of the hall is the first-floor solar block which housed the private rooms of the owner and his family, set over a deep cellar.

The other main building in the first period of the castle's history was the Tower House in the south west corner of the courtyard, but only the lower part of its 7ft thick walls remain. Next to it was the chapel, once again at first-floor level. Only fragments survive of its sculptured decoration – a piscina or sink for washing the holy vessels and the carved head of a woman – but these are enough to show its past splendour.

The eastern range of the castle buildings was never completed. Only its northern half had been built when it was decided to raise the inner wall of the remainder as a curtain wall, leaving the foundations outside. The limekiln used to prepare lime for the building work can be seen next to them.

Sir Rhys ap Thomas, a local nobleman and one of the main supporters of early Tudor rule in Wales, added a grand porch to the hall, but after his grandson was executed by Henry VIII in 1531, Weobley was leased to tenants and became a farm. The castle is popular with visitors to Swansea for its serene and beautiful setting.

IN CARE OF Welsh Office

OPEN at all reasonable times (standard hours)

ADMISSION some charge

LOCATION Off the Llanrhidian – Cheriton road, 7m W of Gowerton

MAP REFERENCE 3 SS4793

COUNTY West Glamorgan

The remains of Weobley Castle are interesting for the variety of shape and size of the towers now left standing

WHITE CASTLE

This castle's walls once gleamed with white plaster. Views from its towers are as memorable as the sight of the towers themselves rising out of the deep moat. Its historical associations range from the Norman Conquest to unlikely-sounding links with Hitler's deputy Fuehrer.

White Castle, one of the Three Castles of northern Gwent, takes its name from the white plaster rendering of its walls, traces of which can still be seen. It began as an earthwork castle of the time of the Norman Conquest. In the 12th century it acquired a stone curtain wall and a small keep but, unlike its sister castles of Skenfrith and Grosmont, it was not rebuilt by Hubert de Burgh in the new defensive style of the early 13th century and had to wait until the 1260s for its magnificent towers and gatehouse.

White Castle was always more a military work than a nobleman's residence, though like almost all castles it was also the centre of a large manorial estate, the yearly agricultural round playing as large a part in its affairs as military matters. By the 16th century it was roofless and empty and, like its sisters, saw no action in the Civil Wars.

EARLY TIMES

The earthworks of White Castle are divided, like Caesar's Gaul, into three parts. The oval inner ward was approached in Norman times across a crescent-shaped outwork, while to the rear of the castle was a large outer ward where troops or supply columns could encamp in safety. Usk has an identical plan, and both castles may have had similar origins in the Anglo-Norman Conquest. In the 13th century, when the castle was re-modelled, it was, as it were, turned back to front, so that the hornwork is now at the back of the castle and the visitor approaches the gatehouse across the outer ward, which was originally at the rear.

During the 12th century the defences of the inner ward were rebuilt in stone with a small square keep and a curtain wall. The keep was demolished during the late 13th-century re-modelling when the round towers were added, but the 12th-century curtain still stands around the ward (and gives it a fine echo). It is dated by entries in the royal accounts which record that Henry II spent £128 16s on work at Llantilio (White Castle) in 1184–86 under the charge of Ralph of Grosmont, the local royal superintendent of works. Llantilio, a royal castle, was granted to Hubert de Burgh in 1201 with Grosmont and Skenfrith, but it was not until much later in the century that it was transformed into the castle we see today.

White Castle's outer ward is the size of a football pitch, enclosed by a stone curtain and flanking towers

This 13th-century flute was found at White Castle, proof of medieval culture

Weobley was constructed as a fortified manor house to protect the interests of a wealthy medieval family

THE CASTLE STRENGTHENED

From 1262 until Edward I's campaign against Wales of 1277, White Castle stood dangerously near the frontier of Llywelyn ap Gruffudd's conquests, and it was probably this threat which led to the strengthening of its defences. In 1254 the Three Castles were granted to the Lord Edward, the king's eldest son and the future Edward I. In 1267 they passed to his younger brother, Edmund, Earl of Lancaster and remained in the hands of the Earldom (later the Duchy) of Lancaster until well into the 19th century.

A CASTLE TOUR

The visitor enters the outer ward through an outer gate, which, like all the stonework of the outer ward, is late 13th century. The pit for the gate's drawbridge and the groove for its portcullis are still visible. Around the ward, one rectangular and three round

White Castle's steep-sided moat

towers helped to give protective covering to the area of the moat. The rectangular tower may have housed the officer commanding the outer ward.

The visitor crosses a high bridge over the waters of the moat and enters the inner ward which would have been lined, as was usual, with minor buildings whose stone foundations supported wooden walls. There are the fountains of two successive halls, both tiny and unimpressive compared with Grosmont or Skenfrith, and appropriate to a garrison commander rather than to a nobleman and his household. Beyond the castle well is an apartment with a fireplace for the constable of the castle, sited next to a large latrine pit.

On the other side of the ward is the kitchen, with a large bread oven. The thick foundations near the arch through the curtain wall are those of the demolished Norman keep. Outside this arched postern gate can be seen the Norman outwork and a

battery of arrow-slits where the 13th-century curtain has been built over the Norman keep. The chapel, part of whose wall painting remains, was in the tower on the opposite side of the keep.

White Castle's place in history did not quite end with the Middle Ages. In the last war, Hitler's deputy, Rudolf Hess, was brought here occasionally from a nearby mental hospital to feed the swans in the castle moat.

IN CARE OF Welsh Office

OPEN all reasonable times (standard hours)

ADMISSION some charge

LOCATION off B4233 at Llantilio Crossenny, 7m E of Abergavenny

MAP REFERENCE 5 SO3816

COUNTY Gwent

KEY TO MOTOR TOURS

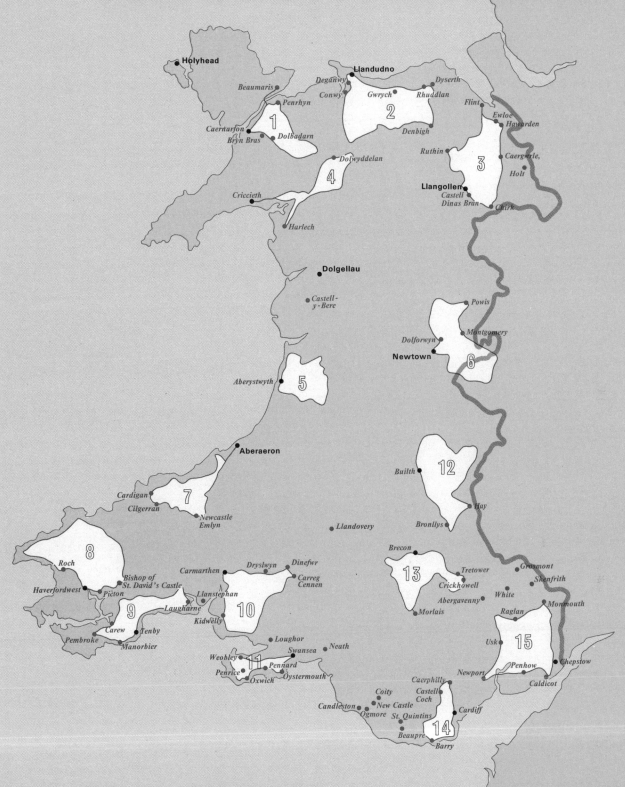

DRIVE 1   53 MILES

SNOWDONIA AND THE SLATE TOWNS

Lofty views of beautiful Caernarfon Castle and the peaks of Mount Snowdon make pleasing contrast to the little slate-bound villages scattered throughout this tour.

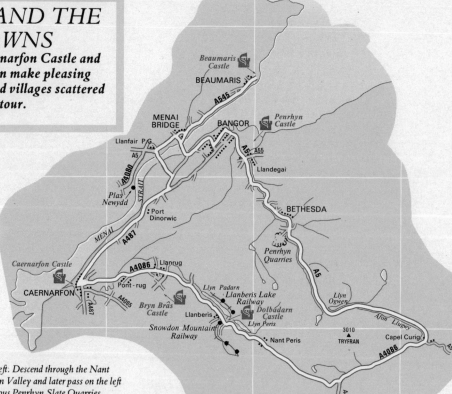

CAERNARFON,
GWYNEDD

Dominated by its famous and beautiful castle where Prince Charles was invested Prince of Wales in 1969 (see page 46), Caernarfon is a pleasant market town with many fascinating historic connections. The Segontium Roman Fort on Constantine Road is an awesome reminder that the Romans recognised the strategic importance of this part of North Wales twelve centuries before the coming of Edward I. From this base Roman auxiliary troops were able to keep watch over a wide area from Anglesey to Mount Snowdon. The internal buildings remain exposed, and excavations started in 1920 uncovered many finds which can be viewed at the Roman Museum.

From Caernarfon follow signs Llanberis along the A4086 to Llanrug.

LLANRUG, *GWYNEDD*

Overlooking this quarryman's village is a piece of architectural romanticism. Bryn Brâs Castle, built in 1830, is a lavish stately home with tranquil pools and landscaped gardens, occupying a wooded hillside. Interior features worth seeing include a Louis XV suite.

Continue to Llanberis.

LLANBERIS, *GWYNEDD*

Home of the vast slate quarries and majestic mountains, Llanberis is generally regarded as the base from which it is easiest for walkers to reach the summit of Mount Snowdon, about 5 miles away. Less energetic visitors prefer to let the train take the strain, and use the Snowdon Mountain Railway which runs from the village. The locomotives gain adhesion to the steep track by a rack and pinion system. Also operating from Llanberis is the Lake Railway, operated by steam trains dating from 1889–1948. The North Wales Quarrying Museum contains original workshop machinery for servicing quarries and maintaining equipment, and also the foundry mill with the famous Dinorwic Water Wheel. Also worth a visit is the CEGB Hydro-Electric Power Scheme and Visitor's Centre. Dolbadarn Castle, native 13th-century stronghold, is fully described on page 96.

Continue along the A4086 and ascend the Pass of Llanberis. From the summit descend and in 1 mile at T-junction turn left signed Betws-y-Coed. At Capel Curig turn left onto the A5 signed Bangor and later pass alongside Llyn Ogwen with Tryfan 3010ft prominent

on the left. Descend through the Nant Ffrancon Valley and later pass on the left the famous Penrhyn Slate Quarries before entering Bethesda. Continue with the Bangor road and in 3¼ miles pass the entrance to Penrhyn Castle.

PENRHYN CASTLE,
GWYNEDD

Built from the huge profits of the Penrhyn slate industry, this neo-Norman Castle dates from 1827. See page 142 for a full description.

Continue along the A5 to enter Bangor.

BANGOR, *GWYNEDD*

Gateway to the great passes of the Snowdonia Mountain region and the Isle of Anglesey, the cathedral city of Bangor bustles with the yachting life centred on the eastern part of the Menai Strait. Worth a visit is the unique garden of bible-mentioned flowers, located near the cathedral, and the Museum of Welsh Antiquities where finds from prehistoric and Roman times are housed.

Follow signs Holyhead along A5 and in 1¾ miles at a roundabout take 2nd exit (no sign) to cross the Menai Suspension Bridge. At far side at roundabout take 2nd main exit A545 signed Beaumaris to enter Menai Bridge (town).

MENAI BRIDGE,
GWYNEDD

The little town of Menai Bridge grew up around Telford's graceful suspension bridge, opened to the public in 1826. The Museum of Childhood, in Water Street, holds many rare and valuable exhibits illustrating the habits and interests of children over the last 150 years.

Continue along the A545 to reach Beaumaris.

BEAUMARIS, *GWYNEDD*

Beaumaris – the name means 'beautiful marsh' – occupies the

eastern corner of the Isle of Anglesey and was once a stopping point for pleasure steamers out of Liverpool. Beaumaris Castle, possibly the most sophisticated example of military architecture in Britain, is fully described on page 36. A few macabre examples of old-fashioned justice can be viewed at the county gaol. There is a wooden treadmill, one of the last to be used in Britain, and on an outer wall is the door through which the condemned would step to their execution, in full view of the congregated townspeople.

Return along the A545 to Menai Bridge (town) and at Berkley Arms, turn right into Dale Street (no sign). Shortly at roundabout take 2nd exit signed Holyhead. In 1 mile turn left to join A5 and cross Britannia Bridge. To visit Plas Newydd (adds 4 miles to tour) go forward

Bangor, Gwynedd

with the A5 signed Holyhead then after ½ mile turn left onto the A4080.

PLAS NEWYDD,
GWYNEDD

Near Llanfair PG stands the distinguished house Plas Newydd (meaning New Place in English) given to the National Trust by the Marquess of Anglesey and opened to the public in 1976. It is worth the short detour from the route to explore the elaborate classic and Gothic architecture of the house and to view the Rex Whistler room, adorned by the painter's largest mural.

The main tour crosses Britannia Bridge and at the far side at roundabout follow signs Caernarfon A487 for the return to Caernarfon.

DRIVE 2 66 MILES

LLANDUDNO AND THE GOLDEN COAST

The sunny side of Wales is represented by the charming resort towns which thrive along this part of the North Wales coast, starting from the architecturally-elegant Llandudno.

LLANDUDNO, *GWYNEDD*

Known as the Queen of Welsh resorts, Llandudno boasts a picturesque seafront, where pretty hotels and guesthouses vie for attention. Spacious boulevards divide the town in the Victorian manner. Holidaymakers can sun themselves on one of two beaches – the north shore or the west. For an unsurpassed view of the North Wales coast and the Vale of Conwy, visitors are urged to take the cabin lift and tramway for the steep climb to the top of Great Orme. This small mountain is traversed by a scenic drive of its own, pointing out places of interest to nature lovers and historians along the route. A 2000 year-old copper mine and the *Alice in Wonderland* memorial can be viewed.

From the pier at Llandudno, a detour may be taken following the Marine Drive (toll). The main tour leaves by Gloddeath Avenue A546 and in ½ mile turn left signed Conwy to Deganwy.

DEGANWY, *GWYNEDD*

This small, south-facing holiday resort holds the sunshine record for the North Wales coast. Deganwy Castle, which has a turbulent history, is described on page 92.

Continue along the A546 and after 1 mile at roundabout, take 2nd exit A55 signed Bangor and cross bridge to reach Conwy.

CONWY, *GWYNEDD*

Many people feel that Conwy can claim to have the three fairest views in Wales – that of the castle, the river and the vale. The magnificent castle, fully described on page 82 was begun in 1283 after the death of Prince Llywelyn and is counted as one of the great fortresses of Europe. The town itself, circled by a walkable wall, has much to offer the visitor with its boat-filled estuary, three interesting bridges and good leisure facilities. Aberconwy House, a picturesque, 14th-century timber-frame property houses the Conwy Exhibition, depicting life from Roman times to the present day. Plas Mawr, a 1577 mansion in Conwy's main street is the home of the Royal Cambrian Academy of Art and houses magnificent ornamental plasterwork. Bodnant Gardens, with its celebrated show of azaleas and rhododendrons and beautiful laburnum archway, is on the east bank of the Conwy Valley. Planned by Henry Pochin, this 87-acre garden is laden with pretty terraces and reputed to be one of the finest in Britain.

Leave Conwy by the B5106 signed

Betws-y-Coed following the west bank of the Conwy Valley to Tyn-y-groes. From here it is possible to visit the famous Bodnant Gardens on the east side of the river, by turning left along the B5279, crossing the river and turning left again onto the A470. The main tour continues south on the B5106 to Trefriw. After another 1¾ miles keep left, passing Gwydir Castle (on right), and cross the bridge to enter Llanrwst.

LLANRWST, *GWYNEDD*

This pleasant market town on the River Conwy is well known for its graceful, three-arched bridge, dated 1636 and attributed to Inigo Jones. In the early 1400s Owain Glyndwr's forces did so much damage to the town that it was said that grass grew in derelict streets and deer grazed in the churchyard. Gwydir Castle, an ivy-covered mansion where peacocks roam in the formal gardens, is south-west of the town near Pant Fawr bridge.

Leave Llanrwst by the A548 signed Abergele. In 7¼ miles at Llangernyw, turn right onto the B5382 signed Llansannan. At Llansannan join the

A544 signed Bylchau then in ½ mile turn left onto the B5382 signed Henllan and in ¼ mile keep left. Ascend and descend to Henllan then follow signs Denbigh to Denbigh.

DENBIGH, *CLWYD*

A walled market town often used as a base from which to tour the North Wales coastal resorts, Denbigh is known as the Queen of the lower Vale of Clwyd. Denbigh Castle is fully described on page 93.

From town centre follow signs Rhyl (A525). In 1 mile at roundabout take 1st exit A525 to St Asaph.

ST ASAPH, *CLWYD*

One of the smallest cities in Britain and the venue for the North Wales Music Festival each September, St Asaph is renowned for its tiny but magnificent cathedral. Founded AD 537 and twice destroyed, it reached its present splendour in 1869 under the direction of Sir Gilbert Scott. The cathedral's museum displays a collection of stone and bronze ware together with a dictionary compiled by the 19th-century scholar-tramp Dic Aberdaron. Outside the cathedral is an 'Eleanor Cross', erected in 1901 to commemorate the translation of the Bible into Welsh by Dr Morgan, who became Bishop of St Asaph in 1601. It depicts eight figures known to have taken part in the translation.

From the cathedral, turn left signed Chester. In ¾ mile take 3rd exit to join A55. In 1¾ miles turn left B5429 signed Rhuddlan. In 2¾ miles a detour may be made by turning right to Bodrhyddan Hall and Dyserth. The main tour turns left (no sign) then left again to enter Rhuddlan.

RHUDDLAN, *CLWYD*

Until a century ago, Rhuddlan counted itself as a busy port, but now most of the action is centred on the main street. It was at Rhuddlan that Edward I announced the birth of a son whom he presented to the people as Prince of Wales. The castle is fully described on page 150. Also worth a visit is Bodrhyddan Hall, which houses an impressive collection of armoury and weapons of war. In the grounds are a sundial and a holy well. Dyserth Castle, also in the vicinity is described on page 98.

Turn left onto the A547 (no sign) then in ½ mile at roundabout take 2nd exit signed Abergele. In 4¼ miles at roundabout take 3rd exit to join A55. Pass Gwrych Castle on a wooded hillside on the left and later reach Colwyn Bay.

COLWYN BAY, *CLWYD*

This attractive resort boasts a splendid waterfront with firm sands and a pleasure pier. Children's attractions include a puppet theatre, miniature railway, donkey rides, amusement parks and boating lakes. The pier pavilion was opened in 1900 by Madame Adelina Patti, the opera singer, and the promenade stretches 3m around the bay to Rhos-on-Sea. From the pier a bus runs to the Welsh Mountain Zoo, high on a wooded hillside. Birds of prey fly free in a daily display and visitors may watch the sealions being fed.

Continue with the Conwy road A55 and after ¾ mile at roundabout take 2nd exit onto the A546 and later pass by Little Ormes Head to return to Llandudno.

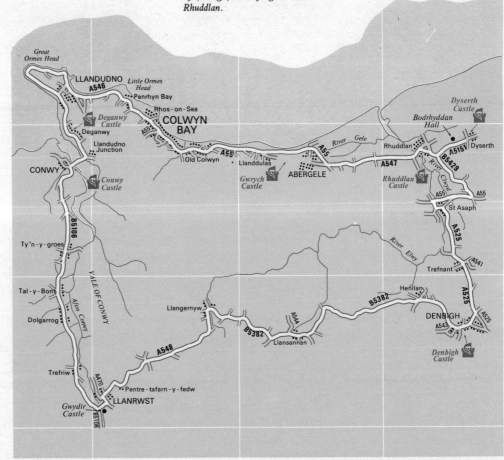

DRIVE 3   61 MILES

THE VALE OF MUSIC

Starting at the home of the International Eisteddfod, Llangollen, this tour has many cultural associations, not least with William Shakespeare, William Ewart Gladstone, four times prime minister, and the landscape painter Richard Wilson.

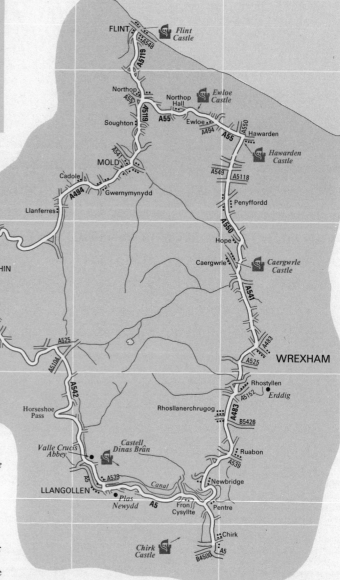

LLANGOLLEN, *CLWYD*

Home of the International Eisteddford since 1947, this small town becomes transformed into a riot of colour and costume for one week every year. High wooded hills and great limestone escarpments shadow the town on the north and south sides and scenic walks from here include the main route of the Offa's Dyke Path. Castell Dinas Brân on the north side of the town, is fully described on page 71, but another building with romantic associations is Plas Newydd, once home of the eccentric 'Ladies of Llangollen'. This charming house, with its eye-catching black and white painted façade, dates in the main from the 18th-century, when extensive alterations were made to the 500 year-old site. Lady Eleanor Butler and Miss Sarah Ponsonby, who left Ireland to make their home at Plas Newydd in 1779, attracted much local interest for their strange and masculine style of dress and behaviour. They became known as the 'Ladies of Llangollen' and received many distinguished visitors at the house. Llangollen Canal Exhibition Centre features exhibits of all the important aspects of the canal era with the use of slides, film and working models.

From Llangollen follow the Shrewsbury road, A5, to Chirk.

CHIRK, *CLWYD*

This well-kept village is the gateway to the beautiful Ceiriog Valley and best known for its splendid castle, fully-described on page 77.

From Chirk return along the A5, then in 1¾ miles turn right onto the A483, signed Wrexham. In 6½ miles, at the roundabout, take the 1st exit to join the Wrexham Bypass, signed Mold. Alternatively, continue forward along the A5152 towards Wrexham. A mile off this road (to the right) is Erddig.

ERDDIG, *CLWYD*

Acquired by the National Trust in 1973, Erddig, a late 17th-century house, boasts a collection of early 18th-century gilt and silver furniture. The outbuildings give a detailed study of the life of domestic staff in the 18th century, with portraits and poetic descriptions of the staff themselves on display in the Servant's Hall. Restored buildings include a laundry, sawmill, smithy and working bakehouse.

The main drive continues along the Wrexham Bypass. After 2¼ miles branch left and at the roundabout take the 2nd exit onto the A541. Three and a half

miles further turn right onto the A550, signed Hawarden. Shortly to the left, on the hillside, are the remains of Caergwrle Castle.

CAERGWRLE, *CLWYD*

Midway between Wrexham and Mold, Caergwrle came into its own during the railway boom when day-trippers from Liverpool made it their destination for day outings. A bronze-age bowl found in Caergwrle in 1283 is now a prized exhibit at Cardiff's National Museum. Caergwrle Castle is fully described on page 45.

Continue with the A550 under the railway bridge, then in ¾ mile at the T-junction turn left and continue to Hawarden.

HAWARDEN, *CLWYD*

Only 6 miles from the very English town of Chester, Hawarden's loyalties are split between England and Wales. Its most famous resident was four-times Prime Minister William Ewart Gladstone, the Grand Old Man of British politics. He lived at Hawarden Castle (fully-described on page 112) after marrying Welsh heiress Catherine Glynne. Memorials to Gladstone abound in the town.

At Hawarden turn left onto the Conwy road A55, and in 1¼ miles at the roundabout take the 2nd exit. After ¾ mile, on the right, is the footpath to Ewloe Castle.

EWLOE CASTLE, *CLWYD*

Above the junction of two streams, near Offa's Dyke, stands Ewloe Castle, fully-described on page 100.

Continue along the A55 to Northop. From here a detour can be made by

turning right onto the A5119 to visit Flint.

FLINT, *CLWYD*

In the heart of a heavily-industrialised region, Flint claims to be the birthplace of municipal life in Wales. Shakespeare used Flint Castle, fully described on page 102, as the scene for Richard II's capture by Lord Bolingbroke in his play *Richard II*.

At Northop the main tour turns left onto the A5119 for Mold.

MOLD, *CLWYD*

Mold, the county town and administrative centre of Clwyd, serves the surrounding farming area with its busy market. The 15th-century church of St Mary boasts a remarkable frieze of animals and the grave of 18th-century landscape painter Richard Wilson. Visitors to Mold should not miss the Theatre Clwyd, an arts complex with its own resident professional company.

Follow signs Ruthin along the A494 to reach Ruthin.

RUTHIN, *CLWYD*

This architecturally-interesting town is situated on an elevated site in the

pretty vale of Clwyd. Town-centre buildings are grouped around a small square, into which run narrow streets with many specialist shops selling traditional Welsh fare. Curfew has been rung here since the 11th century. Ruthin Castle, founded by Edward I in 1281 is fully described on page 152.

Leave by the Llangollen road, A525, and in 4 miles ascend the wooded Nant-y-Garth pass. After 3¼ miles turn right onto the A542 (still signed Llangollen) and later descend the Horseshoe Pass. At the foot of the descent pass the turning, on the left, to Valle Crucis Abbey.

VALLE CRUCIS ABBEY, *CLWYD*

This Cistercian Abbey, founded c1200 by Madog ap Gruffudd, takes its name (meaning Vale of the Cross) from Eliseg's Pillar, an ancient monument to the north of the Abbey, set up by Concenn to commemorate a battle fought in AD 603. Much of its church still survives, along with a cluster of monastic buildings and an elaborately-carved doorway.

Continue along the A525 for the return to Llangollen.

DRIVE 4   67 MILES

INSPIRATION AND INDUSTRY

A contrast of styles, from the Italianate splendour of pastel-coloured Portmeirion, to the grey granite edifices of Harlech, characterize this tour.

CRICCIETH, *GWYNEDD*
This compact Victorian town slopes steeply down to the sea and a mixture of sand and pebble beaches. An acre of flowering shrubs can be seen in the beautiful gardens of Cefniwch, and the town has tennis courts, a bowling green and a miniature golf course. Salmon and sea trout abound in local rivers and lakes. Criccieth Castle is fully described on page 91.

From Criccieth follow signs Porthmadog A497. In 4¾ miles turn right A487 signed Dolgellau into Porthmadog.

PORTHMADOG, *GWYNEDD*
Steadily developing as a holiday centre, Porthmadog was created in the early 19th century by William Alexander Madocks MP. Many tourists come here for a ride on the Festiniog Narrow Gauge Railway, which takes them high into the hills, around Blaenau Ffestiniog, and many others for the extensive beaches in the area. The town's maritime past is recorded at the Maritime Museum, on Oakley No. 3 Wharf, where the sailing ketch *Garlandstone* has been adapted for exhibition purposes.

Leave by crossing the Causeway, and at the far end pass through toll gate, later reaching Minffordd (for Portmeirion)

PORTMEIRION, *GWYNEDD*
A cluster of Italianate, pastel-coloured buildings make up this attractive village, situated on a wooded peninsula. Used as a film set on a number of occasions and setting for the cult television series *The Prisoner*, Noel Coward also found the place inspiring, taking only one week to write his comedy *Blithe Spirit* here. Visit Gwylt Gardens – the finest wild gardens in Wales.

In 1 mile at Penrhyndeudraeth turn right onto an unclassified road signed Harlech (A496) and shortly cross Briwet Toll Bridge. Half a mile beyond bridge, turn right A496. In 2 miles continue forward onto the B4573 to reach Harlech.

HARLECH, *GWYNEDD*
Granite-built houses and narrow streets characterize Harlech, home of the famous castle, fully-described on page 106. Extensive views from the summit of the town's steep hill extend inland to the Snowdonia mountain range and over Tremadog Bay and the Lleyn Peninsula.

From Harlech return along the B4573 and later join the A496 signed Porthmadog. After passing through Maentwrog, turn right onto the A487 signed Dolgellau then immediately turn

left A496 signed Betws-y-Coed. In 1½ miles cross river bridge and keep right B4391 and ascend to Ffestiniog. At Ffestiniog branch right onto the A470. Shortly pass under railway bridge then turn left onto the B4391, signed Bala. After 3 miles, turn left onto the B4407 then in 1¾ miles turn left onto a narrow unclassified road. Later descend from the moorland and continue on a wider road to Penmachno.

PENMACHNO, *GWYNEDD*
This quarryman's village is ringed by mountains. The parish church houses some Early Christian burial stones, but the major attraction is undoubtedly the woollen mill, where weavers of ancient colour patterns in Welsh Woolmark tweed can be seen at work. The mill is scenically situated next to a trout stream.

Continue forward on the B4406 and in 2½ miles, turn left onto the A5 (no sign). One and three quarter miles farther turn left across Waterloo Bridge for Betws-y-Coed.

BETWS-Y-COED, *GWYNEDD*
An ideal base from which to explore Snowdonia, Betws-y-Coed becomes almost overwhelmed with visitors in

the summer. Swallow Falls, a famous beauty spot (especially pretty after rainfall) is particularly rich in natural phenomenon. Conwy Valley Railway Museum, in the old goods yard at the BR Station, has a collection of rolling stock and other items.

Return along the A5, recrossing Waterloo Bridge. On the far side bear right then shortly turn right onto the A470 signed Dolgellau, and follow the wooded valley to Dolwyddelan.

DOLWYDDELAN, *GWYNEDD*
Once a centre for the slate-quarrying industry, this small village nestles in the Lledr Valley. The 16th-century village church, built by Meredydd ap Ifan contains a carved Gothic rood screen and some fine pieces of 16th-century glasswork. Dolwyddelan Castle, birthplace of Llywelyn the Great, is described on page 97.

Continue along the A470 and climb over the steep Crimea Pass (summit 1263ft). On the descent the Gloddfa Ganol Mountain Tourist Centre and the Llechwedd Slate Caverns are passed (see below) to reach the edge of Blaenau Ffestiniog.

BLAENAU FFESTINIOG, *GWYNEDD*
Surrounded by the majestic Moelwyn and Manod Mountains and sometimes rather uncharitably referred to as 'town of slate and rain', Blaenau Ffestiniog appears almost entirely compounded of slate. It was due to the slate industry that the Festiniog Narrow Gauge railway was laid from here to Porthmadog, also a one-time thriving slate port. The trains were originally operated by horses. Gloddfa Ganol Mountain Tourist Centre comprises panoramic views and walks with exhibition and craft demonstrations of slate splitting, and at Llechwedd Slate Caverns visitors are transported underground into massive quarries where Victorian mining conditions are re-created.

Leave by the Porthmadog road A496 to reach the edge of Tanygrisiau.

TANYGRISIAU, *GWYNEDD*
A special bus runs along a corkscrew road to 1,500ft high Cwm Stwlan dam from this industrial village. This reservoir, high in the mountains, supplies water to Ffestiniog Power Station, opened in 1963 and the first pumped storage power station to appear in Britain.

Continue along the A496 and after 3¾ miles, turn right A487. After ½ mile at the Oakley Arms Hotel, turn right onto the B4410 (signed Rhyd) and ascend passing Llyn Mair with its nearby nature trail then pass Tan-y-bwlch station (Festiniog Railway). In 3 miles at Garreg turn right then immediately left signed Tremadog. In 1¾ miles turn left onto the A498 to later reach Tremadog. Continue forward then in ¼ mile turn left. Half a mile further at T-junction turn right for the return to Criccieth.

The Festiniog Railway

DRIVE 5   44 MILES

EAST FROM ABERYSTWYTH

Breathtaking views over the Rheidol Valley, floodlit caves and waterfalls can be seen on this spectacular tour.

ABERYSTWYTH, *DYFED*

Aberystwyth is much more than a popular seaside resort, it is, in fact, the country's academic centre, boasting the National Library of Wales and University College. It also plays an important part in Welsh administration on a local and national level. Historically, Aberystwyth did not become prominent until the 13th century, when Edward I's brother Edmund Crouchback built the castle which was destroyed in 1282 by the Welsh. The king rebuilt the castle but it was again destroyed, this time by Cromwell's forces, and all that remains today are ruins which have been imaginatively laid out as gardens (see page 34). During Charles I's reign Thomas Bushnell was given permission to open a mint here and coins were minted with silver from local mines. Some of these early coins are on view in the University Museum. The oldest of the University buildings is a magnificent Victorian Gothic structure which was originally built as a hotel by railway pioneer Thomas Savin. His was a novel scheme to attract people to Aberystwyth by offering free accommodation in the hotel to anyone who purchased a return ticket from London. Not surprisingly, the project collapsed and the building was sold for £10,000 for use as a university college. Another interesting but more modern building is the Town Hall, built in 1961 and situated in Portland Street. The elegant, crescent-shaped promenade leads from the sea front to the foot of Constitution Hill which can be ascended by funicular railway. Built in 1895 by Croyden Marks it was originally operated hydraulically but today it is electrically operated and fitted with every possible safety device. There are two other railways in the town, the old mid-Wales line from Shrewsbury and the narrow-gauge Vale of Rheidol which travels 12 miles up the beautiful Rheidol Valley to Devil's Bridge.

From Aberystwyth follow signs Cardigan and Aberaeron to leave by the A487. In 1¼ miles branch left onto the A4120, signed Devil's Bridge. This road gradually climbs to almost 1,000 ft, with good views to the left over the Vale of Rheidol, before reaching Devil's Bridge.

DEVIL'S BRIDGE, *DYFED*

Three bridges, built on top of each other, are a peculiar characteristic of this town. The first bridge, built c12th century, attracts the strangest story of origin. This fine pointed-arch bridge was erected by the Devil, so legend tells us, so that a simple

countrywoman, Megan Llandunach, might fetch her cow which was stranded on the other side of the ravine. The condition was that he should have the first living creature to cross the bridge. Megan foiled the Devil by throwing a scrap of bread on to the bridge and a hungry dog leapt across before her. However, those who disbelieve this story claim that Devil's Bridge was erected either by the Knights Hospitallers or by the Cistercian monks of Strata Florida Abbey. The bridge crosses the 500 ft-deep wooded gorge where the Mynach River meets the Rheidol and the two produce a spectacular mass of waterfalls at the Gyfarllwyd Falls. The grandeur of the scene is best appreciated from the valley bottom which is reached via a 91-step zig-zag pathway known as Jacob's Ladder.

Continue on the A4120 to Ponterwyd. From here a detour to the left along the Aberystwyth road, A44, leads to the Llywernog Silver Lead mine (1¼ miles) and the Bwlch Nant-Yr-Arian Forest Visitor Centre (2¼ miles).

PONTERWYD, *DYFED*

At Ponterwyd there are two bridges which span the River Rheidol; one is modern and the other dates from the 18th century. The hotel nearby was named after the famous author George Borrow to commemorate his

Devil's Bridge

stay here in 1847. The view from the front of the hotel overlooks the spectacular Eagle gorge and falls. A mountain road leads from Ponterwyd past the Nant-y-Moch Reservoir to Talybont. A detour to Llywernog Silver-Lead Mine will reward visitors with the complete story of silver and lead-mining in Wales. It is an open-air museum where visitors can explore floodlit underground caverns and watch a 15-minute slide programme, as well as viewing fascinating exhibits such as an engine shaft, cast-iron waterwheel and rock-crusher house. Bwlch Nant-Yr-Arian Forest Visitor Centre, 1 mile beyond, will fascinate those who love the great outdoors.

At Ponterwyd the main tour turns right onto the Llangurig road, A44. In ¼ mile turn left onto an unclassified road, signed

Nant-y-Moch Scenic Route. Take the next turning right and follow this narrow byroad to reach the Nant-y-Moch Dam. Cross the dam and continue with the Talybont road alongside the reservoir. This road passes through forest and moorland scenery, and later there are views ahead to the coast at Borth before the village of Talybont. Here turn right onto the A487 (no sign) and pass through the Taliesin to reach the edge of Tre'r Ddol.

TRE'R DDOL, *DYFED*

Situated half way between Aberystwyth and Machynlleth, Tre'r Ddol has a 19th-century Wesleyan chapel that has been converted into a museum of local history. The village gained national acclaim some years ago when the late Elma Williams established her Valley of Animals home and sanctuary in the hills nearby. The home ran into maintenance difficulties after her death and it has now closed.

Leave Tre'r-Ddol by the B4353, signed Borth. Later this road joins the coast and enters the resort of Borth. At the end of the main street branch right onto the B4572 (no sign) and ascend. After descending to Clarach continue with the Aberystwyth road and ascend again. Later turn right onto the A487 for the return to Aberystwyth.

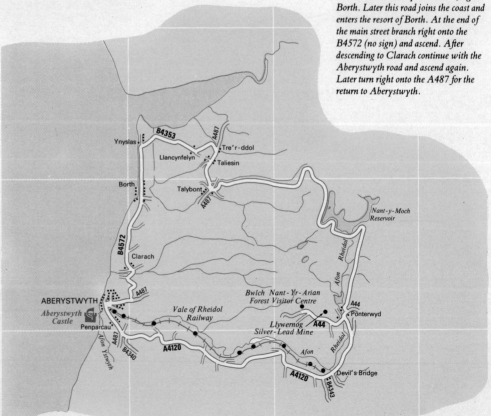

DRIVE 6   65 MILES

ASSORTED ARCHITECTURE

From Newtown with its myriad styles of building to the one-time county town of Montgomery, this tour is loaded with relics of important historical periods.

NEWTOWN, *POWYS*

Black and white half-timbered buildings, notably farms and older town houses, are a distinctive feature of Newtown, aptly-named since acquiring 'New Town' status and becoming the site of new development in recent years. Despite the rise of so many modern structures the olde-worlde charm of Newtown still remains. The styles of architecture range from Tudor, through Jacobean, Georgian, Regency, Victorian, 19th-century Gothic and Byzantine and Fifth Georgian right up to present day. Much of the original character that is lost elsewhere in the town can be seen in the section that lies across the Long Bridge. Of particular interest here is the Newtown Textile Museum. Established in an old weavers' workshop it portrays all aspects of Newtown life in days when the town was the centre of the wool weaving industry. Social reformer Robert Owen was born here and a museum of his life and work can be found.

Leave Newtown by the Welshpool road, A483. In 2½ miles turn left, signed Bettws Cedewain, onto the B4389 (not shown). At Bettws Cedewain cross the bridge and turn left, signed Llanfair Caereinion, then in 2 miles turn right for Tregynon. At New Mills turn left and continue along the B4389, with several ascents and descents, to reach Llanfair Caereinion.

LLANFAIR CAEREINION, *POWYS*

The narrow-gauge Welshpool and Llanfair Light Railway is a star attraction in this sleepy little town. Built on a hillside above the River Banwy and Einion Llanfair, Caereinion is a popular place for anglers and those seeking a peaceful retreat in the heart of the Welsh countryside. The 19th-century Church houses the stone figure of a knight which is said to date from pre-Reformation times.

Follow the Welshpool signs and continue along the A458 to Welshpool.

WELSHPOOL, *POWYS*

This town used to be called simply Pool but was prefixed with Welsh to distinguish it from Poole in Dorset. Built originally on a series of pools or marshland, this cramped little town is squeezed in between Powis Castle Park and the triple barrier of canal, railway line and river. The impressive Powis Castle (for full description see page 145) lies 1 mile south of the town. Welshpool is the market town and administrative centre for the district with a Monday market dating from the 13th century. A wall plaque in the town indicates the one-time residence of Gilbert and Ann Jones who claimed to be descendants of the 'original Jones'. Half-timbered houses on the road leading to the Castle bear nail-studded inscriptions, relics of political feuds, with words like 'God Damn Old Oliver'. The date, 1661 leaves no doubt which Oliver was intended. The parish church of St Mary of the Salutation stands high on a bank and its foundation dates from the 13th century. The church's proudest possession is a gold chalice made in 1662 which was in use at festivals until fairly recently. It now rests in the safety of the bank vaults. A boulder in the churchyard was once regarded as a Wishing Stone. Down from the church in St Mary's Street some interesting cobblestone work can be seen with the date 1846 and initials 'EM' worked into it. On land once known as the Field of Blood is an ancient cockpit house, where cock fights used to take place. A particularly heated disagreement between bird owners resulted in the murder of a man here. Being a border town, Welshpool has always been a highly-anglicized town and when Owain Glyndwr sought support for his wars against the English here he was rejected. Modern places of interest include the row of almshouses opposite the railway station and the attractive war memorial garden at the bottom of Severn Road.

Leave Welshpool by the Newtown road, A483, and in 6 miles turn left onto the B4385 for Montgomery.

MONTGOMERY, *POWYS*

One-time capital of the old county of Montgomeryshire, Montgomery is a town of charm and distinction. Tudor, Jacobean and Georgian architecture abounds and there are some fine Regency windows. It is a town of winding streets, slopes, steps and quaint corners all waiting to be explored. Broad Street is literally one of the widest streets anywhere – almost an enormous square closed off at one end by the red brick town hall. A fairly recent addition to the town is the charming little parterre garden alongside Arthur Street, set out with seats in the continental manner. The 13th-century parish Church of St Nicholas is situated on a high bank east of the town. It was restored during the 19th century but several pieces of the original building such as the two nave roofs dating from the 15th century, and the double screen, remain intact. Robber's Grave in the churchyard carries the fascinating tale of John Newton Davies who claimed that he was innocent of the murder for which he was hanged. He said that proof of his guilt would be shown by the fact that no grass would ever grow over his grave for 100 years. Today, more than 160 years after his death there is still a bare cruciform patch to be seen. Ruins of the early 13th-century castle still stand on Castle Hill.

Continue with the Bishop's Castle signs (still B4385) and in 3 miles cross the A489. On entering Bishop's Castle keep left, then turn right into Bull Street for the town centre. Follow the Clun signs and at the end of the town turn right onto the A488. At Clun turn right, signed Newtown, then cross the river bridge and turn right again onto the B4368. The road then follows the Clun Valley to Newcastle where the tour bears left and gradually ascends to over 1,400 ft. A descent is then made to reach the junction with the A489. Here turn left for the return to Newtown.

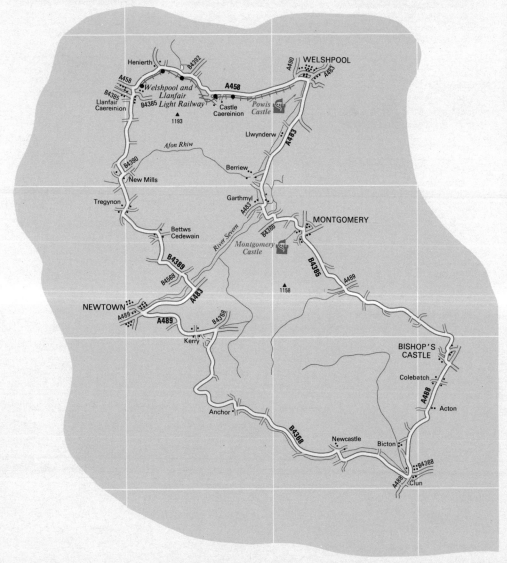

DRIVE 7   67 MILES

AROUND THE WATERFRONT TOWNS

Towns with crowded harbours and busy markets and villages that buzz with the workings of the Welsh woollen industry feature on this tour.

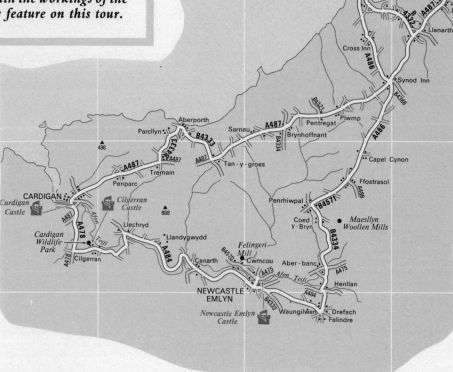

ABERAERON, *DYFED*

Aberaeron is a popular coastal resort with a neat appearance that owes much to careful planning during the 19th century, when the town came into being. The attractive harbour that once echoed to the sounds of schooner building is now a haven for sailing boats. There is much to attract the holidaymaker including a safe beach of mainly pebble and the Aberaeron Aquarium.

Leave Aberaeron on the Cardigan road A487 and pass through Llanarth after 4¼ miles. Two and a half miles farther at Synod Inn turn left onto the A486 signed Llandyssul to Ffostrasol, where at the Ffostrasol Arms Public House turn right onto the B4571 (no sign). In 2 miles at Penrhiwpal turn left onto the B4334, signed Henllan. In ¾ mile at Coed-y-bryn, pass on the left the road leading to Maesllyn Woollen Mills Museum. Continue along the B4334 crossing a main road at Aberbanc and continue with Henllan signs. On the far side of Henllan, cross the Afon Teifi and turn left then immediately branch right onto an unclassified road (no sign) over main road to reach the joint villages of Drefach and Felindre.

DREFACH FELINDRE, *DYFED*

This double village is the home of the Museum of the Welsh Woollen Industry which occupies part of a working mill. On show is a collection of textile machinery which dates back to the 18th century. There is also an exhibition tracing the development of the industry from the Middle Ages to the present day. A mill shop sells local crafts as well as Welsh flannel made on the premises.

At the end of the main street turn right onto the Newcastle Emlyn road (no sign) and shortly pass through Llaungilwen. In 1 mile, join A484 to reach Newcastle Emlyn.

NEWCASTLE EMLYN, *DYFED*

A typical Welsh market town, Newcastle Emlyn consists of one main street which turns right and then left before reaching a bridge across the River Teifi. The river forms a natural moat around the castle ruins (full description on page 128) which was a 'new' castle in the 13th century. The prefix 'new' was used to distinguish it from an earlier fortification close by. An attractive avenue of lime trees leads to the church which was built in 1840 and incorporates local slate. Two famous writers lived in Newcastle Emlyn, Theophilus Evans, vicar of Llangammarch and author of *Drych y Prif Oesoedd* and Allen Raine (Mrs A

Puddicombe) who was born here in 1836. At Adpar, across the river, the first Welsh printing press was built by Isaac Carter in 1718. To the north-west of the town, near Cwmcoy, is the interesting Felin Geri Mill. The Teifi is noted for its trout and salmon fishing.

The tour leaves Newcastle Emlyn on the Cardigan road A484 to reach Cenarth.

CENARTH, *DYFED*

Popular with anglers, not only because of the good fishing hereabouts, this village is also the site of the Cenarth Fishing Museum. Coracles, traditional and ancient fishing craft are still seen on the River Teifi and in the 12th century beaver were found here. Cenarth has fine waterfalls and an old four-arched bridge crosses the river.

Cross Afon Teifi with Cenarth Falls to the right and in 4½ miles at Llechryd turn left onto an unclassified road across an attractive old bridge. In ½ mile turn right signed Cilgerran and ½ mile farther turn right again to reach Cilgerran.

CILGERRAN, *DYFED*

Turner and de Wint are just two of the many painters and poets who have been inspired by the majesty of Cilgerran Castle (AM) perched high on its crag overlooking the beautiful Teifi. A full description of the castle appears on page 79. Each August local fishermen test their skills in coracle races on the river.

Keep forward through village passing the Wildlife Park on the right and in 1¼ miles turn right onto the A478 (no sign). One and three quarter miles farther, turn right onto the A487 to enter Cardigan.

CARDIGAN, *DYFED*

An important seaport before the River Teifi silted up, Cardigan is now a busy market town and seaside resort where numerous sandy bays beg exploration. Cardigan Castle (full description on page 62) was the site of the first National Eisteddfod in 1177. An outstanding feature of the town is Cardigan Bridge, a Norman construction which was rebuilt in 1640 and yet again after the Civil War when it was damaged by Roundheads. There are two notable chapels in Cardigan; the 19th-century Bethania is in William Street and the Tabernacle in the High Street dates from 1760.

A detour from Cardigan Bridge ¾ mile west leads to St Dogmaels Abbey. Founded in 1115 for monks of the French order *Tiron*, the abbey

boasts a notable north door with beautiful moulding which dates from the 14th century. In the north transept the corbels are carved with three figures; the Archangel Michael, a lion representing St Mark and an angel for St Matthew.

Follow signs Aberystwyth A487. In 5 miles turn left B4333 signed Aberporth and later descend to Aberporth. From Aberporth turn inland to continue until the B4333. In 2¼ miles at crossroads turn left onto the A487 signed Aberystwyth and continue along this road for 8¾ miles then turn left onto the A486 signed Newquay and later descend into Newquay. In town bear right along the Aberaeron road B4342 and after 3 miles turn left onto the A487 for the return to Aberaeron.

Newcastle Emlyn

DRIVE 8

69 MILES

TO THE CITY OF SAINTS

Seafaring towns in the heart of magnificent coastal scenery lead to St David's, city of Saints, through Welsh-weaving villages and back to Haverfordwest.

HAVERFORDWEST, DYFED

There is a distinct English flavour to this quaint market town situated on the valley slopes of the Western Cleddau River. The town is built on a medieval pattern with the steep main street dominated by the stately pile that is Haverfordwest Castle (for full description see page 112). A one-time port, Haverfordwest had an influx of Flemish settlers during the Middle Ages, sent to the town by the first two Henrys. Its early links with Bristol and Ireland were less important by the 19th century when the South Wales Railway was opened and when Milford Haven, whose situation was closer to the sea, developed into a town. Places of interest include Foley House, designed by John Marsh and lived in by Admiral Sir Thomas Foley, one of Nelson's officers; the County War Museum in Salutation Square, and Market House, where high-quality Welsh weaves may be bought. The town's proximity to the Pembrokeshire Coast National Park and Coastal Footpath, which runs 167 miles from Cardigan to Amroth, make it a popular base for tourists.

From the north side of the Haverfordwest one-way system follow signs Hayscastle and Croesgoch to leave by the B4330. In 3¾ miles branch left over the crossways onto an unclassified road, signed Roch. In 2¼ miles at the T-junction turn left, then take the next turning right for Roch.

ROCH, DYFED

This tiny village nestles in the shadow of its imposing castle with large pele tower which dates from the 13th century (for full description see page 152). Roch lies some 2 miles from the coast.

At the far end of the village turn right onto the A487, signed St David's and continue to Solva.

SOLVA, DYFED

This picturesque village of typically-Welsh cottages perches on the hills surrounding the north shore of St Bride's Bay. A place of mysterious coves and magnificent scenery, Solva was once the territory of smugglers and later was in use as a port for coal

and lime. Disused lime kilns dating from the 19th century stand near the road bridge as a monument to the past. Cliff scenery surrounds Solva and the village itself is best viewed from Gribyn Cove where rare flowers are to be found.

Remain on the A487 to St David's.

ST DAVID'S, DYFED

Patron saint of Wales, Dewi Sant, or St David, was born in this tiny city in the 6th century. Architecturally, St David's is not a particularly impressive city but St David's Cathedral and the Bishop's Palace are of note. One of Christianity's greatest historic shrines, the cathedral suffered much through the centuries from the ravages of war. St David's shrine, damaged through centuries of neglect, can now be seen. The beautiful nave is the embodiment of three centuries of craftsmanship, combined to produce a scene of medieval splendour. Fine examples of the wood carver's art can be seen in the Misericords. Bishops Palace (AM) lies close to the cathedral and was built in c1340.

Leave by the Fishguard road (still A487) and after 10½ miles bear left, signed Fishguard Harbour. Half a mile farther turn left onto an unclassified road, signed Abermawr. In another mile, at the crossroads, turn right (signed St Nicholas) and shortly pass the turning to Tre-gwynt Woollen Mills (on the left).

TRE-GWYNT WOOLLEN MILLS, DYFED

Visitors are invited to walk around the mill and watch the processes involved in the making of fabrics, wools and flannels. Knitting-wool and other items are on sale in the shop.

Continue along the narrow lane and in ½ mile turn left to enter St Nicholas. Keep forward and in 1½ miles at the crossways turn right, signed Fishguard. In ½ mile turn left, signed Strumble Head. Ascend and descend (narrow in places) to reach a T-junction. From here a detour to the left can be made to visit Strumble Head.

STRUMBLE HEAD, DYFED

Some of the finest stretches of coastal scenery in Wales are hidden away in the rugged recesses of the Strumble headland.

The main tour continues with the Fishguard road. In 1¾ miles turn left and later descend into Goodwick. At the Rose and Crown PH turn right onto the A40, then go forward at the roundabout and ascend to Fishguard.

FISHGUARD, DYFED

This little port on Fishguard Bay is well known today for its ferry service link with the Republic of Ireland. The harbour was constructed in 1906 to cope with heavy Atlantic trade, after World War One, this traffic dwindled as did the once-thriving industries of herring fishing and pilchard curing.

From the roundabout in Fishguard follow the Cardigan road, A487, then take the 1st turning right onto the B4313, signed

Gwaun Valley. Take the next turning left and continue to Llanychaer. Remain on the B4313, signed Maenclochog, and across the Mynydd Preseli. Later, at the New Inn, cross the main road (now signed Narberth) and continue to Maenclochog. At the end of the village turn left then in 5¼ miles pass under a railway bridge and turn right onto an unclassified road, signed Llawhaden. Shortly cross a river bridge and turn left. Two miles farther turn left and continue to Llawhaden.

LLAWHADEN, DYFED

Llawhaden enjoys a picturesque location by the banks of the East Cleddau River. An 18th-century bridge and mill are notable aspects of the river. The Bishop of St David's Castle (for full description see page 42) was originally a wooden structure built in Norman times.

Leave by the southwards unclassified road to reach the A40 and turn right, signed Haverfordwest. In almost 3 miles turn left, unclassified, signed Graham Sutherland Art Gallery, Picton Castle. One and a half miles further, at Rhos, turn left for Picton Castle.

PICTON CASTLE, DYFED

Picton Castle (OACT) dates from the 13th century (full description on page 145). The attractive gardens are occasionally open to the public in aid of the National Gardens Scheme.

Return to Rhos and turn left (no sign). In ¾ mile bear right, signed Haverfordwest, then in another ¾ mile turn left onto the A40 (no sign) for the return to Haverfordwest.

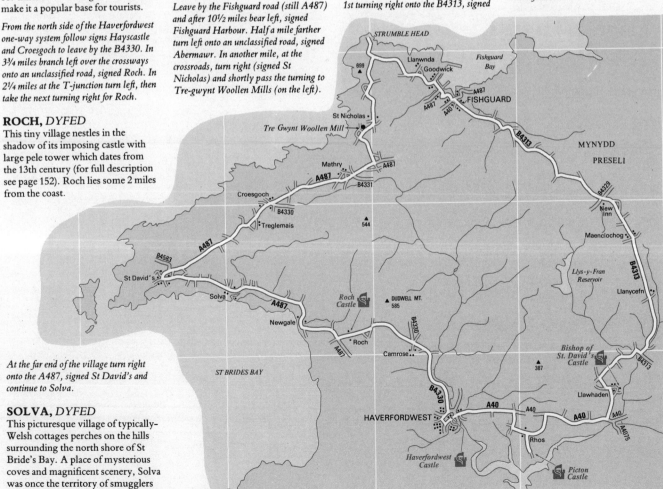

DRIVE 9
57 MILES

'LAND'S END' AND POET'S REST

On to the Pembrokeshire Peninsula, past historic parish churches to the home of poet Dylan Thomas.

TENBY, *DYFED*

This popular holiday resort possesses a distinctive charm that owes much to its medieval origins. The ruins of a 13th-century town wall still encircle old Tenby, although the present town has outgrown this line of fortification. Elegant Georgian houses, perched on the cliffs, overlook extensive golden sands and a harbour crowded with yachts. The harbour was once an important link with Bristol and Ireland, because of its ideal situation on a narrow rocky promontory on the west side of Carmarthen Bay. The ruined walls and keep of the 13th-century Tenby Castle (see page 155 for full description) stand high on Castle Hill. The keep now houses Tenby Museum which holds exhibits on the archaeology, natural history, geology and medieval history of Pembrokeshire. The Tudor Merchants House (NT, OACT) on Quay Hill is a fine example of 15th-century architecture with gabled front and carbelled chimney breast. From the same period and adjacent to the Merchant's House, is Plantagenet House (NT). Modern attractions for the holidaymaker include two cinemas, a dance hall, amusement arcades and facilities for angling, golfing, bowls and water-skiing. Just off the coast is St Catherines Island, which features a zoo and a 19th-century fort. Near Tenby is the Manor House Wildlife and Leisure Park.

Leave Tenby by the Pembroke road A4139 and continue through Lydstep then in ½ mile beyond village turn left onto the B4585 to Manorbier.

MANORBIER, *DYFED*

Manorbier is a tiny seaside village where the houses cluster in the shadow of Manorbier Castle (OACT), whose impressive Norman ruins (see page 122 for full description) look out across Manorbier Bay. The parish church is also of Norman origin with a 13th-century tower and some later additions.

In village keep left (one-way) then turn sharp right with the Pembroke road. In ¾ mile at the T-junction, turn left to rejoin the A4139 to Lamphey.

LAMPHEY, *DYFED*

This fast-growing village is the site of Lamphey's Bishop's Palace, one of seven palaces in Wales dedicated to the Bishops of St David's. Built between the 13th and 15th centuries, the palace has a great hall constructed by the 'building bishop', Bishop Gower. During the 16th century the palace was owned by the Earls of Essex who used it as a family mansion. Eventually the building was abandoned and fell into ruins until it was acquired by the DoE who are presently carrying out extensive restoration work.

Pass the church and bear left for Pembroke.

PEMBROKE, *DYFED*

The name Pembroke is a corruption of the Welsh name *Penfro* which means 'Land's End', and is an apt description for this town at the head of the Pembrokeshire Peninsula. Standing stones, cairns, tombs and hut circles are plentiful in this area, evidence that Pembroke had a fairly large population in ancient times. Pembroke Castle stands guard over the town as it has done since 1090, when a Norman gentlemen called Lord Grimly de Montgomery erected a structure of wood and earth. The foundations of the castle we see today, were built during the 12th century by William Marshall (for a full description of the castle see page 134). Parts of the old town walls can be seen in the town, and also of historic interest are the two churches.

From Pembroke follow signs Carmarthen then St Clears along the A4075. In 2½ miles turn right onto the A477 and in 1¾ miles turn left again onto the A4075 to reach Carew.

CAREW, *DYFED*

The two main attractions in this village are the castle and the cross. The latter is a Celtic Cross (AM) dating from the 11th century, which stands 14 ft high and is decorated with an intricate series of designs. Inscribed on it in Latin are the words 'Maredudd the King, son of Edwin'. Carew Castle is of Norman origin and was lived in by Gerald de Windsor in 1095 when he married Nest, a very beautiful woman and daughter of Prince Rhys of Tewdwr. (For a full description of the castle see page 64).

Continue along the A4075 for 6 miles then at the Cross Hands PH turn right onto the A4115 signed Templeton. In 2¾ miles turn left A478 to enter Templeton. At end of village turn right onto the B4315 signed Tavernspite and

Whitland. *In 1¾ miles at Princes Gate keep forward onto the B4314 to reach Tavernspite. At end of village bear right for Red Roses. At Red Roses turn left onto the A477 signed St Clears. In 5¾ miles at roundabout take 2nd exit A4066 to enter St Clears.*

ST CLEARS, *DYFED*

St Clears is a busy agricultural town standing at an important road junction on the A40 where holiday traffic in the summer months is intense. The church of St Mary Magdalen boasts an impressive west tower and a few examples of Norman work, including an elaborately carved chancel arch. In the 19th century St Clears was the centre of the Rebecca Riots which resulted in toll-gate reform. World War One flying ace Group Captain Ira Jones is remembered by a war memorial in the main street.

Follow signs Laugharne, Pendine A4066 to Laugharne.

LAUGHARNE, *DYFED*

This little town's main claim to fame is in its connections with Welsh Bard Dylan Thomas. The Boathouse, a Georgian dwelling which stands on a narrow cliff walk near the castle was his home and place of work, and a simple cross marks his grave in Laugharne churchyard. Some say that Laugharne was the inspiration for *Under Milk Wood* and the play is often performed in the town.

Continue to Pendine then from seafront ascend (1 in 6) along the B4314 (no sign) and at top turn left onto an unclassified road signed Amroth. Later descend to Amroth and keep forward and ascend then in ½ mile turn left signed Tenby and descend again passing through Wisemans Bridge then ascend through a wooded area and at top keep left and descend to Saundersfoot.

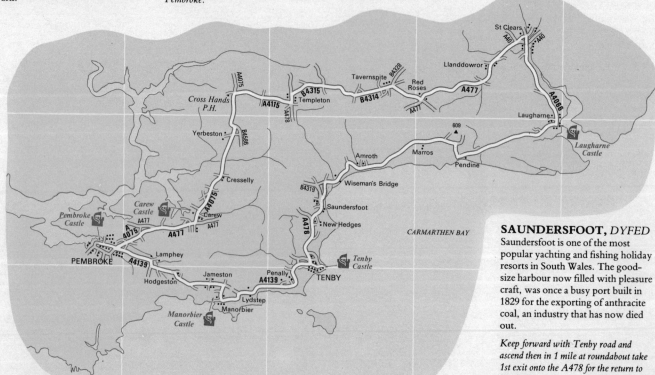

SAUNDERSFOOT, *DYFED*

Saundersfoot is one of the most popular yachting and fishing holiday resorts in South Wales. The good-size harbour now filled with pleasure craft, was once a busy port built in 1829 for the exporting of anthracite coal, an industry that has now died out.

Keep forward with Tenby road and ascend then in 1 mile at roundabout take 1st exit onto the A478 for the return to Tenby.

DRIVE 10   *61 MILES*

THROUGH FERTILE FARMLANDS

This tour undulates through rich farmland to the heart of industry at the British Steel plant at Llanelli and to popular Llandeilo.

CARMARTHEN, *DYFED*

Modern traffic has been a major problem for Carmarthen, whose steep and narrow streets are more suited to a bygone era, although a long-awaited bypass is now under construction. Despite this, Carmarthen is a market and county town of repute, which forms the centre for some of the finest farming land in Wales. There is much to excite the historians in this little town. In Roman times it was an important settlement as excavations have revealed, and many Roman exhibits can be seen in the museum in Quay Street. Legend has it that Merlin, that great Arthurian enchanter, was born in the Carmarthen area. One of Wales' most valued treasures was written here; known as the *Black Book of Carmarthen*, it is the oldest manuscript written in the Welsh language, and is now housed in the National Library of Wales in Aberystwyth. Carmarthen Castle was once the main seat of the Princes of Wales, and was therefore the subject of countless attacks. Today, there is little to be seen of the original structure (see page 66 for full description) and much of the site is now occupied by the County Hall. The most venerable of Carmarthen's buildings is the 13th-century St Peters Church. The Guildhall, dating from 1767, stands next to composer Brimley Richards' birthplace – his most famous work was *God Bless the Prince of Wales*.

From Carmarthen follow signs Llanelli A484 to Kidwelly.

KIDWELLY, *DYFED*

Situated at the head of the Gwendraeth inlet off the sandy Tywi estuary is Kidwelly, one of the oldest boroughs in Wales. The earlier, once-walled section of the town lies on the west bank of the River Gwendraeth Fach below the castle, while the later part with its prominent church stands on the east bank. Both are linked by a bridge which dates from the 14th or 15th century, although it has been widened considerably since then. The pride of the town is Kidwelly Castle (for full description see page 115), the best preserved of all of Carmarthenshire's nine strongholds. The local church was originally a Benedictine Priory founded in 1130 by Bishop Roger of Salisbury, who also built the castle. The 13th-century tower with its tall spire, the chancel and the large span of the nave are among its more notable features.

Continue along the A484 towards

Llanelli later passing on the right the entrance to Pembrey Country Park.

LLANELLI, *DYFED*

A mainly industrial town with a population of around 28,000, Llanelli stands on the estuary of River Loughor. A major market town during the late 16th century, the town turned to industry in the 19th century, when Alexander Raby established the first ironworks. The coal industry once flourished here but it has since given way to steel. The British Steel Corporation opened the Trostre works in 1951. One of the largest tinplate works in the country, this complex covers 270 acres. Bryncaerau Castle is a museum with a fine collection of Llanelli pottery and exhibits depicting the history of the tinplate industry. The castle also houses an art gallery devoted to the work of local painters. Bryncaerau Castle stands in Parc Howard, a present to the town from Sir Stafford Howard, its first mayor. Near the town is Pembrey Country Park, a popular tourist spot.

From Llanelli, follow signs Llandeilo to leave by the A476. Later pass through Cross Hands then in 1 mile, at Gorslas, turn right onto the B4556 signed Llandybie. Continue on this road to Llandybie and cross main road onto an unclassified road signed Trapp. Shortly at church, turn right into Church Street

and go over level crossing. In 2 miles turn right then left to reach Trapp. In village turn left then cross the river bridge and turn right. In ¾ mile turn right for Carreg Cennen Castle Car Park.

CARREG CENNEN CASTLE, *DYFED*

Perched 300 ft above the River Cennen on a formidable limestone crag (the 'carreg' in its name) is the imposing grey stronghold of Carreg Cennen Castle. The present structure, built in the 13th century was a popular subject with 18th and 19th century artists and engravers. (For a full description see page 66.)

Return to Trapp and keep right and ascend. In 2¼ miles turn left and pass under railway bridge then at crossroads turn right onto the A483 for Llandeilo.

LLANDEILO, *DYFED*

A popular touring and fishing centre, Llandeilo is essentially a market town standing as it does amid rich farming lands by the side of the River Tywi. The bridge over the river dates from the 19th century and measures 365 ft in length, with a central span of 145 ft. The 13th-century St Teilo's

Church was virtually rebuilt in 1840 and contains two Celtic cross heads, which date from the 10th century. One mile west of the town lie the privately owned ruins of Dinefwr Castle. (See page 95 for full description.) Nearby is Golden Grove Mansion and Country Park.

Return along the A483 to Ffairfach then turn right onto the A476 signed Llanelli. In ¾ mile turn right onto the B4300 signed Carmarthen. In 4¼ miles turn right onto the B4297 (no sign) for Dryslwyn Castle.

DRYSLWYN CASTLE, *DYFED*

The ruins of this 13th-century stronghold are situated on top of a hill overlooking the River Tywi. It played an important part in the struggles between the Welsh and the English during the 13th century. Today, the ruins comprise mainly remains of the chapel and hall.

Return for ½ mile along the B4297 then turn right onto the B4300 passing through Llanarthney and Capel Dewi before turning right onto the A48 for the return to Carmarthen.

Kidwelly Castle

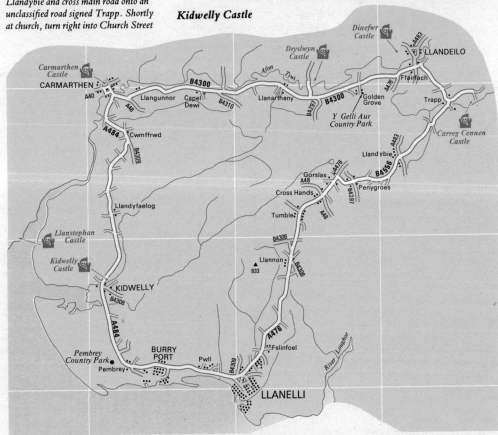

DRIVE 11   41 MILES

SURF AND CLIFF SCENERY

Picturesque thatched cottages give an almost English atmosphere to this mostly coastal tour from busy Swansea.

SWANSEA, *WEST GLAMORGAN*

Although Swansea's origins can be traced back to Viking times, World War Two and industrialization on a grand scale have left little of historic interest in this, Wales' second-largest city. The notable 15th-century St Mary's Church suffered bomb damage in 1941 and was rebuilt in 1955, and the remains of a 14th-century manor house (AM) can be seen in Wind Street. Today's city is very much a product of the Industrial Revolution with ironworks, chemical factories, steelworks, mills and a host of other industries, all sited here. However, not all of Swansea is built over or polluted by factory waste; inhabitants and visitors can enjoy over 900 acres of well-tended parkland. Swansea University was formed in 1919 and occupies many buildings in the town. Some fine examples of Swansea and Nantgarw Porcelain are housed in the Glynn Vyvian Art Gallery in Alexandra Road. The city's most famous sons are the poet Dylan Thomas and Beau Nash, the 17th-century gent who dictated the lifestyle of the fashionable people of Bath. Offering complete contrast to the sprawling city is the nearby Gower Peninsula.

From Swansea follow signs Mumbles, Gower along the A4067 to The Mumbles.

THE MUMBLES, *WEST GLAMORGAN*

The 13th-century ruins of Oystermouth Castle stand on a hilltop overlooking a holiday and residential area. See page 132 for full description.

From The Mumbles, leave by Newton Road B4593 (signed Caswell Bay). In ¼ mile turn left and ascend then ½ mile further bear right. In another ½ mile turn right then left and descend to Caswell Bay. At Caswell Bay continue forward onto an unclassified road and in 1 mile turn left and pass through Bishopston. Later turn left onto the B4436, signed Port Eynon. In 1 mile turn right and in ½ mile at T-junction turn left onto the A4118 and shortly reach Parkmill where a footpath may be taken on the left to Pennard Castle.

PENNARD CASTLE AND PARC LE BREOS BURIAL CHAMBER, *WEST GLAMORGAN*

Flowing through this attractive village is Ilston Stream which passes the ruins of Pennard Castle (described on page 141), en route to its outlet at the beautiful Threecliff Bay (NT). Sand, blown from the extensive dunes in the area, has completely buried two churches and threatened to engulf the castle. The fine megalithic tomb of Parc le Breos (AM) is situated in woods nearby.

Continue along the A4118 and in 3¼ miles turn left onto an unclassified road signed Oxwich passing on the right the entrance to Penrice Castle.

PENRICE CASTLE, *WEST GLAMORGAN*

The ruins of Penrice Castle, described on page 144, date from the 13th century. It was built to replace an earlier structure which stood on the mound close to Penrice Church. Castle open by written application only.

Oystermouth Castle

Continue along unclassified road down steep descent and pass a Nature Reserve to reach Oxwich.

OXWICH, *WEST GLAMORGAN*

This delightful little village has the appearance of the traditional English counterpart complete with thatched and whitewashed cottages, and pleasant country church shaded by sycamore trees. The Norman-rooted family who once owned Oxwich Castle (AM) installed the exquisite de la Mare tomb that can still be seen in the church. In 1541 the castle was rebuilt as a Tudor manor house but many of the relics from the original 14th-century stronghold still remain. See page 132 for full description.

At the crossroads turn right (no sign). In ½ mile at the T junction turn right, signed Horton, and in another ½ mile turn left. Continue on this road for 2 miles then turn left onto the A4118 to reach Port Eynon.

PORT EYNON, *WEST GLAMORGAN*

This picturesque village takes its name from the 11th-century Welsh Prince Einion. Its appeal lies in the old thatched cottages, still well-preserved, and the narrow leafy lanes that defy any car. Today Port Eynon is a noted surfing centre with a fine beach, and it lies east of some breathtaking cliff scenery (NT).

From Port Eynon, return along A4118 for 2½ miles then branch left onto an unclassified road signed Burry. Keep forward on this road for 2½ miles then at Burry Green turn left signed Llangennith. In a little over ½ mile, turn right, signed Llanmadoc and later descend to Cheriton. Here turn sharp right (no sign). Continue forward and in 2 miles pass on the left a track leading to Weobley Castle.

WEOBLEY CASTLE, *WEST GLAMORGAN*

The impressive Weobley Castle (AM) dates from the 13th and 14th century and enjoys a beautiful setting overlooking Llanrhidian Marsh. More of a fortified manor house than a castle, the building is worth a visit for the glimpse it gives of domestic life at the end of the Middle Ages. See page 158 for a full description.

Continue along unclassified road to Llanrhidian then turn right onto the B4271 signed Swansea. Later cross Fairwood Common before joining the A4118 and proceed through the suburbs of Killay and Sketty for the return to Swansea City Centre.

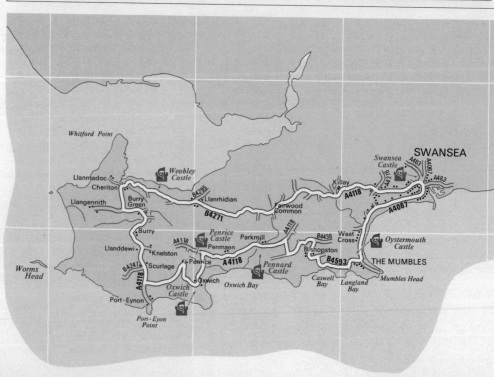

DRIVE 12   65 MILES

THE OLD SPA TOWNS

Taking in some old spa towns and a 'bookbuyer's paradise' this tour winds through the county of Powys.

BUILTH WELLS, *POWYS*

The Welsh name for this town is *Llanfair yn Mault* which means 'St Mary's in Builth'. It grew up in Norman times around a castle of which nothing more than a mound exists today. Builth became a popular resort during the 18th century, when spas became fashionable; the two sources known as the Park Wells and the Glanau Wells are no longer in use. The main shopping street is called Broad Street for part of the way, and the High Street for the rest, forming a large thoroughfare which snakes its way through the town. A riverside park known as the Groe lies between the main street and the River Wye. The Alpha Chapel is an interesting grey stone building, which stands beside the main entrance to the Groe. The Wyeside Arts Centre has much to offer lovers of theatre and the arts.

From Builth Wells, follow signs Brecon A470 to Llyswen then continue forward on the A479 signed Abergavenny. In 2 miles at T-junction turn right onto the A438 to Bronllys and in village turn left onto the A479 shortly passing on the left Bronllys Castle.

BRONLLYS CASTLE, *POWYS*

One and a half miles south of the village lies Bronllys Castle (AM) which dates from the 12th century. For a full description of the castle see page 43.

Continue with the A479 to Talgarth then turn left onto the Three Cocks road A4078. In 2¼ miles turn right onto the Hereford road A438 (no sign), and proceed through Three Cocks (Aberllynfi) to the edge of Glasbury on Wye. Continue forward onto the Hay road B4350 following the Wye Valley to Hay-on-Wye.

HAY-ON-WYE, *POWYS*

This attractive market town occupies the north-east corner of the Brecon Beacons National Park on the River Wye. One-time centre for the flannel industry, Hay-on-Wye is now a local farming focus. The older part of town is most interesting – a maze of narrow, winding streets with numerous little shops. The town is known as a 'bookbuyers paradise' and the Richard Booth bookshops are of particular note. The parish church of St Mary dates originally from the 13th century, but was largely rebuilt in 1834. The early-English south entrance still survives and the church contains a silver chalice inscribed 'Oure Lady Paris of the Haia' which dates back to 1576. On the river there is a treacherously-deep section known as the 'Steeple Pool' for it is here that the old bells of St Mary are said to have fallen in.

Hay Castle (for full description see page 113) dates from the 13th century and was built by William de Braos. Alongside the castle ruin is a privately-owned Jacobean house which replaced the castle.

From Hay on Wye leave by the Clyro road B4351 by crossing River Wye. In 1¼ miles bear right over main road onto an unclassified road into Clyro. At the church turn left signed Painscastle and in ½ mile turn left again and up long ascent. In ½ mile bear right continuing ascent and proceed to Painscastle.

PAINSCASTLE, *POWYS*

This quaint little village of cream and yellow cottages takes its name from a courtier to Henry I, Pain FitzJohn. He was responsible for the building of the castle or the rebuilding in stone of an earlier motte-and-bailey fortress. Of this structure only a mound remains.

In village, turn right onto the B4594 signed Newchurch and pass through the quiet villages of Rhosgoch and Newchurch and continue with Gladestry signs. Pass through Gladestry and in 2¼ miles bear right, then 1 mile farther turn left onto the A44 signed Rhayader. Continue on this road to Cross Gates where at the roundabout take the 1st exit A483 signed Llandrindod Wells to reach Llandrindod Wells.

LLANDRINDOD WELLS, *POWYS*

Foremost among the Mid Wales spa towns, Llandrindod Wells first emerged as such in the late 17th century, but did not reach its peak until well into the 19th century. With the advent of the railway in 1866, visitors were flocking to 'take the waters' in tens of thousands each year. Eventually spa treatment went out of fashion and in the 1960s the Pump Room was closed down but that was by no means the end of Llandrindod. It became the ecclesiastical capital of Wales when the first Archbishop of Wales was elected here in the 19th century. In 1974 it took on a new lease of life as the capital of the newly-formed county of Powys. Visitors still clamour to the town, but nowadays they are attracted by magnificent scenery and outdoor pursuits such as pony trekking and fishing. From an architectural point of view the town is a fairytale of towers, turrets, cupoles, balconies, oriels, colonnades, ornamental ironwork, loggias and balustrades. The ubiquitous grey stonework is transformed into a confection of strawberries and cream, and the whole scene is brought to life with the sparkling greenery of parks, gardens, green banks and commons. There is much to see in the town and places of interest include the museum with its fascinating collection of dolls from all over the world, the Llandrindod Wells Lake and Rock Gardens, and Tom Morton's famous cycle collection at the Automobile Palace. One mile north of the town is Castell Collen, possibly the site of a Roman fort known as *Magos*.

From Llandrindod Wells, follow signs Builth Wells along the A483. In 7 miles at roundabout take 1st exit to cross River Wye into Builth Wells.

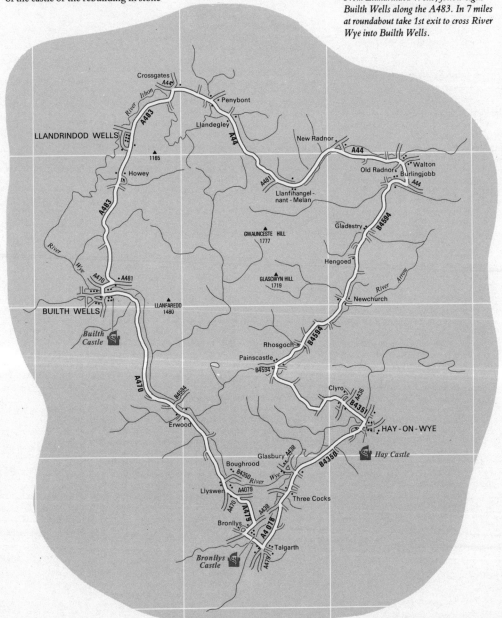

DRIVE 13

AROUND THE BRECON BEACONS

64 MILES

Panoramic views of the internationally-famed Brecon Beacons highlight this historically-important tour.

BRECON, *POWYS*

The Welsh name for Brecon is Abberhonddu and its situation is at the confluence of the rivers Honddu and Usk. This beautiful Cathedral city was accorded the status in 1923 when the 13th-century Benedictine priory church of St John became a cathedral. Streets lined with Jacobean and Georgian houses do much to enhance the character of Brecon, while outside the city the Brecon Beacons National Park is an added attraction.

Situated on the northern outskirts of the city, the cathedral displays many outstanding features of architectural interest; notably a choir in Early English style and a nave in still-later Decorated style. Several of the priory buildings have been restored, including a fine tithe barn. Beyond the cathedral there is a charming walk along the banks of the Afon Honddu. The Castle Hotel incorporates remains of Brecon Castle (see page 43) and sections of the medieval town walls can be seen at Captain's Walk. Places of interest include St Mary's Church, a greatly-restored medieval building in the heart of the city, the Brecknock County Museum in Glamorgan Street and the Museum of South Wales Borderers which is sited on the Watton. Christ College, a public school situated across the River Usk, was originally built as a Benedictine friary and was restored in the 19th century.

From Brecon follow signs Merthyr A470 to Libanus then turn right onto an unclassified road, signed Mountain Centre. In 1½ miles pass the turning (on the right) to the Brecon Beacons National Park Mountain Centre. Continue with unclassified road and in ½ mile turn left. One and three quarter miles farther turn left onto the A4215. In 3 miles turn right onto the A470 signed Merthyr. Ascend to 1,440ft then descend into the wooded Taff valley. On reaching Cefn-coed y-cymmer turn left onto an unclassified road signed Pontsticill. (In 1½ miles along this road a detour can be made by branching right at the Aberglais PH to visit Morlais Castle.)

MORLAIS CASTLE, *POWYS*

Gilbert de Clare built Morlais Castle as a borderland stronghold in the 13th century and still today its location atop a 1,200 ft hill affords panoramic views of the Brecon Beacons. For full description see page 126.

The main tour bears left for Pontsticill. Continue with the Talybont road and beyond the village keep left. Pass alongside Pontsticill Reservoirs and in

1¾ miles turn left. One mile farther turn right and continue through woodland to reach Talybont Reservoir. Pass the dam then in 1¼ miles bear right and later cross canal bridge and turn right onto the B4558 into Talybont. Continue on the Crickhowell road to Llangynidr. Here turn right and cross the canal, then in 1 mile turn right again on to the B4560 signed Beaufort and up long ascent. Beyond the summit turn left onto an unclassified road and descend to Llangattock. In ¼ mile beyond village turn left onto the A4077 then right to cross ancient bridge into Crickhowell

CRICKHOWELL, *POWYS*

The name of this Usk Valley country town is derived from Crug Hywel or Howell's Mount, an iron-age camp. Spanning the River Usk at Crickhowell is a splendid 13-arched bridge which dates from the 17th century. The town boasts some attractive buildings, not least the local church with its fine 19th-century broach spire. An uninspiring mound and some broken masonry is all that remains of the castle which was largely destroyed by Owain Glyndwr in 1403. Porthmawr, an interesting 15th-century gatehouse, can be seen to the west of Crickhowell.

From Crickhowell, leave by the Brecon Road A40. (In 1½ miles a detour may be taken by turning right onto the A479 to Tretower Court and Castle.)

TRETOWER, *POWYS*

Lying amidst the unspoilt charm of water and woodland Tretower enjoys a peaceful location in the upper reaches of the Usk Valley. The remains of Tretower Castle (AM) (fully described on page 156) comprise a sturdy keep surrounded by a many-sided wall. The nearby Tretower Court is a 14th-century mansion considered to be one of the finest early fortified mansions in Wales. It was the home of the Vaughan family for three centuries. A notable member of that family was Henry Vaughan, one of the outstanding metaphysical poets of the 7th century.

The main tour continues along the A40 and later ascends to Bwlch. Beyond the village at War Memorial turn right onto the B4560 signed Llangorse. Pass through Llangorse and turn left into an unclassified road signed Brecon. At Llanfihangel Tal-y-llyn turn left and 2½ miles farther turn left again. Shortly pass under road bridge then turn right to join A40. In ¾ mile at roundabout take 2nd exit B4601 for the return to Brecon.

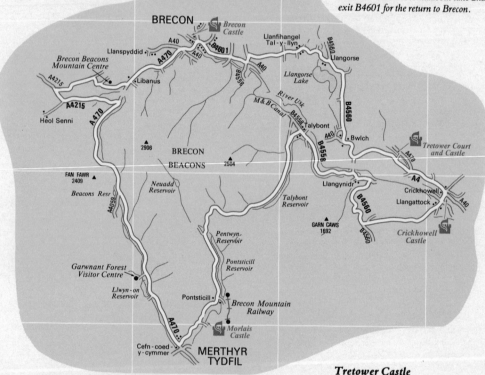

Tretower Castle

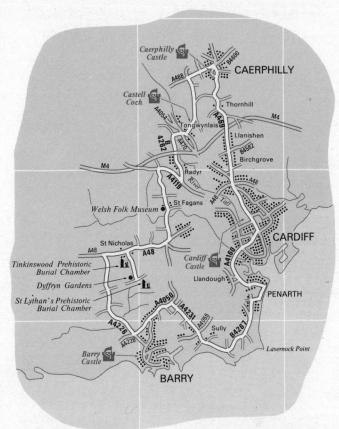

CARDIFF, *SOUTH GLAMORGAN*

This beautiful city was created the capital of Wales by Queen Elizabeth II in 1955. A large industrial seaport, Cardiff's history goes back at least as far as Roman times when they established a fort here in AD 75 to control Welsh tribesmen. Although always a place of importance, Cardiff's real expansion took place in the 19th century when it was a busy port shipping coal from the Welsh mining towns. The modern city centre, with its attractive shopping arcades, is dominated by the regal splendour of Cardiff Castle. This fairy-tale stronghold is of ancient origin but in the 9th century it was extensively rebuilt and redesigned by architect William Burges, who created a masterpiece of Victorian opulence (for full description see page 59). Several fine examples of Victorian architecture remain in the town, notably the Great Western Hotel in St Mary's Street and Park House (1874) in Park Place. The City Hall and Law Courts are 20th-century additions to the city; built in extravagant baroque style, they do much to enhance their magnificent surroundings in Cathays Park. Also in Cathays Park is the National Museum of Wales. One of the largest museums in Britain, it houses a rich variety of objects illustrating all aspects of Welsh culture as well as an outstanding collection of European art and sculpture. Another fine museum is the Welsh Industrial and Maritime Museum, situated in the heart of Cardiff's dockland. Its treasures include a beam engine and a triple-expansion steam engine. The word Cardiff, to many people, is synonymous with rugby football and the ground at Cardiff Arms Park is world famous. Near the banks of the River Taff on the city's west side is the beautiful Llandaff Cathedral. Of 12th-century origin it was very nearly destroyed by the effects of wars and the passage of time but it has now been restored to its former glory.

From the Central Station area of Cardiff, follow signs Penarth to leave by the A4160. In 2½ miles at roundabout take 1st exit. Half a mile farther pass under railway bridge and at mini roundabout forward to enter Penarth.

PENARTH, *SOUTH GLAMORGAN*

Once only a small fishing village whose harbour was busy with the coal export trade, Penarth has now become one of the major water ski-ing and sailing areas of South Wales. A little sand can be found at low tide. The town is now geared towards the tourist and the harbour is busy with yachts and cruisers. The slopes,

behind the promenade, bedecked with flowerbeds and fine lawns, have earned Penarth the name of 'Garden by the Sea'. The beach is mainly pebble and shingle and bathing is considered hazardous due to strong currents. Some think Coleridge's *The Rime of the Ancient Mariner* was inspired by a Penarth seaman. There are fine cliff walks behind the beach, leading to nearby Ranny Bay and St Mary's Well Bay. Turner House Art Gallery, in Plymouth Road, was founded in 1888 and is part of the National Museum of Wales. Both classical and modern works of art can be seen here.

At roundabout go forward signed Sea Front and descend to the Esplanade. At far end ascend and keep forward into Raisdale Road. Shortly cross the railway bridge and at next crossroads turn left (no sign). In just over ¼ mile turn left again onto the B4267. Three and a half miles farther at roundabout take 2nd exit onto the A4231 signed Cardiff, Wales Airport. (At this point a detour into Barry may be taken by taking 1st exit at the roundabout onto the A4055.)

BARRY, *SOUTH GLAMORGAN*

This popular seaside resort is an ideal base from which to explore the Vale of Glamorgan and its Heritage Coast which extends westward from the town for some 18 miles. Tourism apart, Barry is also an important industrial town and port. Massive docks were built to cope with the export of coal as it poured out of the Rhondda Valley and other mining areas, in the 1880s. Today the town is the site of large chemical industries. Barry Island is linked to the town by a large causeway and it is this area that draws the greatest amount of holidaymakers. Butlins Holiday Camp, at the south end of the island, includes a 5-acre pleasure park, seafront restaurants and gardens which flank Whitmore Bay. Knap Lido includes a boating lake, gardens and the largest open-air swimming pool in Wales. Nearby is Porthkerry Country Park covering 225 acres of valley through which runs an impressive railway viaduct. Glamorgan (Rhoose) Airport has regular flights within Britain and Europe.

Continue along the A4231 for 1¾ miles then at roundabout take 1st exit onto the A4050. In 1½ miles at roundabout take 2nd exit A4226. One mile farther at roundabout take 3rd exit (signed Port Talbot). In 4¼ miles turn right onto the A48 signed Cardiff and shortly pass through St Nicholas. (A detour can be made here by turning right onto a unclassified road signed Dyffryn Gardens to reach Dyffryn Gardens, and Tinkinswood and St Lythan's prehistoric Burial Chambers.)

TINKINSWOOD AND ST LYTHAN'S BURIAL CHAMBERS, *SOUTH GLAMORGAN*

A pleasant pathway through fields leads to Tinkinswood, an ancient chamber rectangular in shape and enclosed by five upright slabs, where the bones of at least fifty people were found. Nearby is St Lythan's, the site of another chamber which dates from c6200 BC. Also in this area are the beautiful Dyffryn Gardens which are open to the public and form the grounds of the 19th-century Dyffryn House. The 100-acres of garden include many rare trees and shrubs and of particular interest are the collection of Chinese plants.

Continue along the A48 and in 1¾ miles at roundabout take 1st exit signed Cardiff then take next turning left onto an unclassified road (no sign). In 1¼ miles forward over level crossing. Immediately on the left is the Welsh Folk Museum and St Fagans Castle.

ST FAGANS, *SOUTH GLAMORGAN*

Set in the grounds of the many-gabled Tudor mansion of St Fagans Castle is the National Folk Museum of Wales – but this is a museum with a difference. Within the 100-acre grounds are historic buildings which have been carefully dismantled and brought here from all over Wales to form a living monument to the past. Exhibits include an 18th-century whitewashed cottage with slate roof, a 15th-century farmhouse, a woollen factory, a tannery and a cockpit. The mansion itself is filled with furniture and household equipment which spans the centuries and the whole effect is to give the visitor a taste of life in bygone Wales. To complete

the picture a wood turner and basket maker are at work at St Fagans displaying the traditional skills.

Continue into St Fagans village and keep left. In 1¾ miles at T-junction turn right A4119 signed Cardiff. One and a half miles farther turn left onto the B4262 signed Radyr. Keep forward through village and pass beneath the motorway, then ¾ mile at a roundabout, take 2nd exit and cross the River Taff. At the large roundabout on the far side follow signs Tongwynlais onto the A4054 and shortly reach Tongwynlais. By the church, turn left onto a unclassified road signed Castell Coch and shortly pass on left the entrance to Castell Coch.

CASTELL COCH, *SOUTH GLAMORGAN*

Castell Coch is a magnificent reconstruction of a 13th-century Welsh castle, built in c1870 by William Burges. For a full description see page 68.

Continue along wooded lane and up long ascent. In 1 mile turn left and continue ascent. At top keep left and descend to reach a roundabout and take 4th exit B4600 to enter Caerphilly.

CAERPHILLY, *SOUTH GLAMORGAN*

Caerphilly, the home of the famous cheese, is an attractive town and best viewed from the 800 ft-high ridge of Caerphilly Common. Although the tradition of cheesemaking has largely died out in the town its castle lives on with dignity. Constructed in the 13th century, Caerphilly Castle is the second largest in Britain after Windsor Castle. For full description see page 52.

Follow signs Cardiff A469 via 14% hill and ascend out of Caerphilly and cross Caerphilly Common to return to Cardiff.

DRIVE 15   65 MILES

GUARDIAN OF THE WYE

Towns such as Caerwent and Caerleon reflect the strong Roman influence throughout Gwent. Wordsworth found inspiration in the last town on the tour, Tintern.

CHEPSTOW, *GWENT*

Once an important port and shipbuilding yard, Chepstow is situated on the River Wye near its confluence with the River Severn. A border town, it is sometimes known as the 'gateway to Gwent'. There is evidence of Roman presence here and in c1067 the Normans built the first castle. The remains (AM) are located between the town and the River Wye (for full description see page 74). Remains of the town walls, known as Port Walls (AM), lead from the castle and through the town. A fine 19th-century iron bridge spans the Wye.

From Chepstow follow signs Newport to leave by the A48. In ¾ mile at the roundabout take the 3rd exit, signed Caerwent. Two miles farther turn left onto the B4245, signed Caldicot, then bear right. In another 2 miles turn right, unclassified, and enter Caldicot. At the roundabout take the 3rd exit and shortly pass the entrance to Caldicot Castle.

CALDICOT CASTLE, GWENT

Popular banquets are held here recreating an evening of typical medieval revelry. The castle has been restored and dates back to the 12th century (full description on page 57).

Continue with the unclassified road to Caerwent.

CAERWENT, *GWENT*

Beneath the peaceful fields and old cottages of this attractive little town lie the remains of a Roman settlement named *Venta Silurum*. A large town, *Venta* was inhabited by some 3,000 people. Most of the city wall still stands and is particularly impressive in the south where it reaches a height of over 15 ft in places. Caerwent itself stands within these walls and the main street marks the approximate line of the Roman central avenue.

At the crossroads in Caerwent turn left and in ¾ mile turn left again onto the Newport road, A48 (not shown). Two and a half miles farther pass the entrance to Penhow Castle (on the left).

PENHOW CASTLE, GWENT

Atop a steep hill stand the 800-year old remains of Penhow Castle. The living quarters, tower, courtyard and curtain wall can still be seen. For a full description see page 140.

Continue along the A48 and in 4¼ miles at the roundabout take the 3rd exit to enter Newport.

NEWPORT, *GWENT*

Newport is the largest town in Gwent. Steelworks and docks are the main employers in Newport and today it is one of the major metal-exporting ports in Britain. As with many of the Welsh docks, Newport established itself during the coal trade boom of the 1800s. Newport Castle was built as a Norman Lordship in c1126. It was the victim of many a siege, but some remains still stand (for full description see page 130). On the four walls of the Central Hall of the impressive civic centre are a series of remarkable murals. The subjects of the panels include *Celtic Settlement*, *The Roman Settlement at Caerleon*, *The Arrival of the Americans* and *Building of the New George Street Bridge*. Another modern mural can be found in St Woolos Cathedral which stands on Stow Hill. Among the 500-plus acres of park an pleasure ground in Newport is the 58-acre Tredegar Park, which stands in wooded splendour on the west side of the town.

From the centre of Newport return across the River Usk, then at the war memorial (traffic signals) keep left onto the B4596, signed M4 and Caerleon. In 1 mile at the roundabout take the 2nd exit and later recross the Usk and turn left (one-way) into Caerleon.

CAERLEON, *GWENT*

One of the most historic towns in Wales, Caerleon has strong connections with the Romans and King Arthur. From AD 75 to the 4th century BC it was *Ixa Silurum*, chief fortress of the second Augustan legion. An amphitheatre seating 6,000 was constructed in AD 80 and, before excavations discovered its real identity, it was reputed to be King Arthur's Round Table. Today the legionary museum, part of the National Museum of Wales, stands on the spot where the legionary commander's building would have been.

At the end of the main street go forward onto a unclassified road, signed Llangybi. After 7¼ miles turn right onto the A472 and cross the River Usk to enter Usk.

USK, *GWENT*

A notable angling centre and old market town, Usk is situated on the river of the same name. A Roman settlement called *Burrium* lies beneath the town and the ruins of Usk Castle overlook it. The castle was founded as a Marcher Lord's stronghold in the 12th century (for full description see page 157).

In Usk turn left onto the B4598 (signed Abergavenny A471). In 6¼ miles at the T-junction turn right, unclassified, signed Raglan. Four and a half miles farther at the roundabout take the 1st exit onto the Monmouth road, A40, and shortly pass the entrance to Raglan Castle.

RAGLAN CASTLE, GWENT

The present 15th-century castle with its impressive hexagonal tower is built on the side of an earlier motte-and-bailey structure. For a full description of the castle see page 147.

Continue with the A40 and ¾ mile farther branch left (still signed Monmouth). In 5¾ miles pass through a tunnel, then turn left onto the B4233, signed Rockfield. At the ensuing roundabout turn right and cross the Monnow Bridge to enter Monmouth.

MONMOUTH, *GWENT*

From its strategic position at the meeting places of the Wye and Monnow rivers, Monmouth played its part in subjugating South Wales from Roman times until the Middle Ages. Its network of streets hold many interesting Tudor and Georgian buildings, but the Monnow Bridge (AM) is perhaps Monmouth's most prized possession. Monmouth Castle is described on page 124.

From Monmouth follow the Chepstow signs and cross the River Wye to leave by the A466. This road follows the picturesque Wye Valley to reach Tintern.

TINTERN, *GWENT*

Immortalized by William Wordsworth in his famous poem about Tintern and 'the sylvan Wye' the setting for the majestic Tintern Abbey (AM) is one of the most beautiful in Wales. This famous Cistercian Abbey was founded in 1131 by a member of the de Clare family and its substantial ruins are the main attraction in this lovely village.

Continue on the A466 and in 4½ miles at the roundabout take the 1st exit onto the B4293 for the return to Chepstow.

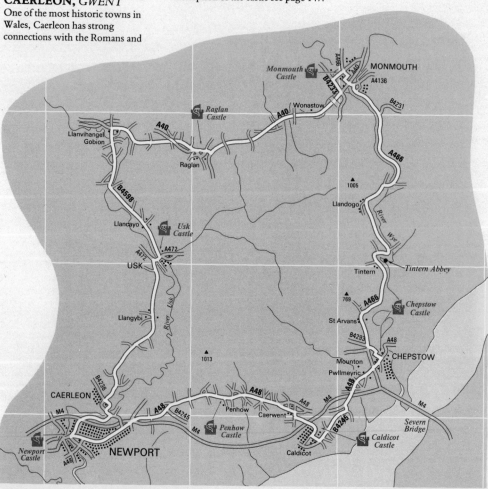

ROAD MAPS

NATIONAL GRID

To locate any of the castles, using Tenby as an example, look up the reference in the gazetteer- 2 SN 1301.

2 This is the number of the page on which Tenby Castle lies.

SN These first two letters show the major relevant area in which Tenby Castle is situated. They relate to an area labelled SN which is bound by lines numbered in all cases 0. (It can be seen that Pembroke Castle lies in the next area labelled SM).

13 The first set of numbers refer to the thin blue grid lines labelled along the bottom of the page. The 1 relates to the line of that number while the 3 is an estimated 3/10ths of the division between the 1 and 2.

01 The second set of figures refer to the numbers on the side of the page, the 0 relates to the line of that number, while the 1 is an estimated 1/10th of the division between 0 and 1.

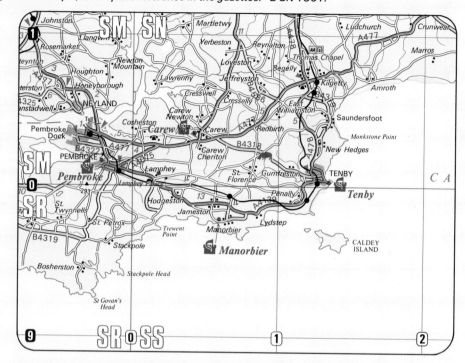

If a line is drawn, from 13 vertically and from 01 horizontally, Tenby Castle should lie where the two intersect. It may be noted that, in every instance, it is the first set of figures after the area letters that applies to the number of the bottom of the grid. Therefore the second set will relate to the figures up the side of the page.

The National Grid

The National Grid provides a reference system common to maps of all scales. The country is divided into major grid squares (100kmsq), which are outlined on the map by heavy blue lines and each is designated two letters (eg SN) as its reference code. Each of these squares is then sub-divided into 100 10kmsq, thus forming a finer grid which is numbered from 0 to 9, west to east, and south to north within each of the major lettered squares.

Thus each location can be referred to by first, two letters; showing the 100km square in which it lies, then a set of figures representing co-ordinates within the forementioned square, which gives precise location.

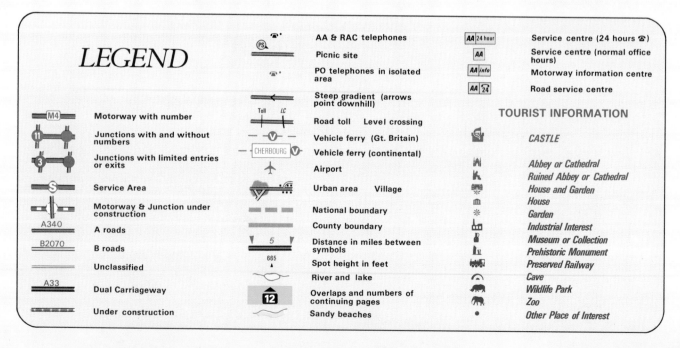

KEY TO MAPS

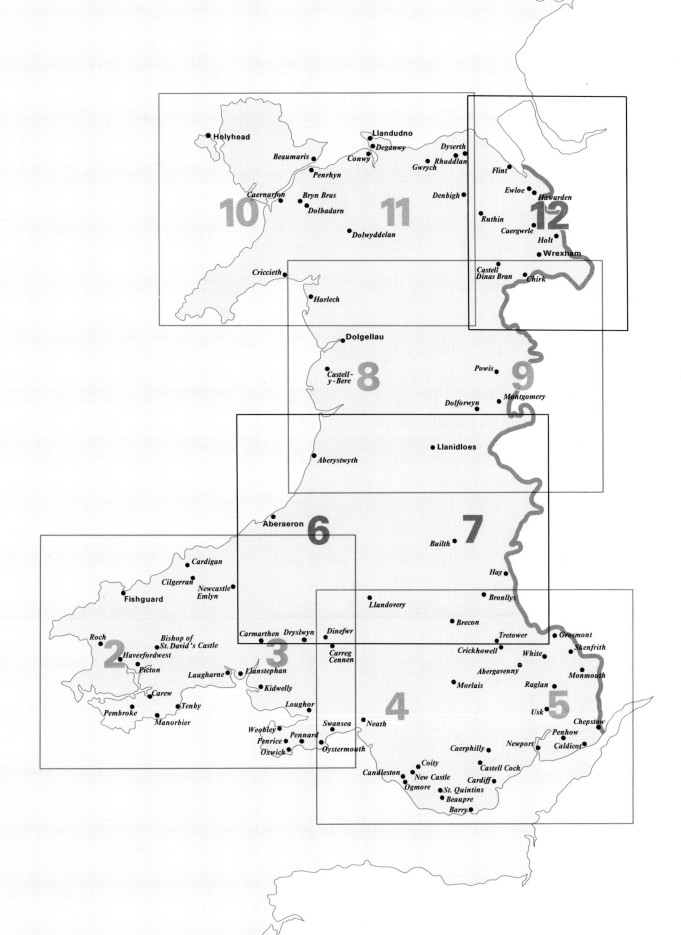

- Holyhead
- Llandudno
- Deganwy
- Beaumaris
- Conwy
- Dyserth
- Rhuddlan
- Gwrych
- Penrhyn
- Flint
- **10**
- Caernarfon
- Bryn Bras
- Denbigh
- Ewloe
- Hawarden
- Dolbadarn
- **11**
- Ruthin
- Caergwrle
- **12**
- Holt
- Dolwyddelan
- Wrexham
- Castell Dinas Bran
- Criccieth
- Chirk
- Harlech
- Dolgellau
- Castell-y-Bere
- **8**
- Powis
- **9**
- Dolforwyn
- Montgomery
- Llanidloes
- Aberystwyth
- Aberaeron
- **6**
- **7**
- Builth
- Cardigan
- Hay
- Cilgerran
- Newcastle Emlyn
- Bronllys
- Fishguard
- Llandovery
- Brecon
- Carmarthen
- Dryslwyn
- Dinefwr
- Tretower
- Grosmont
- Roch
- Bishop of St. David's Castle
- Crickhowell
- White
- Skenfrith
- **2**
- Haverfordwest
- **3**
- Carreg Cennen
- Abergavenny
- Monmouth
- Picton
- Laugharne
- Llanstephan
- Morlais
- Raglan
- Carew
- Kidwelly
- Usk
- **5**
- Pembroke
- Tenby
- Loughor
- **4**
- Chepstow
- Manorbier
- Swansea
- Neath
- Penhow
- Weobley
- Pennard
- Caerphilly
- Newport
- Caldicot
- Penrice
- Coity
- Castell Coch
- Oxwich
- Oystermouth
- Candleston
- New Castle
- Cardiff
- Ogmore
- St. Quintins
- Beaupre
- Barry

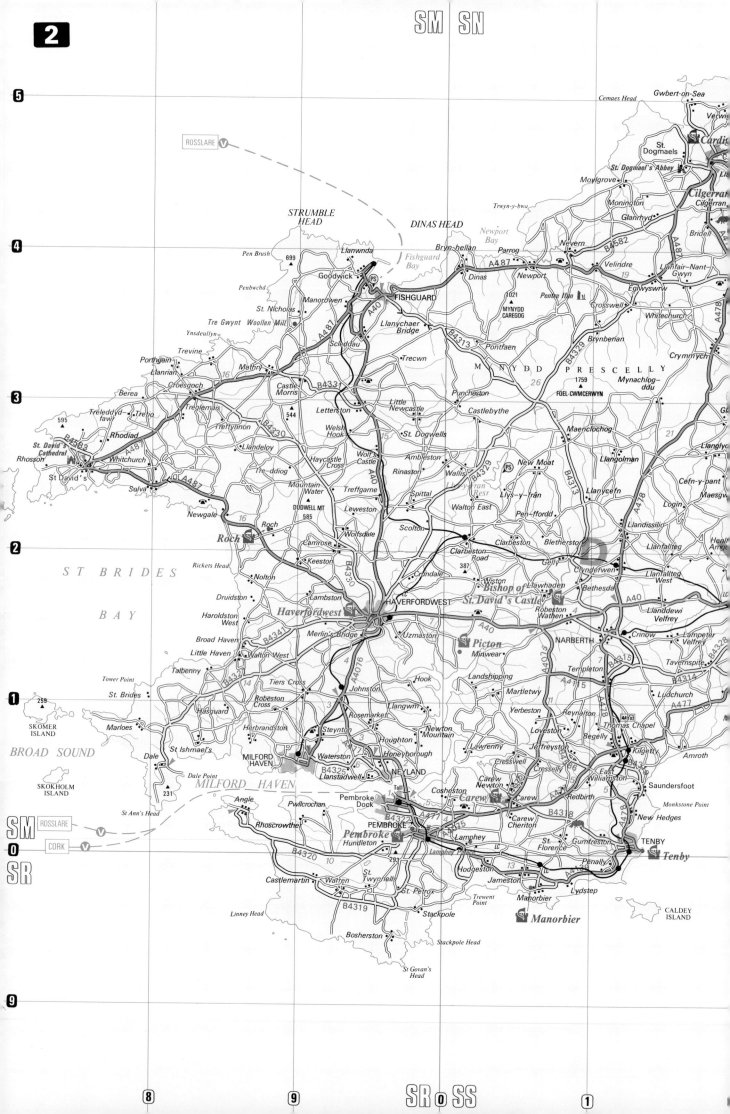

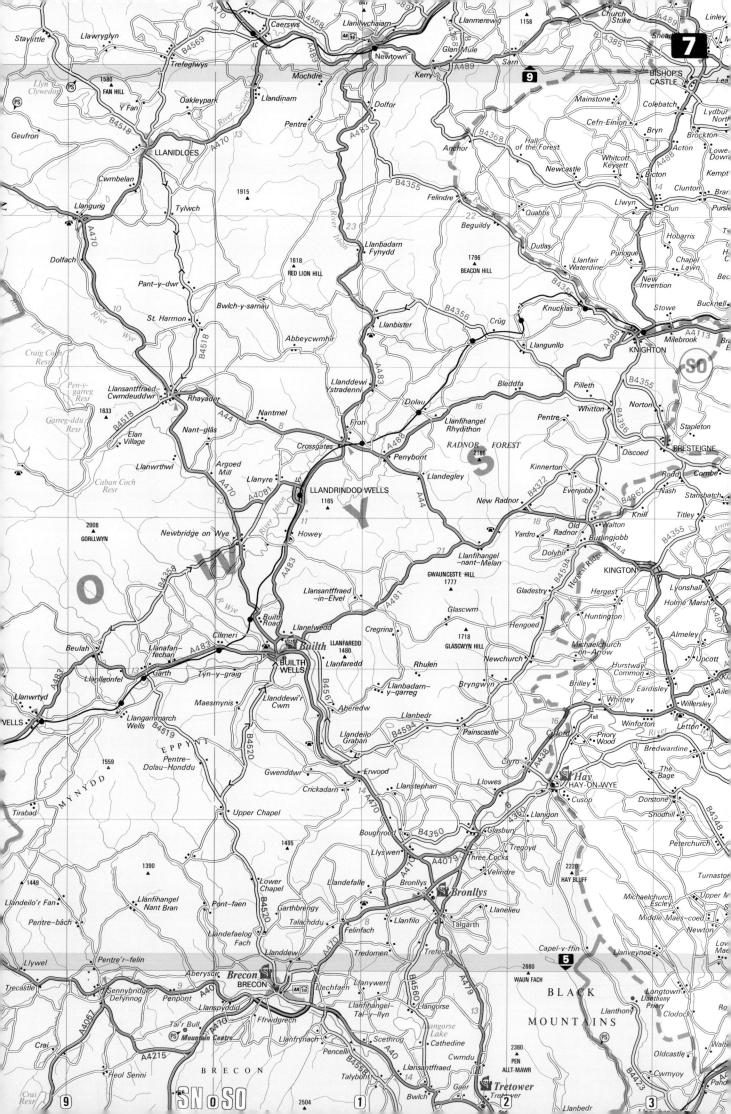

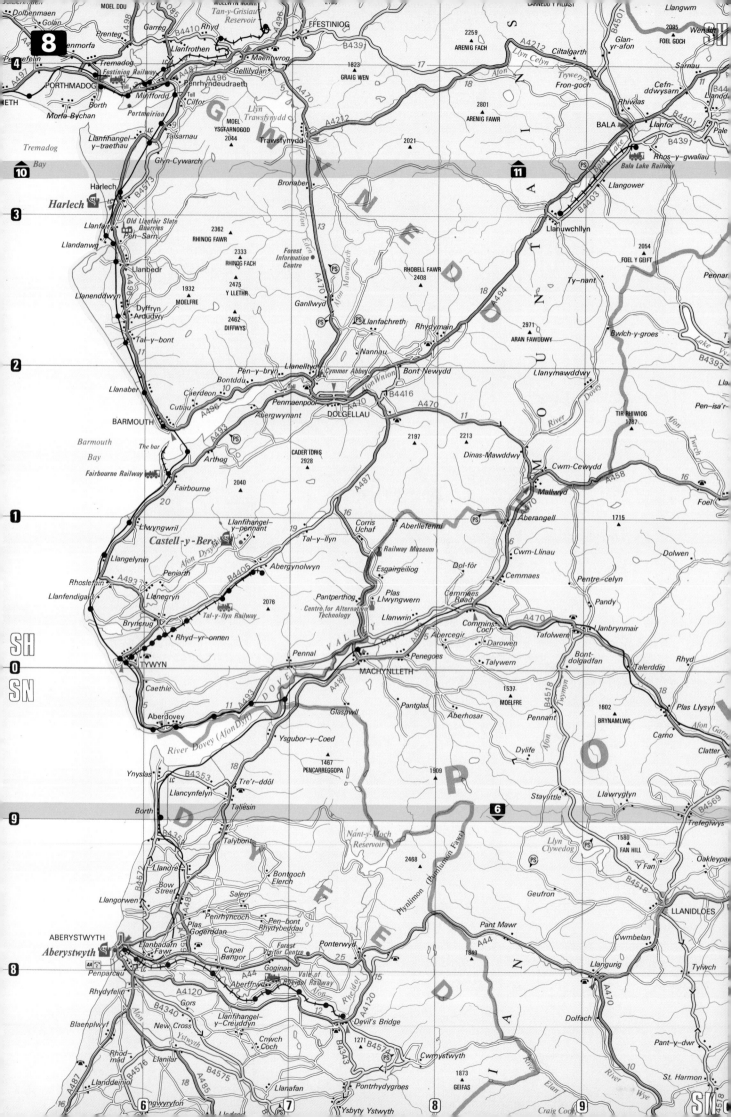

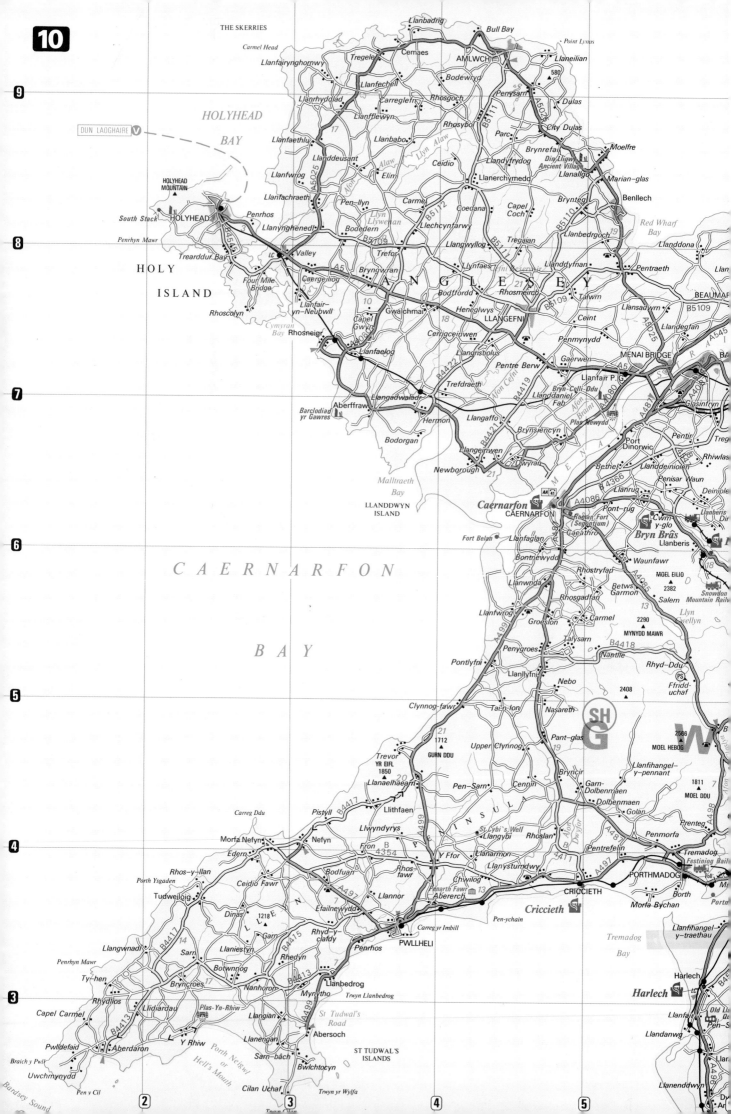

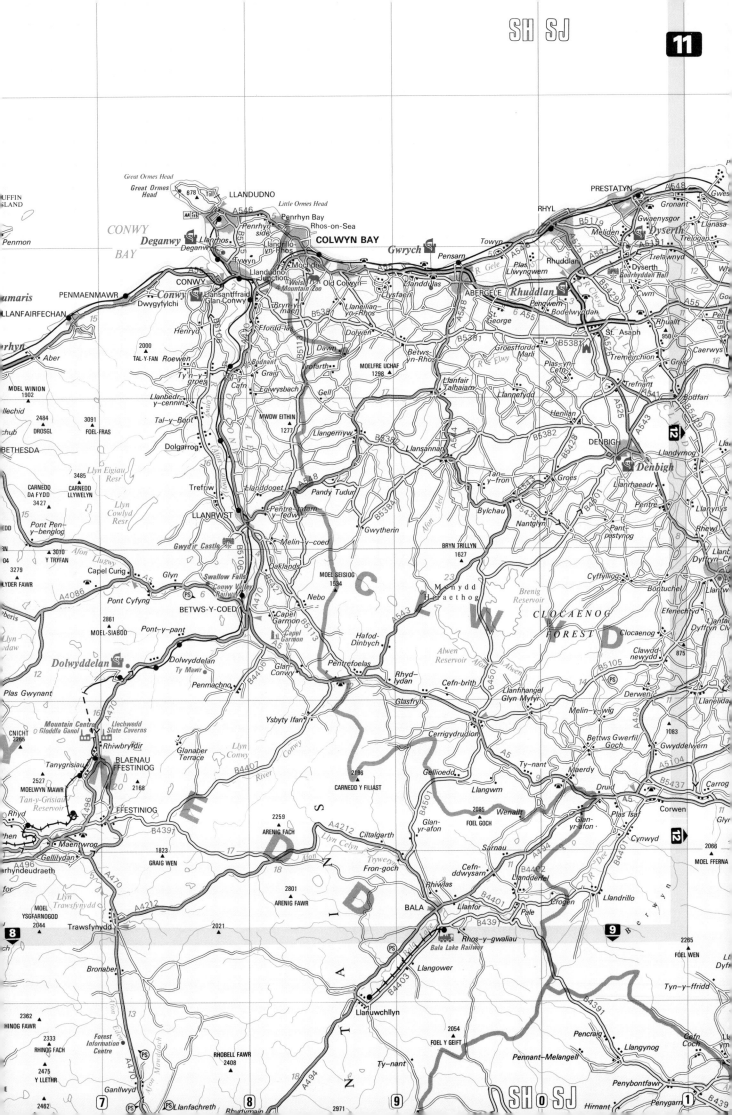

INDEX

Page numbers in bold type denote the location of the main castle entry.

ACKNOWLEDGEMENTS

All photographs are copyright Wales Tourist Board except those listed
Automobile Association: Cardiff Castle pp5, 59 & 62, Aberystwyth Castle pp34/35, Museum pp48/49, Caernarfon Castle pp50/51, William Marshall p57, Conwy Castle pp84/85, 86 & 86/87, Harlech Castle pp106/107, Llandovery Castle p119 & Monmouth Cap p124.

The publishers gratefully acknowledge the following for the use of photographs and illustrations:
Bibliotheque Nationale, Paris (Ms Fr 9084, folio 20v): mounted knights pp16/17. British Library – Crown Copyright Reserved. Luttrell Psalter manuscript – crossbowman p2, serving at the table p4, scenes from medieval life pp114/117. Also Royal ms 14 E III – two knights pp14/15; Cottonian ms Nero DI folio 23v – building scene p88; Royal ms 15 DIII – building a castle p89. Dictionnaire Raisonné de l'Architecture Française du XIeme an XVIeme siècle, by Viollet le Duc: medieval warfare scenes pp18, 20 & 24/25. Graham Rickard: Battle scene, Montgomery Castle p125. Industrial and Maritime Museum, Cardiff: 19th-century Merthyr Tydfil pp28/29. John Speede Map, The National Library of Wales, Aberystwyth, endpapers. Mary Evans Picture Library: archive engravings of Conwy Castle p5, Beaumaris Castle pp39 & 40, Caernarfon Castle p50, Caerphilly Castle p55, Pembroke Castle pp136/137, Bangor p162, Ffestiniog Railway p165, Devil's Bridge p166, Newcastle Emlyn p168, Kidwelly Castle p171, Oystermouth p172 & Tretower p174. Mrs E Sorrell and Mr G A Tanner: Alan Sorrell self-portrait p111. National Museum of Wales, Cardiff: prehistoric farming settlement p12, Offa's penny p13, 3rd Marquess of Bute p68. Items depicted on pp23, 56, 71, 121, 128/129, 154 & 158/159 are on display at the Museum. Peter Humphries: Castell Coch p3 & p70, Tomen y Mur p73, Tomen y Rhodwydd p73 & Montgomery Castle p125. RIBA Journal (2 June 1934): William Burges p29. Royal Library, Windsor Castle – Reproduced by Gracious Permission of Her Majesty the Queen: Edward, Llywelyn and Alexander – an imaginary scene p23. Welsh Office, Cardiff – Crown Copyright, reproduced with the permission of the Controller of Her Majesty's Stationery Office; Castell Coch p3, Caerphilly Castle p55, Carreg Cennen Castle: A Sorrell p66, Castell-y-Bere p72, Cilgerran Castle p80, Conwy Castle – A Sorrell p84, Caerphilly Castle p88, Dolbadarn Castle p96, Dolwyddelan Castle p97, Harlech Castle – A Sorrell p109, Kidwelly Castle – A Sorrell p116, Laugharne Castle pp118 & 119, Llanstephan Castle pp120/121, Caernarfon Castle p139, Raglan Castle – A Sorrell p147, Raglan Castle p149, Dolforwyn Castle p149, Rhuddlan Castle – A Sorrell p150 & Rhuddlan Castle p150. Whitworth Art Gallery, University of Manchester: Conwy Castle by J M W Turner p1.